GURDJIEFF AND THE WOMEN OF THE ROPE

Notes of Meetings in Paris and New York
1935–1939 and 1948–1949

Photo Credits:
Gurdjieff, from the Archives Department,
University of Wisconsin-Milwaukee Libraries.
Elizabeth Gordon, from the archives of GJ Blom, Amsterdam.
Solita Solano and Margaret Anderson, courtesy of the Library of Congress.
Jane Heap, MSS 258 Florence Reynolds Collection related to Jane Heap and The Little
Review, Special Collections, University of Delaware Library, Newark, Delaware.
Alice Rohrer, 1920s, by Consuelo Kanaga (American, 1894-1978). Gold toned gelatin
silver photograph, Brooklyn Museum. Gift of David and Marcia Raymond in memory
of Paul Raymond, 2002.85.2. Copyright transferred to Brooklyn Museum by the Estate
of Wallace Putnam.

Grateful acknowledgement is made to Solita Solano, the Library of Congress;
Kathryn Hulme, Beinecke Rare Book and Manuscript Library, Yale University;
University of Wisconsin-Milwaukee Libraries, and Special Collections, University
of Delaware Library. Special thanks to Frank Brück for his assistance and for
proofreading the text.

British Library Cataloguing-in-Publication Data.
A catalogue record for this book is available from the British Library.

CONTENTS

CHRONOLOGY 1866–1935

1866 January 13: Gurdjieff is born in Alexandropol (now Gyumri), Armenia.

1869 February 8: Georgette Leblanc is born in Rouen, France.

1883 November 1: Jane Heap is born in Topeka, Kansas.

1886 November 24: Margaret Anderson is born in Indianapolis, Indiana.

1888 October 30: Sarah Wilkinson (Solita Solano) is born in New York.

1900 July 6: Kathryn Hulme is born in San Francisco.

1908 Margaret moves to Chicago.

1912 Gurdjieff begins teaching in Russia.

1914 March: Margaret publishes the first issue of the art and literary magazine, *The Little Review*.

1915 Summer: Margaret and Jane meet in Chicago.

1917 Margaret and Jane move *The Little Review* to New York.

1920 Spring: Margaret and Jane meet Georgette Leblanc and Monique Serrure in New York.

1922 Solita settles in Paris with Janet Flanner.
Gurdjieff moves to the Château du Prieuré in Fontainebleau and founds the Institute for the Harmonious Development of Man.

1923 Jane, Margaret, and Georgette attend A. R. Orage's presentation of Gurdjieff's teaching in New York.

1924 January: Gurdjieff visits New York to introduce the teaching to America and holds public demonstrations.
June: Gurdjieff returns to France.
Impressed by the demonstrations, Jane, Margaret, Georgette, and Monique follow Gurdjieff back to France to attend the institute.
July 8: Gurdjieff is seriously injured in a car crash—work at the institute is suspended and he decides to transmit his ideas by writing.

1926 *The Little Review* suspends publication.

1927 February 19: Margaret and Jane meet Solita and they invite her to visit the institute.

vii

It was in 1927 that I first met Mr. Gurdjieff. Margaret Anderson and Jane Heap had invited me to go with them to the Prieuré at Fontainebleau, saying, "There you will see not one man, but a million men in one." The magnitude of this integer excited me. I hoped for a demigod, a superman of saintly countenance, not this "strange" ecru man about whom I could see nothing extraordinary except the size and power of his eyes. The impact everyone expected him to make upon me did not arrive. In the evening I listened to a reading from his vaunted book. It bored me. Thereupon I rejected him intellectually, although with good humour. Later in the study-house (how annoyed I was that women were not allowed to smoke there) I heard the famous music, played, I believe, by Monsieur de Hartmann. This, almost from the first measures, I also rejected. A week or so later in Paris I accompanied Margaret and Jane, who had not quite given me up, to a restaurant where *écrevisses** were the speciality which Mr. Gurdjieff was coming to eat with about twenty of his followers. He seated me next to him and for two hours muttered in broken English. I rejected his language, the suit he was wearing and his table manners; I decided that I rather disliked him.

Years passed.

In the autumn of 1934, in a crisis of misery, I suddenly knew that I had long been waiting to go to him and that he was expecting me. I sought him out and sat before him, silent. . . . He was then living in the Grand Hôtel, over the Café de la Paix—his "office," while waiting for a flat to be found. The Prieuré group had dispersed, there were no followers or pupils near him except Elizabeth Gordon who sometimes came to the Café. Three friends of mine, who had previously met Mr. Gurdjieff, also began to go to the Café to see him. Within a few days he gave us chapters of "Beelzebub" to read aloud to him. And thus, by such an "accident," we four formed the nucleus of a new group which was to grow larger year by year until the end of his life.[†]

1927   Kathryn meets Alice Rohrer (also known as "Madame X," "Wendy," and "Nickie") in New York.
Jane establishes a study group for Gurdjieff's teaching in Montparnasse.

1929   The final issue of *The Little Review* is published.

---

* Crayfish.

† Anderson, *The Unknowable Gurdjieff*, 28–9. (Solita Solano's account of her first meetings with Gurdjieff.)

1930 *My Thirty Years' War* is published.

1931 April: Kathryn and Alice sail to France. A chance encounter aboard the ship with an American artist leads to a meeting with Solita, Janet, and Djuna Barnes in Paris. Solita leads Kathryn and Alice to the place where "the only important thing in Paris" is going on—Jane's study group. The group expands to include Kathryn Hulme, Alice Rohrer, Margaret Anderson, Georgette Leblanc, Solita Solano, and Louise Davidson.

1932 February: Kathryn collects Alice from the docks of Le Havre on her return from a trip to California and they go directly to Café de la Paix (knowing in advance that it is Gurdjieff's "Paris office"). By chance, Gurdjieff is there; they introduce themselves as members of Jane Heap's study group, and he invites them to visit Fontainebleau.

May: Gurdjieff leaves the Prieuré and moves into the Grand Hôtel above Café de la Paix.

1933 *The Herald of Coming Good* is published.

1935 October 18: Jane moves to London leaving a small group of students high and dry.

Jane Heap left for London on October eighteenth . . . Her train pulled out, and our group dispersed in different directions. I stood alone for a moment, then a self I had never seen or heard, the self that Gurdjieff was to name Crocodile that same evening, propelled me to the Café de la Paix, through its heavy revolving door and directly to Gurdjieff's table.

He gazed up at me without a trace of recognition. My heart pounded as I recited my sketchy credentials for the intrusion, reminding him that I had once driven behind him to Fontainebleau, later met him in a Child's Fifth Avenue and now had come from Gare St. Lazare after seeing Miss Heap off for London. His boring eyes seemed to be sampling my inner state as I chattered; then, when I had come to the end of my rope, he mercifully invited me to sit for a coffee.

After a period of easy-feeling silence he looked at me and remarked that I had changed; I was "thin in the cheeks," he said. "Now I think you smell my idea, you smell so-o . . ." he inhaled deeply. . . .

Then he asked me if I had ever heard of his "crayfish club" where he took people and "sheared" them. Shearing, I knew, was his colorful term for getting contributions toward his Work. Would I like to be

ix

a "candidate for shearing" that night? he asked, and I was nodding in advance of his statement of what it would cost me. . . .

The coffee finished, he gathered up his notebooks and told me to come with him to his hotel. . . . Right after lunch, he indicated I was free to leave and escorted me to the door. He reminded me of the crayfish dinner that night to which, he said, I could invite one friend and he would invite one. We would meet in the café at seven.

I sorted out my excited thoughts walking home to the Left Bank faster than a bus could have taken me. Was this possibly the end of our long siege of café sitting? I heard every word he had spoken to me, exactly as spoken, rumbling, meditative or jocose, heavily accented. How quickly one got used to his extraordinary simplified English when one listened to it with head and heart! I rehearsed his words for Solita and Louise as I flew through narrow streets lined with picture galleries and antique shops where formerly I loitered for hours. Though he had said "one friend," I intended that both of them accompany me to that crayfish dinner.

We were in the café promptly at seven, as instructed. Gurdjieff was alone at his table and appeared glad to see three of us. His friend had not come, he said without regret.[*]

---

* Hulme, *Undiscovered Country*, 73.

NOTE ON THE TEXT

Solita Solano prefaces her typescript with a handwritten note: "My Gurdjieff notes daily—in Paris 1935–1940 and account of his death at American Hospital, Paris. Buried at Avon near Fontainebleau next to his mother, brother, wife, and Katherine Mansfield."

Kathryn Hulme, in her autobiography, *Undiscovered Country*, recollects the genesis of the record that began after their first dinner with Gurdjieff on October 18, 1935: "In a small café around the corner, we stopped off to review our night's adventure, to make notes on every word Gurdjieff had spoken, pooling our memories, squabbling amiably . . . 'The way I heard it . . .' 'Nonsense, he would *never* have used that word . . .' beginning then the documentation of the master's spoken words which was to run to over a hundred typescript pages before it ended, utterances stranger (and, to the uninitiated, more incomprehensible) than anything to be found in the new school of surrealist literature that flourished in Paris at the same time."

On a day when Gurdjieff gave an especially long talk, Solita, "remembering but a fraction," wrote of her method, "My habit was to rush out to the café across the street everyday and write down everything while still fresh in my mind. Katie also, when she was in Paris, did the same. We would then combine our recollections and establish sequences." Kathryn also, commented on her ability to recall the dialogue—"My memory, which had always been good, developed the accuracy of a tape-recorder in Gurdjieff's company. For the first time in my life, I was listening to words rooted in reality. I could take an entire evening of his talk and reproduce it afterwards on my typewriter, word for word."

Solita and Kathryn wrote interchangeably in the first person and the third, referring to themselves and each other by their first names or the names Gurdjieff gave them, spelling them either correctly or as Gurdjieff pronounced them. To preserve the integrity of the text, the original spellings and the phonetically spelled words used by the writers to capture Gurdjieff's unique style of expression have been retained. Therefore, some seemingly misspelled words appear in the dialogue, for example, "aftomatic" (automatic), "be-gind" (behind), "toll" (tall), "nervious" (nervous), "garmony" (harmony), and so on.

Instances in which Solita used Kathryn's notes or combined them with her own have been retained in the footnotes with any other annotations made to the original typescripts. Additional notes by Kathryn have been footnoted in the same fashion.

All comments in brackets and parentheses are by the two writers.

1935

Friday, October 18

Katie, Louise, and I went to the café tonight. He said, "You very much changed—if before worth one hundred dollars, now worth thousand." He took us to his l'Écrevisse* restaurant for dinner and when he gave the toasts he called in the patron and the cook to drink with him, and the waiter too. He said to Louise, "Never mind idiot doctors, drink, good for you." When he said to me, "Drink, drink," I emptied my glass. He said, "No, no. Woman must drink only half glass for toasting. All she wants, but in half glasses. Now you not drink next toast."

He said Katie and I had "Jewish" psyche; I was "Jewish" and canary combination and Katie was "Jewish" and crocodile combination. (Three years later, he said suddenly one day, "Kanari, you remember what I first tell about Jewish and canary? Well, now you are just canary. You astonished my memory, I see on your face. Many things I forget, but not such thing.") To Louise he said, "You are sardine and wart. You know how sardine struggle to get back in water when left between sea and sand?" Louise asked, "But what is wart?" He would not reply except to say, "I once knew priest who prayed for one." (A year later he explained that "wart" was not the right word; he had meant "carbuncle.")

Later at the café he said, "I now am old idiot; both feet in galosh, moreover old Jewish. I need now some church mouse again. Wednesday I take you and Sardine to Fontainebleau and we can read book on the train and see machine for music."

Wednesday, October 23

Last night he came to my hotel with the book and we read aloud to him in Katie's room until 2:00 a.m. This morning we met him in the café and waited while he read some proofs, then we took the train to Fontainebleau. I read all the way in his book. He took us to his

---

* Brasserie Excelsior. See Hulme, *Undiscovered Country*, 75.

brother's little house and showed us the machine. It looks like a radio. Beside it is a rod that emits moans, music, buzzing or shrieks according to who has approached; its tone changes for each person's vibrations. His invention.

Lunch and the idiot toasts. He's angry if one doesn't remember the sequence of idiots. He's been mad at Krocodile a lot, but not with Sardine. She said the right one once and he said, "I am astonished." (I had written them down and learned them as precautionary measure.)

We read the book again, took the 4:00 p.m. train back and fetched him later at the café for dinner. No one had any money for l'Écrevisse, so we went to a small Greek restaurant near my hotel. Gurdjieff spoke Turkish to a man at next table and Greek to the patron. Said he knew forty-eight languages well and twenty more as well as he knows English! Said he is planning a group here and that we three are to start it. He said, "You very dirty but have something very good—many people not got—very special." When I began to cry, he said, "Must not cry." I said, "But I *must*." He said, "Must—but must not." He made a tirade against A. Once he laughed at me and said, "You have a screw loose."

We returned to the hotel and read again until midnight. Janet came downstairs from our rooms. I introduced her—"Old friend, we live here ten years." He said, "Oh, sometimes such friendship very bad, great hate comes out, then love, then more hate." When I said, "I'm too old to begin this work—it's too late," he replied, "Never too late, but now it is twice as hard." When was it he said, in the café, "The only difference between me and other men is that I know more"? Another time—"I am small man compared to those who sent me."

Saturday, October 26

Another session last night. I walked alone with him from the restaurant to the hotel. He said, "You wonder why I so good to you?" "Yes. Why?" "I not tell you yet," and smiled under the electric light. "Is it bad for you that I am good to you?" I said, "No, I am sure not," and he said, "I think so too." In the restaurant he said to me, "You are lopsided," and twice when he offered the others a drink, he said to me—"Except you. You cannot have this time." He said, "I see all your quintessence."

To see him every night is a miracle. During the reading he said, "Ah, human nature. You give something to someone. First time he prostrates himself, second time he kisses your hand, third time he gets familiar, fourth time he merely nods at you, the fifth time he insults you because not enough what you give, and in the end he sues you."

Sunday, October 27

At dinner I had the misfortune—no, good fortune—to ask a "mental" question. Thunderbolts fell. "Now you know your illness, your sickness. It is curiosity—American curiosity. Always you want to know more and more without understanding what already I have said to you. For that you will die merde." Tears from me, of course. He asked, "You angry?" I said, "No, it's true."

When he left, he said, "Tonight you were bitten by your flea. You be careful not to catch more fleas or you cannot sleep in your bed." Back at the hotel, he talked to Miss Gordon, who came for the first time to the reading. He told her she had not much time left, it was now or never. She must do something special now. "If you do not; merde you have been, merde you are, and merde you will perish, like dog." He said to us, "Miss Gordon will be like Mother Superior for you and you must treat her as such. Now all listen carefully to what I tell. Here is special exercise, first of seven, and tomorrow Miss Gordon must bring me seven questions about this. Think of legs and try to imagine emanations that flow from them. Then try to think you are holding them back so they will not escape. Now I advise you not sleep all night but think about this, then I will tell more. Now Miss Gordon, by telling this I have made myself an obligation to you and I must be your slave, at your service any moment you command me. But if you not do, I have obligation to stop."

Poor Miss Gordon was rigid with fear. Then he talked about emanation of all bodies. He said, "We emanate. This is an active function; a dirty process, as dirty as making merde. But sometimes there can be something else but dirt in emanations." I was waiting to hear what, and he looked at me and said, "No. That I not tell."

He went on. "The earth emanates. The atmosphere around planet is its emanation." Again he looked at me, hanging breathless in mid-air, and said, "Many more things like this I know but can never tell." He says that curiosity about all this unknown knowledge

3

"stinks." To EC whom Katie brought to dinner, he said, "Two things I like about you—three things I hate." He said, at table, "Sometimes God is unique merde."

Sunday, October 27[*]

We meet Gurdjieff by arrangement at La Coupole at one o'clock— Solita, Louise, and myself. "You make plan," he said, "Now what we do? Place you know here, go?" I suggested Oasis which once he said he liked. He had a plan. "We go gastronomic shop, buy hors d'œuvres, go your place, eat." He went to the Russian shop next to Oasis, leaving us to finish our coffee on the terrace. He came out after a while with two large bundles. We join him and take a cab to the hotel. Elaine joins us—now we are five around the table.

He has bought a great spread—caviar, salmon, meat cutlets, sausage from Latvia, animal feet in jelly (a favorite weekly dish of Priory he says), black bread, white bread, cheese, olives, pickles, vodka, and a bottle of white mustard, and one of horseradish which he mixes together. We eat.

We read afterwards but we have stuffed our tapeworms and are sleepy. He is most sleepy. He leaves us around half past three and we will meet that night at Excelsior Brasserie for crayfish.

At 8:30 p.m. the four of us arrive for crayfish. He is already there. He tells us he has already drunk four large Vieux Armagnac at Café de la Paix. He doesn't seem affected. But tonight he is going to let loose lightning, the first time with us, at us. I get it first. The peppery soup around the crayfish—he says, "Eat it, good for cold, take much bread in mouth, then sauce." I think he says breath, and proceed to fill mouth with breath. He says, "Bread"—but still it sounds like breath, and I take soup (without bread). Then he roars—and I am unable to stop the flush from the crayfish pepper soup plus his raving at me for stupidity. And later, I cannot stop the alibi—"I thought you said breath, not bread." By that time he had gone away from my subject. Solita next—she asks a wrong question—he tells her her curse is curiosity . . .

Miss Gordon awaits us in the hotel room. Solita and I go ahead in the taxi—we are one hour late. We have among us, drunk two whole bottles of Armagnac. Gurdjieff will follow with Louise and

---

Elaine. Gurdjieff has learned a new word at dinner. He tells me I am "kind born seven months—not nine—what is that?" "Premature," we say—and so he says I am Miss Premature. Later he asks me to tell Miss Gordon what my new title is.

In the room he tells Miss Gordon she must drink brandy, because we are all drunk and her vibrations are cacophonous with ours— "For garmony, you drink"—and she does.

Tonight he has no book to read. He talks. He tells Solita she is a slave to functions, any function—he doesn't name it, but a function. He says, "Tonight I make arise on you one flea—which bite, yes? And she has had those fleas always—sometime he make arise all her fleas, and all bite, and she never sleep again.

"Now Miss Gordon I tell you something, for you specially, you can understand. They can listen—for some other day they can remember this. But you will know now what I mean.

"Emanations—everything has emanations. Earth, dog, that bottle, me, you—emanations are automatic, must go out from us, from every separate part, from all total, part go out automatically from every living thing. We each one surrounded by atmosphere of our emanations—some scientific apparatus can see these emanations. We each have atmosphere around us all the time—dog also, also bottle, also earth.

"Now then, think of your leg. Emanations go out from leg also. Try now think. This is first step—this is first thing can do so that you die not like dog but can become part of god. Good formulation— born like dog, die part of god, is it not good?

"When I tell you this beginning thing you can do, tonight your most big moment in life—more important for you than God—more important than your birth. Why? Because you born like dog. After tonight, you have responsibility, because I tell you this. Your leg emanations go out—now you think—not all emanations go out of leg, you save some of them, you accumulate emanations in your leg, not let all go out. Let some for necessary reasons, but you accumulate some also, you begin accumulate in you some of emanations which go out automatically. This is what I tell you. This is a beginning, to be not dog but part of God. After this, I tell you more. There are seven ways to accumulate emanations—this is first. To do this you must remember yourself. But you cannot do without asking me questions—think of questions—I give you twelve hours. You meet tomorrow morning. Must ask seven questions before can understand what I mean. Seven questions *must* ask, otherwise I know you not understand."

Three days ago we were at Fontainebleau with him—Solita, Louise and myself at lunch in his brother's house. He turns on me and gives me a terrible test I cannot understand. I need no notes, for I cannot forget. Only this—to make the picture always complete—he says, "Me in room, ten men, guns pointed at me. A plate of sh— on table. Kees her or eat that." I do self-observation while his attack goes on and stop flushes or tears and keep my eye on him—eye to eye with him.

Afterwards, looking me in the eye, he laughs, then turns to the others and says, "See, she stare at me like cow stare at new-pan-door." We all have to think what new-pan-door can mean. Finally we realize he means newly painted door.

"Cow in morning, goes out from barn—live always in same barn, go down same road to field, stay all day and eat. Man, while cow gone, paints door of barn. At night cow come home. Same road he knows, to same barn but now barn has new paint door. Cow stands looking at new paint door. That how she stare at me now. You see?"

I have thought of many interpretations of this but the one that seems most right to me is this: His sudden attack of me on a most personal and near theme was the painting of the door, and I, who had felt that he was "my idea of home," suddenly find myself staring at the door he had deliberately painted, behind which door I still knew "home" was, but staring, confounded.

Since then he has used this picture several times—he told me last night I could write many articles on new-pan-door and sell them in America (and give him ten percent).

"Many new-pan-door in America," he says. "Roosevelt when he have expenses list in front of him, costs of his programs etc., stares down at list they give him like cow stare at new-pan-door."

This may be a form-thought for what you think you know and then discover abruptly you don't.

When he left last night we all stood around and thanked him. Our vibrations were high, it has been the biggest evening we had had with him. Outside my door he turned to Miss Gordon and said, "Now Mees Gordon, you see? You smell something here?" (As if he meant that among us there was a start of something which pleased him.)

Above and below: Le Château du Prieuré des Basses Loges, Fontainebleau-Avon

Above and below: Café de la Paix

*Monday, October 28**

Miss Gordon telephones at 7:30 p.m. to say, "He will be there at 9:30 p.m." I do not know where all of us are, I say so and promise to call her back at Café de la Paix in half an hour. However, Elaine, Louise, and Solita are ready for the evening. We gather together like gangsters in long coats saying, "he is coming—coming." And from beds and café terraces, we gather, feeling almost too exhausted to stand. A quick Italian dinner to absorb cocktails. At 9:31 p.m. and sixty seconds, he comes coughing up the stairs.

Miss Gordon is a few minutes late. We have coffee in the room, lemon for him. Then we read the chapter on League of Nations.

Late in the evening, he turns to Miss Gordon to ask if she has seven questions—a continuation of the emanation accumulating talk of the previous night. First he goes the rounds with us and asks if we thought about this, and what we say to each other—he insists. Each in turn must say what she said to the other. Principally, we had all tried to imagine seven questions, such as Miss Gordon would have to ask.

All we have done together is titillating, still, he sees we had interest, and decides to interview Miss Gordon with us present.

Miss Gordon then asks a question—she tells him she tried the exercise but thinks she had her mind on it too much. "Where, Mr. Gurdjieff should the center of gravity be for this? In mind? In leg?" She explains to him how there came a stoppage when she tried.

Gurdjieff then says that "stop come because you have too much mind on this—*must* have *attention*. What is attention? Attention is working together of association of thought with association of feeling. Memory working together with sense makes attention. But feeling have two centers—solar plexus feeling, solar plexus brain and spine brain. Must have attention which means memory and sense working together on it. But must *not* philosophize—very dangerous philosophize. Be simple like monk, a monk given a task. You do with faith, not try knowing (with head) but *sure*-ing. (Gurdjieff touches his solar plexus region.) Not knowing, but sure-ing.

Miss Gordon then asks about time—should one force oneself to do it for a long time, without stopping?

---

* Written on the 28th.

Gurdjieff says, "One third of waking state must be active—for active mentation or active in sense that the real 'I' functions. One third of waking state be active, one third be actively relaxed, one third be automatic. Can do this exercise at any time. Example—you go water-closet, know have twelve minutes there, then you give four minutes this exercise. Have three hours free, you *know* about, know for sure have three hours—then give one hour this exercise, etc."

Man has three worlds, he says. One; the outer world, the world of impressions, everything that happens outside of us. Two; the inner world, the world of the functioning of all our organs, the totality of organ functioning. Three; the world of the soul, which was called by the ancients, *the* world of man.

"Three worlds have man—this exercise of leg is exercise for inner world of man. Mentation of inner world."

Miss Gordon then asked (following the emanation accumulation task) if she should do it when in life or should do it sitting quietly alone.

Gurdjieff says, "First at beginning, do it when *not* in life, when lie in bed, sit in chair. Important not make mistake at beginning, not occupied with outside life, etc. Important do it first outside of life, then, when sure that doing right, do it *in* life. Can make mistake at beginning and that can be dangerous, then you have only psychopathic attention—mental center attention—not totality of memory-sense attention. Later, must do in life. Must do *all* in life—not be like monks, isolated from life. Monk all psychopathic. This must be full thing."

Later, he says that when you start accumulating emanations, you find that there is a place in you for them, like that place in automobiles where power is accumulated. "When you have many emanations accumulated, you find they will crystallize, then you have force. Not force that can go out of you like water, but emanations crystallized. Then can do many things with. And when do this (in reply to another question of hers), it best to have all muscles relaxed. Weak. Have all muscles weak. *No* tension."

Miss Gordon asks, "How can one know which is sense brain and which is feeling brain?"

"Can know that when come to you those stops—maybe you have no spinal brain working at this task and you can know that by the absence of feeling in the spinal cord."

He says again, "Memory working together with sense, makes attention. Important—sense have two meanings—in English no two words—but is something like feeling and sense—feeling in solar plexus region and sense in spinal cord."

After the meeting ends at 12:30 a.m. we go with him to Café de la Paix for coffee. After we order and start drinking coffee, he says, "But tonight we not be parra-seet (parasite) maybe now we have Armagnac because we not be parraseet tonight." We have Vieux Armagnac. We start the toasts "A la santé des idiots ordinaires," then divide later for second and third toasts—both Louise and Elaine not being able to drink the whole of a big glass of Armagnac (having had chocolate first). Louise endeavors to give Solita and me more than the half out of her glass, Gurdjieff stops her and says, "You have more need this than they." He taps his head. "You psychic weak, they have some, maybe only tail of donkey psyche, but better than nothing what you have." And makes her drink the amount he ordained for her.

"I cheeck-make" is one of his expressions, meaning, he cracks like a louse under his nail all things that do not please.

"Tail of donkey" is something very low but nevertheless a little on the way—many things are *not* tail of donkey to him such as good old Armagnac, a good formulation, crayfish, etc.—people, too.

There's a paragraph in his book about persons who in one state of being will give him their soul, and in another state of being, with their hate, drown him in a teaspoon of water. This love and hate which he arouses—there was, a thought I could not get accurately, to the effect that the force of the hate is directly proportionate to the time spent in proximity to him. (He explained this last part in the cab going to the café.) Proximity has to do with atmospheres of emanations brought close—like me here. He says, "I helpless. You three so close—your emanations *keel* (kill) me almost." And that remark followed some of his previous talk in the room about emanations of people who are forced to live in close proximity. Their emanations merge and find corresponding emanations in those of others. Many people close together—emanations all fuse like the colors of the spectrum and corresponding emanations find each other and mix.*

---

* End Katie's Notes.

11

Monday, October 28

Miss Gordon asked about exercise, "Where must center of gravity lie, in mind or in leg?" She came to a stop and wished to know why. He said, "Because too much mind; instead must have attention, association of mind with association of feeling. Memory plus sensing makes attention. But feeling has two centers—solar plexus feeling plus spinal brain. Must not philosophize about it but do with faith like monk. Not try to know with the head, but *sure-ing*." She asked, "How long should I do this exercise?" He said, "One-third of waking state must be active—for active mentation or for making real 'I' function. One-third active, one-third actively relaxed, one-third automatic living. Have three hours you know will be free, do the exercise one hour. Man has three worlds; the world of impressions which is the outer world, the inner world which is the totality of organ functioning, and the world of the soul which the ancients called 'The World of Man.' The leg exercise is for the mentation of the inner world. Just as the physical presence of man can arise, so can the soul world of man arise. Between the physical world of man and the soul world there is an intermediate state." (I believe that here he mentioned the astral body, but I did not understand him.) "Miss Gordon, you first do this exercise when not in ordinary life; later you can do anywhere. When man begins to accumulate these emanations, he finds there is a place in him waiting for them, like the place in a motor where power accumulates. When you accumulate emanations, they will crystallize and you will have a force that does not pass from you like water."

He said to Louise, "You are psychic weak." To Katie, "You are like cow who comes home at night and stares at new painted barn door. Not know home because just was painted." To me, "I have thought of seven things about you and one I tell now. You have eye of suffering wolf. Only eye, very special thing. I have seen wolf, female wolf, attacked by herd, hungry, tired, bitten; in agony they turn look on me, like look in your eye."

"Dirty" also means the result of mixed bloods, he says. Scotch very dirty, Irish very dirty, Spanish worse than Italian; mixed blood gives less chance for individuality. He illustrated this with Jews; never straight Jew, always German Jew, Armenian Jew, Spanish Jew, French Jew. He doesn't like altruists or egotists, but didn't say what he did like. He said he always knows what a person is thinking and feeling by the way their muscles are "composed." He said, "My mind not squeamish but my body very squeamish."

Yesterday, Sunday, he telephoned us to meet him at the Coupole. He shopped for our lunch, bought caviar, Vodka, Russian cold foods, and we all lunched in Katie's room at the hotel. Afterward we read for hours. At night, we met him at l'Écrevisse where he spent three hundred francs for dinner and two bottles of Armagnac. He scolded Katie and me, and Louise for treating her dog like a human being.

Friday, November 1

He telephoned at 6:00 p.m. to say he would come at 9:30 p.m. We all were so depleted that no one could hold herself in her chair. Nevertheless we read until 3:00 a.m., mostly Katie, as she is the best reader. The strain was unendurable. He watched us as never before and the room was charged with his dynamo and our super-effort. Tonight we dined at the Greek restaurant and read until 2:00 a.m. Katie brought FS to dinner and the hotel. When Gurdjieff saw her, he called for the chicken soup chapter.

Saturday, November 2

At dinner tonight, he said to me, "I think on you today. This evening is for you—you are hero of evening. I bring special chapter for you." (It was the one on Time.) When he heard Louise was sailing, he said, "Now I think you are spoiled for American company." He again scolded her for attention to her dog and inattention to him. He said morning sun is best for us, the only time of day when the rays contain certain properties necessary for our understanding. He said, the stronger physically a man is, the weaker his brain; that E. and F. are too tall for good brain; if women have very long hair that also means very short brain. Donkey is stronger than horse because donkey is more stupid.

Wednesday, November 6

Last night we read from 8:30 p.m. to 3:00 a.m. without a break. He said he planned to write on for two months, finish his last book, then start classes. After that we can never see him alone, only from a distance; how we are with him now, is an accident. We're reading second series now, the portraits.

Saturday, November 9

Tonight he came an hour early, just as I was going out to join the others at dinner. So I had none. He talked with me about my personal problems until the first steps arrived. It was F.

He said, "Oh, it is Mees-Understanding."

"What?"

"Mees-Premature, like seven months baby." She looked angry.

He said, "You are hopeless, you are empty and always will be; you have no brain, no possibilities of being."

During the reading he said, "I can pronounce four hundred consonants for your thirty-six. Sound-producing organs in man are more important than his eyes. Americans worst nation for sound-producing."

Thursday, November 14

Sitting with him in Café de la Paix, he said, "I make special program now for you. You badly organized—too much here, too little there, one place empty, good physical, fourth center wrong. First will give you piqûres,* then initiate exercise for which you must take vow. On what you choose take vow? What is most important for you?"

"My eyes, Mr. Gurdjieff."

"Then let be so. Kanari, would you believe could exist such type man who would give eyes before his arms or legs? Yet it is so."

Later E. came in with Katie.

He said to E., "You have zero attention. For ones like you with such dirty life, exists special kind of hell." He described it. All souls there must sit in a lake of merde up to their mouths. They must sit very still, for at the slightest movement, the liquid goes into their mouths. Whenever a newcomer approaches, all the souls call out, "Get in gently, please, be slow and careful." Once a year to commemorate Jesus Christ, a great stone is thrown into the lake and all souls receive the liquid in their mouths."

E. was very angry and left the café.

---

* Injections.

14

He said he had just finished his book and that he wished to celebrate tonight. "After tonight I drink no more."

Saturday, November 16

I went to him at noon for my first piqûre and my first exercise. In the evening when I saw him, he asked how many times I had forgotten. At my reply, he said, "If so hot at first, afraid later will be cold."

Wednesday, November 20

Fourth piqûre today. Last night Alice gave us dinner at l'Écrevisse restaurant and Miss Gordon came. She said suspiciously, "Have you been seeing Mr. Gurdjieff?" I said, "Yes—every day, sometimes twice a day." She turned red and said to me, "That's a lie!" I did not answer. Alice said, "Yes—today we've been with him since noon." During dinner he reproached me for not knowing a Greek root he wanted and Miss Gordon was pleased! He has found a new apartment, rue Labie, number eleven.

Sunday, November 24

We now go to lunch every day in his apartment. He cooks the food himself and we each put fifteen francs in the kitchen box (except Miss Gordon) and Katie washes the dishes. He calls her "kitchen boy"—"I like such kitchen boy, he not make me nervous." I set the table and wait on him. Finished first seven piqûres—now a "pause" before the next series.

Monday, November 25

I had luncheon alone with him. He said, "Exercise I gave you is to instill in you a new kind of data you will need for what is to come later."

He gave me the Good and Evil chapter to read—first to myself, then to the others, then to read again alone. I asked him if it was true that once man had a tail in which was a continuation of the denying brain. (I had thought of this in the night.) He said yes.

Gurdjieff

Alice Rohrer

Kathryn Hulme

Solita Solano

Louise Davidson

Elizabeth Gordon

Monday, December 2

All day and evening with Mr. Gurdjieff. After we had read again the Good and Evil chapter, he said men have never seen angels in the world but always thought they had seen devils. The more "good" men thought they were, the more devils they could see—they see devils where a really good man does not. He said the only devil in us is self-calming. I dare not ask "curiosity" questions, so asked E. to ask him, "Is man the result of evolution from animals?" He replied, "No—man is a different formula." Miss Gordon was there for lunch. She is friendly to me now. He stopped drinking three days ago—says he cut off everything—Armagnac, Calvados, Vodka. No more nightly readings. I am the only one who goes twice a day.

Tuesday, December 3

He is in black moods and has money difficulties. I waited in vain at the café last night and dined with Miss Gordon. He said he would give her piqûres also.

Friday, December 6

I had the idea of learning Russian yesterday and today Gurdjieff was very angry. "Idiot, you waste time idiot language while I your future prepare. You already late your future, now this important time and you must idiot language learn. Svoloch!"*

At lunch he said, "I know you give me all your heart. Soon you must decide if all give up in world." Another kind of piqûre today. I look better, I *am* better.

Wednesday, December 18

Have gone every day, twice a day. Today I told him I must go to London for an article. "How long?" "Five days." "Well, three days all right, but I must know exactly when you go and when return."

---

* Russian for garbage pail.

Saturday, December 28

"Happy to see you again, Mr. Gurdjieff." "Ach, happy must not be. Happy is psychopathic." Another series of piqûres, then a special diet for "quality blood" and second exercise. "Your psychopathia much better." He said never to say "in the world" that he is teacher, I pupil. "I used also to be idiot, but finished when my accident was. Now I writer and you reader. If I special thing do for you, you not speak." In the café he said to Katie, "I have made over one-seventh of Kanari's seven parts—the rest will proceed automatically."

When we were alone, he began to explain my new exercise. I was listening with all my being. Suddenly he stopped. Then he said, "The way you receive my instruction is with very bad expression. People who are watching us would think I am telling you something quite else. There are spies for me everywhere. You must always keep your inner world for yourself alone. This is a serious matter for you. There is no correspondence between your exterior and your interior. Lucky for you I can read your interior or I would not be able to judge you. Often you have not corresponding expression of your inner life. The world cannot always judge you correctly. Sometimes when even a good effort at understanding you make, you have quite idiotic expression. But I see because I have knowledge of these things. You must always watch yourself, always remember yourself. You are a bad case of lopsided. Always you have been for mind and nothing you find for understanding, because that is quite another thing and for that you must have teacher—but not in your idiot American sense." He sat in silence and I feared he might not give me my exercise. Finally he explained it. I must do it three hours a day.

"And remember yourself before the world. They must nothing see."

"Why have I no correspondence, Mr. Gurdjieff?"

"Heredity and bad education."

"Why do I now menstruate so frequently?"

"Quite natural. Piqûres change all processes, that one too. New adjustments necessary in all organs. Now you not try to think. You must catch up to your thinking; your mentation will come later when I have given you data for understanding."

1936

I sat in the café alone with him. Katie and Alice were in the further room. He said he would not see them; they were not "serious." He asked me why I had been crying.

"Afraid to tell you—you will say again I am psychopathic."

"No, no, tell me."

"Today is anniversary of my mother's death and I always have guilt and remorse about her."

"How long ago she die?"

"Fourteen years."

"Then not psychopathic. Very good thing. Mother very important—you get fire from mother. But not think about her only once a year—but think often."

He asked about the exercise. I said I couldn't manage it very well, it made me sleepy. He waved his arms and said, "You must struggle, struggle all the time. This exercise is very important. Your whole future depends from this. It should be even more for you than God. Even get angry, if necessary. Every day struggles, little by little make data, and from this data your future depends. You must think of yourself as a baby you take care of and lead by hand. After you do, necessary you rest twice as long as you have done exercise. Be passive afterward." I asked if that meant sitting still or could I do my work on the typewriter? He laughed. "Oh, yes. You passive then. You well asleep then." There was much more, but I can't remember. He said to Miss X, "You not have brain. Brain very important to have in head and not manure."

Sunday, January 12

He invited Alice, Katie, and Miss Gordon to lunch today. We read three chapters.

He said to me, "You always have a purpose and you are always looking for something unusual or wonderful. I think after you go water-closet you look in to see if by chance there is something wonderful."

Monday, January 13. His Birthday.

He has begun to talk to us like a teacher. He sat on his big divan cross-legged, we sitting like a class before him. Today he talked for an hour and a half, continuously, "the search for a soul." I remember but a fraction; as follows. (My habit was to rush out to the café across the street everyday and write down everything while still fresh in my mind. Katie also, when she was in Paris, did the same. We would then combine our recollections and establish sequences.)

"You have heard my horse and cart representation; I will make another to represent man. This one in his search for a soul.

"Man in his history has always believed he had a soul and sought for it. This is the aim of all religions. If in ordinary life I were asked if man has a soul, I would say *no*, because in general, man has not. Before man can have a soul, he must have an 'I.' Only when he achieves an 'I' can he develop a soul.

"There are four ways. Let us compare ordinary man with a three-room apartment. The dining-room will represent his organism, his moving center, the place where he eats and attends to the needs of the body's maintenance and development. The drawing-room represents his feeling center and the bedroom is his mental center. But this apartment lacks a bathroom, which we will call the 'I' room. In this man's ordinary three-room apartment there is disorder. The roof leaks in the dining-room or there is no floor in the drawing-room or the window panes are broken in the bedroom. Nothing has been washed or painted or repaired. Perhaps only one room is furnished. Or the articles of furniture that belong in the bedroom are scattered about the dining-room or are on the table in the drawing-room. The building itself may be in the slums.

"Man has tried three ways to find the soul. The first way is by living only in the dining-room—develop the body, give it great tasks and sufferings. This way is called Fakirism, practiced by uneducated men. If by some accident one of these fakirs finds a way to a soul, it would be only one man out of a thousand and it would take him fifty years.

"Another way is via the drawing-room, or Monkism. Here by the feeling center and psychic experiences, men have tried to find a soul via religion.

"Only one from a thousand might succeed, but it would take him, if he did, only twenty-five years. Then he could pass to the bedroom. The best way of the three is the third room, the bedroom, or mental center, via knowledge. Here, *if* he succeeds, it would take him about ten years. This is called Yogism.

"But there is a Fourth Way. This also is called Yogism, but it is different because this kind of yogi has a secret by 'heredity'—initiate secrets. By this way, with a teacher, a man with the possibility can do the work in six months and then be his own teacher.

"I am the representative of the Fourth Way. And I have no *concurrent* (rival). For instance, ordinary yogis who do not know these secrets lie for three hours a day to learn how to use air. With my secret short-cuts they could do this in five minutes—in fact, like magic, drink the active elements they need from air out of a glass.

"Man as he is has three or four personalities instead of one 'I.' Each day he is a different person, depending on which center is the day's center of gravity. Only after he has made his 'I' can he begin to develop a soul; and unless he does this, he will die the merde he was born."

He interrupted here to give the example of the rivers again, and concluded:

"Before man can make a bathroom, his 'I' room, he must first repair his old apartment. Sometimes it is cheaper to make a whole new one, throw out all the furniture, furnish each room again, with each new object in its proper place. Then the bathroom can be made and it will be a place to bring up a baby in, with ordered rooms for the purpose of living in order.

"I am the architect for apartments—I examine old apartment, the neighborhood, I tell what reparations must be made and the estimate of the work."

Miss Gordon said that our experience with him now is incredible—he has never in twelve years spoken directly to anyone. He said to me, "You must stop automatic personality gestures." Twice when he saw tears in my eyes he said, "That process proceeds automatically." He also said, "No good when *not* cry sometimes. Your stink-source (he spoke of Alice who was being recalcitrant) never cry except for self."

21

Miss Gordon brought a woman for lunch—tall, spare, French, but lives in England and India; interested in yogis, vegetables, against alcohol and tobacco. He said, "You are stupid. You not understand what I say, you not even listen." She said, "I didn't hear the last part of what you said." He said, "Not even first part, no intelligent look on your face. Even when man not understand, he can have lively look for trying." He made her eat meat and drink Armagnac with him. He said, "Every thinking man—and by man I also mean woman—*must* be occupied only by this interest—to develop a soul." And, "It is as important to compose a dish in its correctly-blended elements as a composition of music or the colors in painting. Harmony in scale. Must have much knowledge to be a good cook. A culinary doctor."

Friday, January 17

He said at luncheon, "There are three kinds of onanism; the Greeks called them onanism, Platonism, and Socratism. Now you, Miss Gordon, if you were sick from too much of this, a doctor who knew you would look at you and say which kind it was before he could cure you. Each center has its onanism. Man lost his tail because of titillation in three centers." Speaking of intensity he said, "Kiss till last breath."

He said he might add one more person to our group of four. (He did not, however. We are all tied to one rope and together we must climb the mountain, he said. Miss Gordon is becoming a professional squelcher at table—she doesn't care for levity, even his! He took a tube of blood from my arm for "detailed examination." We all brought him urine in bottles wrapped, at his instruction, in black paper and a sample of our saliva. He gave us all an exercise together which we do from one to five hours a day! Besides I have the other to do also.

Tuesday, January 21

His toast to us for journey up that mountain: "Let God—not your Jewish God—or devil—not *your* devil—help you return from your journey with feeling all body deserving." At night he talked:

"Man has wish or desire but not possibility of doing what he wishes or desires. This is not his fault for such he is made. Even if he makes a promise and breaks it, it is not his fault. Either not his fault or we are all guilty.

"For wishing and doing, man is made in two separate parts. And such is the law concerning the operation of these parts that the more he may wish to do with one part of him, the less he can do in this doing part, even with constant struggles.

"For a young person, boy or girl, nature will help in the effort to *do*, so the person will not have to struggle as will a person of responsible age. After a certain age, this effort is very difficult and often impossible. But there is an artificial aid by means of physico-chemical substances. By the way, for example, a substance can be injected which will furnish artificial help for effort, for prayer. Or artificial help for effort in some other place. For everyone a different quantity necessary which must correspond with the amount of effort made by the individual. If the effort and the amount of this chemical are not balanced, it becomes a dangerous poison for the organism.

"If each of you decide to work on with me, you must now be ready to give up all outside life—no engagements, no cinemas. You must always be ready to be here with me at all times, at any moment I call for you."

Thursday, January 23

He said, "I am colleague of life. Only two things not spoiled by age— Armagnac and carpets."

He asked each what she had experienced from the exercise.

Alice said, "Confusion."

He said, "You mean shame? Real meaning of this is shame. You find out with shame you are not like what you thought you were like?"

"Yes."

"Very good, that tells me much about your new beginning. Already you make twenty-five percent advance. You know about new birth, the resurrection religions speak about? You must first die to be born, and now you begin that."

Katie said she had found out things about herself in the exercise that she had not known before and she thought it was because he had deprived her of cigarettes.

He said, "Then you already know that a million dollars not buy what you find out from not having just one cigarette. You must now put the wish for cigarettes into your wish for being. And this is useful for all of you. Say four times daily, 'I wish the result of this suffering to be my own for being.' "

To me he said, "Kanari, your result bad, very bad. That can be psychopathic and I even must measure take. Tomorrow when I get analysis of blood I can tell what element necessary. If some years from now you have result such you tell me, that means you could cure wound in few hours. But now you could know nothing, it must be your imagination."

Friday, January 24[*]

First task.

GURDJIEFF: We emanate all the time. This flows out from us—task is to keep from flowing out.

At first, can only *imagine* you not let emanations flow out—but this imagination makes begin data for second body and all this will pass over into the real thing, later.

We must have within us, *unchangeable source*.

This holding-in of emanations will make energy for unchangeable source. Now, as average man, we have many sources instead of just one from which flow all active initiative. Unchangeable source for which we work can be compared to the "I," though not same thing. Just as we have many I's which each day, each hour, take the initiative with us, so we have many sources which give many kinds of impetus and so we have disharmony. We have not one strong central aim with one strong corresponding impetus, but many aims, many sources for impetus. Unchangeable source important, also for garmony.

Questions after twenty-four hours of trying to achieve withholding emanations: I said, "Very very difficult for me—cannot do even forty seconds of this work without having associations start and so must stop work in order to cope with associations."

GURDJIEFF: Can *never* make stop associations; as long as you are breathing there are associations, these are aftomatic. Therefore, in this task, must not try stop associations—let them flow but not be active. With other part of mind you work at new task and this is ac-

---

tive. Pretty soon you find you have beginnings of new kind of brain, a new one for this new kind of mentation and that other one becomes entirely passive.

SOLITA: In this work, it's difficult for me to be aware of my body as a whole, it seems the center of gravity for me is always in the solar plexus and so I am more aware of emanation from that part of the body.

GURDJIEFF: Very important you know body as a whole, for this work, very important. If divide attention then not good. What you do is this: imagine center of gravity on shoulders—*theenk* it there.

He talks about sensing the body *as a whole*. He leaves the room: "Now you all titillate until I come back." When he returns, he hears Alice saying, "And my eyes close when I do this exercise, and *I look inward* . . ."

He tells us about *inner vision*—something very important in this work. Alice has this faculty psychopathically—he tells her she must do it exact from opposite. "Do this only when you have conscious wish to do, as now is, you do aftomatically. Just do opposite way around." He tells Miss Gordon she must begin to make data for this kind of thing.

GURDJIEFF: How begin—look at an object, then suddenly shut eyes and go on seeing it, without any break. Any break in attention when shutting eyes, means you must begin again. Must without break in attention, go on seeing inwardly exact details of what last saw . . . and this all makes for inner vision, which becomes power in time. Was time, thirty years ago, when I could split that table with thought.

I geev toast, not idiot toast, first time in long time I geev such toast: "Whom God (not your Jewish God, but God you not know about) and devil (not devil you know about but other devil)—Whom God and devil help, *may he return with feeling, all body deserving*." (Start of "journey" toast.)

And these small begin things that we do, make data, and we on our part have taken a vow, *not to be average*, not to be man in quotation marks, but be real man, *one who can do . . . and then can be what is*.

You like my formulation? Good formulation, don't you think? Look Canary, a writer, but all her life cannot think phrase like that.

And so is Crocodile writer—different kind. Canary she write with delicatesse; Crocodile, she write with axe.

Saturday, January 25

Noon meeting, discussion first.

GURDJIEFF: What you find now?

[*Alice says she finds within herself, since beginning the holding emanations exercise, "a great confusion."*]

What confusion? What mean thees word? Maybe you mean shame?"

ALICE: Yes, shame—that expresses better . . .

GURDJIEFF: Ah, thees very important theeng. She have shame—shame with mind for how is all of self. Now perhaps this shame will go in all centrum and then she realize how is? She realize *her insignificance as man.*

And what is? Ees sheet. Then she die—man must die to resurrect. But cannot die until realize insignificance. So I say that she have twenty-five percent possibility—is twenty-five percent along way to die, because she have shame, and if this shame proceed from mind to other centrum, then she will know what she is, how is *her* insignificance. Know insignificance of self is extremely difficult; example, like try imagine one's own death. Can imagine Mr. Smith being killed, but never self being killed. So it is with insignificance. Can know this about other person, but not about self.

I tell Gurdjieff that in the exercise, I get mixed with my task about cigarettes (not smoking for a week to see what new flow of associations results) and that I seem for the moment to learn more of myself through cigarette abstinence. Example: I discover I have wild animals, I discover "it" is very crafty, never once has even the word cigarette come up in my mind, imagination never produces a picture of a cigarette, and I can look on friends smoking without feeling anything. All while "it" is suffering for a cigarette—but a very cunning crafty animal I have, which spends great craft covering up its desires.

GURDJIEFF: This can be thing for power. I tell you one very important thing to say each time when longing come. At first you say and maybe notice nothing. Second time, maybe nothing. Third time, maybe notice something. Say, "I wish that the force of my wishing be my own, for being." [*Then he thinks.*] No, better another way. Force such as this have special results—make chemicals, have special emanations. Better say, "I wish result of this my suffering be my own for being." Yes, can call that kind wishing suffering, because *is* suffering. This saying can maybe take force from animal and geev to being . . . and can do this for many things—for any denial of something that is a *slavery.**

Saturday, January 25

Another examination and the following talk from him:

"We have three tapeworms, one organic, one in feeling center, and one in mental center. Miss Gordon has English tapeworm. That is why I say to her every day, 'Ah, this food is not like your English frozen beef, your kippers.'

"We must make preparatory work to have one 'I' not three. The work you will do now will give you unchangeable source for achieving one 'I,' for taking the quotation marks from your 'I.' Then you will not be a different person every day, but always one person with one aim.

"Active mentation and later pondering come just from the new processes you are about to exercise and from which you will receive results. Active of mind cannot be without taking this exercise in new feeling. And together with it, the mind. But not mind meditating like monk or philosopher. A little of this new process put in the mind and you already will have beginning of active mentation. Discussion with others is no good. Only discussion with yourself on this new activity is important. But you must not philosophize. Later I will explain everything. You cannot keep out associations. Let them flow on. You can never be without or you would die. But put them in separate place. Pay no *attention* to them, but put your *intention* on new activity. For each one it will be different and you must each ask questions so I can direct you differently. For instance, Alice has too much of one psychopathic thing. This same thing Miss Gordon not have enough of. They must just opposite make. Kanari has too much in solar plexus. She must put attention on shoulders for this exercise. All parts must be made harmonic or bad results will be received.

---

* End Katie's Notes.

"Two kinds of vision we have—outer world and inner, the inner world of man. There is an exercise of looking at an object, closing the eyes and still seeing it go on. This, for example, is for Miss Gordon very important, and if she forgets when she closes her eyes, she must leave off and begin again. This one is not for me. The kind of power I have, does not need that exercise. Thirty years ago I had it so much that I could split that table in two from a distance, if I so wished, and kill a large animal like a yak.

"Religion says believe, and uses words like love, hope, faith. I say to you, believe nothing, trust nothing, hope for nothing, love nothing. Yet I am a very religious man."

About this time I saw two examples of Mr. Gurdjieff's "power" which I have decided to disclose. One day after luncheon, he led me into his room and told me to stand at the window with my back to him. He remained at the door.

He said, "Relax all body. If head or any part wishes to move, let move. I wish make experiment and at same time give you something."

In a few seconds, my head began to move from side to side and up and down, slowly. Then a wide hot ray or wave struck my neck with force and moved down, then up my spine. Startled, I said, "Oh, you're touching me!"

"No," he replied from the door.

A minute later he said, "Now enough."

He left the room with no explanation and never referred to this again.

Another example—I brought him a woman with creeping paralysis who had been given up by all doctors in London and Switzerland. They said she would die within the year. Mr. Gurdjieff said he could not cure her because "screw" was broken, but he could save her life. Every day he or I gave her injections and he taught me how to treat her with a complicated electric machine that had to be polarized differently on different days. She walked with great difficulty, dragging her feet. One day he told me to bring her into his room. I helped her in a chair and started toward the door.

He said to me, "Not necessary go."

I turned at the moment his arm stretched toward her and downward in a swift gesture.

"Dormez, madame," he said.

Her eyes closed at once. For perhaps three or four minutes he stood before her, passing his hands from her head to her feet, at the distance of two feet, or less. Then he called, "Madame!" and she opened her eyes. After a question or two about her health, he told me to take her away. I went to assist her, but she rose from her chair and walked quickly to the door, to the front door, down the stairs and into the street. I caught her up and walked by her side.

"Je me demande pourquoi il n'a rien fait pour moi aujourd'hui," (I wonder why he didn't do anything for me today) she said. *She did not know she had slept, she did not notice she was walking.*

In the taxi she scarcely spoke, left it without my aid (usually it was necessary for me and the chauffeur both, to get her in or out of a car) and at her hotel she easily climbed the stairs.

Finally I said to her, "You seem to be walking better today."

"*Tiens*, why so I am."

The next morning she was as before. Part of this mystery is that she never once, then or later, asked me what had happened. She did not ever walk again, nor did she die. She is living in Switzerland today.*

Sunday, January 26[†]

Last night, dinner at Gurdjieff's apartment. Solita, Jane Heap, Alice, Miss Gordon and myself—Gabo as always. He has made special boiled potatoes for Jane, also an egg dish—a kind of omelette with asparagus stuffing (sugar on our portions, none on Jane's).

One thing comes up towards the end of dinner.

GURDJIEFF: How is tapeworm?

JANE: Tapeworm lie down exhausted.

GURDJIEFF: No, you know what tapeworm do? He shake head, like thees [*and he shakes his head slowly back and forth*] and you know what happen? Vibration from head-shaking go to stomach nerve, start stomach nerve vibrating and then tapeworm, because stomach nerve vibrating, want food again.

A time later, Gurdjieff turns to Alice and starts the story about the "lake in hell" where should sit in water-closet liquid, up to chin level, crying "come slowly, oh please come slowly" to each new

---

* Died August 1954.
† Katie's Notes.

29

Jane Heap

Gurdjieff in the mid-thirties

soul coming into the lake, who might stir up ripples on the surface (which comes to lip level of those condemned to sit in it).

Gurdjieff says at the beginning of this story, "Vibration of tape-worm head-shaking make me think of thees lake, you know thees lake?" . . . he proceeds with the story, and I proceed to question my-self—is there any connection between this frightful "lake in hell" story and the tapeworm?

Today, Sunday, I go to Café de la Paix to see if there are plans. I find him sitting alone and I'm invited to sit at his table. He tells me the Ford car deal is off, money arrangements are too complicated "and thees too bad because it was car which correspond very good for me." Then he asks how Jane survived his food, what we talked about afterwards, "how titillate" and his word "titillate" brings back what he said last night, how he likes this word, how it can be used always "censor-ly" in his book, but no one realizes this (except him) because no one realizes it means masturbate.

And words, philology, another association flows. Last night at the dinner table—how he tells us about the phrase he especially likes—"tail of donkey" and how in the Third Series he wrote much about this phrase which has no equivalent in French . . . how he cannot say "queue de l'âne" in French because it means something dirty "and this phrase for me very lovely." "Very perhaps" is his phrase that Jane likes. "First-able" is Miss Gordon's special favorite.

Today at lunch he spends a full quarter hour trying to find from Gabo the exact meaning of a Russian word he has used talking with Miss Gordon. He has told her she is —— because she sneak up and steal from his store of food . . . and he works and works with us all to get the exact meaning. Finally he gets the dictionary but it is "old Russian word" and not found in his Russian dictionary, though he does find a root that means "infamous wretch." He says, "Does that mean *small-false*? This word I use, old Russian, mean small-false, mean make false in small ways. All I can think of in English is *dirty-dog-ness*, that perhaps exact meaning in English. In Russian is a *big* word, only old Russian."

Today at lunch we ate "twenty-first salad in Third Series," the "visa on your passport for journey," said Gurdjieff. I could identify tomatoes, parsley, leek, onion, horseradish and preiselberry sauce, some curry . . .

Today we read Arch Absurd and part of Arch Preposterous. Gurd-jieff explains about Okidanokh the common-cosmic-Active-Element

31

and at table tells us that his cabbage soup is very important for Okidanokh, for Active Element, more important than all rest of the meal. So I "keep company" with him for a second bowl.*

Thursday, January 30

He says that half our waking hours must be spent on his exercises. Jane Heap came from London and went with us to dinner. The Rope had piqûres. He said his work would soon be done and then he would go away, travel, dance the fox-trot and we could all suffer as he has suffered. Said how he hated to take people's stink money. To me he said, "After this if I ask you for your left eye, you must bring me it in paper, and your last teaspoon of merde." Tomorrow Katie's drinks go the way of cigarettes. No more Armagnac for me in four days. Toward the end of the dinner, I casually brought out my puff and powdered my nose. Mr. Gurdjieff nearly leaped from his chair. The gist of what he said to me:

"I am Oriental and man. Never can I see woman making prostitute thing without my insides turning over. Never has woman sat my presence and painted face. I see you make now six times and each time if I had had knife in my hand, I wish send it through your heart. This is seven times and finish. At Prieuré no woman even dare smoke before me. This idiot fashion put paint on face exist only New York and in territory around Place de l'Opéra. Only prostitute make in other places. If you wish make this thing, you must in water-closet go as if to make merde, and not make merde in my salon. What your father and your brother say to you ten years ago if you paint face in their presence? Now you must remember that you are one of Mr. Gurdjieff's people and pupil. Me, I am Gurdjieff, and compared me you are merde nonentity." He made himself look terrifying, veins stood out on his forehead as he shouted. Then he made a ceremony of apologizing to me, Miss Gordon, Jane Heap, and Alice in turn. He said, "Now Kanari hate me, she hate me for two days."

Sunday, February 2†

First ride in Gurdjieff's new car—Paris to Rouen in nothing flat. Speedometer at one hundred and ten per hour nearly all the way.

---

* End Katie's Notes.
† Katie's Notes.

Once I constated a speed of one hundred and twenty and Gurdjieff himself promised one hundred and thirty-five after he has had the car a week. Every possible kind of motor-accident death passed us by—I had to decide categorically to non-identify with all I knew and felt about cars otherwise I would have been wrecked. Alice says she did the emanation-holding exercises en route.

Once, Gurdjieff stopped for a view over a wide valley beyond Orgeval, where Normandie begins and said, "It gives a feeling of *wide*"— and that was exactly what happened to one when one looked.

Lunch in the farmhouse at Pont de l'Arche with his two friends, Papavitchka and the Doctor. Such charm and such goodness and reality in these people, we felt odd and strange, painfully unaccustomed. I told Gurdjieff that they made me want to cry "because forget was this kind of real people on earth."

We left Paris at half past eleven and were back at quarter past seven—Rouen and return in something like five hours, for we had about three hours out for coffees, shopping in St. Germain market, shopping and coffee-ing again in Rouen and lunch at the farm.

In Café de la Paix Gurdjieff started talking about roses, roses, how he felt. How next week would be thorns, thorns when the fourteen thousand francs becomes due on the car. But thorns, thorns in outer world were good because then there were roses, roses in inner world. "Is law—for one dissatisfaction, always a satisfaction." Then he asked which I think would he rather have roses, roses in his inner world or in his outer world . . . then when I answered, he decided that was too complicated a question. He said, "Better I tell you one thing. This make you rich for life, richer than your Mr. Rockefeller. There are *two* 'struggles'—inner world struggle and outer world struggle, but never can these two make contact. To make data for third world, not even God can give this possibility for contact between outer world struggle and inner world struggle, not even your heredity. Only *one* thing—must make *intentional contact* between outer world struggle and inner world struggle. Then can make data which crystallize for third world of man, sometimes called world of soul. Understand?"

We said, "Not quite, but get the taste."

I said, "One thing I cannot think about—cannot think about this *intentional contact*."

Gurdjieff shook his head and said, "Ah, that too far ahead, too far ahead for you yet."

33

But later, he said, "I can geev small example which maybe give you *taste* of this *intentional contact*. You, for example, your cigarettes. You have outer world struggle—not take, not buy, remember always, break habit, and also, you have inner world struggle about same thing. With inner world you can imagine how it was when you smoke—you imagine in a different way, more keen, and with more longing, and it seem even, with this inner world imagining, even more desirable than it ever could be. You have made this cigarette intentional contact between the two struggles, and even by this small thing will you make data for third world, for world of soul as is sometimes said. This not exact example—I have chapter on intentional contact in Third Series but this enough to give you taste of what is.*

Tuesday, February 4

Katie and Alice returned from a motor trip with him, haggard with fear. Katie reports he said, "Which would you choose—all roses, roses or all thorns, thorns? One for inner life, the other for outer? If both thorns you choose, an intentional contact can be made."

At dinner he said, "Just like home" about something.

Jane said in low voice, "Home Sweet Home."

He pounced, "What's that you say?"

"Just a song we have in America."

"Song—ugh—idiot song—sweet home—ugh—just like your America. Not know what home is. Only in Orient know what is home, what is real hospitality. When in my house you sit, it is yours, even my soul is yours, such is guest in Asiatic country."

At table Alice remarked, "I am simple."

He said, "No one simple. One kind of person says 'I am simple,' another kind feels he is simple, another kind tries to act simple. No simple person—all are idiots. Simple idiots and complicated idiots."

Alice said, "I liked that man who was here last night. He had a kind face."

"Yes, he is kind. When he is asleep. Everyone kind when he has a need. But see what he is when you tread on his tender corns."

He said, "Two kinds of nerves—high and low." He gave Alice medicine for high kind. After piqûres and reading, he said, "Kanari

---

* End Katie's Notes.

writer of delicatesse but I think Krocodile write with axe." He talked again about man as "apartment."

Said the exercise we are doing "will let fresh air in the rooms and drive out stink; for years apartments not aired; people use dining-room for water-closet, leave there on floor, have dirty banquets, break furniture. And in every room there are also many other compartments—all stink."

About now, it may be of "subjective" interest to note that I feel slightly mad from those two meals a day, my two jobs, these notes I keep, the exercises; I'm unkempt from head to foot, no sleep, look drawn and quartered, hurt all over. I've refused to go on the trip to Evian and Geneva . . .

Thursday, February 6

Reading before and after dinner. Mr. Gurdjieff talked about proper mixing of food and showed us a scale of seven notes in spices—brought out seven bags from the store room and named them do, re, mi, etc. This scale is very bad for all but me. Alice in bed, Katie "upset"; he told both to take enema last night and gave a talk on proper method. "Even cleans up psyche. First must inject four glasses, then eight, then sixteen, last time twenty-five. One time I injected fifty-four glasses, held while chopped tree.

"Everybody astonished," he said. (Katie bravely tried the sixteen but she burst on twelfth.) He said all "lower" floors purified by this process, as much law as bath or washing face. In the midst of dinner he stopped and looked at a guest. "I can't eat my pudding—I swallow and it stick half way. Must wait for new process to make go down. Such is effect on me of Mees X's vibrations."

Monday, February 10

We went to the café to say goodbye, but the car was out of order (already) and he invited all to the flat for lunch. After he gave us a new exercise. "If ever you tell this, terrible punishment for one who tell will happen. Don't know how or why this happens, but always is so, like a law." After piqûres, he packed cold food, bought a sweater, and we found a sweater, scarf, and gloves for the old "Senator" he was taking along—also Nicholai. The car wasn't ready until seven o'clock, so we had to go again to the café to say goodbye. Finally he got off into the bitter cold night, bound for Sens without even a blanket in the car. While he's gone, I'm reading all the alchemists and catching up on work and sleep. Xenophon defined the "I" as the compound result of consciousness, subconsciousness, and instinct. Certainly simpler than "a relatively transferable arising depending on the quality of the functioning of thought, feeling, and organic automatism."

Saturday, February 29

Noel Murphy, friend, handsome, chic, Park Avenue type, went to the café with me to see him.

"Why do I have headaches all the time?"

He looked at her through his glasses and said, "Liver. Come lunch."

At lunch he said to her, "You are combination camel and sparrow. I not understand why Kanari call you friend. I know very well psyche Kanari. Also I have made special study of camel properties during forty years. Never can two such animals be friends—is not basis of friend. Now I look to see if you are male camel or female camel. I not know yet. But I know even what kind of merde you make. You ever see camel merde? Small hard rounds, no scientist ever understand why merde like that. But I know. I also study strange sex organ female camel have."

Poor Noel turned red and white, but took it well. Later she said she was going to the Opera that night.

"No, not go, such music only titillation."

"What's that?"

He told her.

She said, "Oh, I don't mind that, do you?"

He looked at her a long time and did not reply.

We're having a pause in the piqûres and taking two medicines each, all different. The day he stopped the piqûres he gave us an examination on "How feel?"

Katie said, "Oh, wonderful, body gladness, I get up in the morning and sing."

He said, "Well, I often hear of crocodile tears but never before of crocodile song. And you, Kanari?"

"Stronger, but sad all the time."

He was delighted. "I have been expecting that from you; is as I thought. This is remorse of conscience and only the beginning. You will be much more sad later, as should be for your merde life you have lived."

Later he said, "High sex combined with laziness of organism." And, "Even God cannot tell where will find what lost."

Wednesday, March 25

At the café he said to me, "You must now live in suffering between two worlds, the two worlds of man. You must die in first, be resurrected in second, and only then live in both."

"If only I had something solid to build on. Cannot even explain inner state."

"Yes, no words for these things. But say anything you wish and I will understand from intonation . . . I have made first stone foundation. You can be objectively happy now. Look at those people there in street. You have something they not have. Later I will put second gravity stone. Then third, up to seven. You need no longer say you will try. That is over and now you have only to do and do. Later I can tell you what I must not yet tell. Imagination has always been your weakness and your enemy. Must now take off quotation marks (imagination), forget it and hate it. And you must see what your old friends are like. No one who liked you before must like you now—must hate you. Your friends are all special merde. Seeing their merdeness will help you see your own. Man has two mentations and you know what kind I wish for you. Only now is being-data being crystallized in you. In past, everything rolled off like water from back of goose. All went in and out again."

At dinner my toast was, "Although past was merde, let future not be."

Then he said, "Take exercise, but not one-part exercise like horse or bicycle. Swim in water or climb mountain—climb with two watermelons under arms." He said, "The total sum of vibrations from all organs in whole person makes a subjective chord." And, "Good wishing is effective from great distance—bad wishing also." And, "Here is old Russian prayer: 'May God kill all people who not make merde in the morning, loud noise at noon, and *so*-so in evening.' Krocodile, you make good translation for this—find words. I not ask Kanari, she too naïve."

He described the great storehouse of food in his childhood home—butter was kept underground (he used to steal it) and fresh vegetables were buried in the sand.

He gave a talk on objective and subjective satisfaction which I cannot reproduce, such was my emotion for its beauty. I only remember the sheep. "Poor sheep never have husband—except in passing, a by-the-way husband—never knows a life with husband by her side in old age; and if she does not have subjective satisfaction from him from making lamb, she will be unhappy all her life. Then often she is killed before the lamb is born and cheated of that too." ... "Woman is like leaf—responds to nature in the spring if she is nine years old or ninety-nine."

GURDJIEFF: Do you know first property of monkey?

KATIE: Perhaps imitation?

GURDJIEFF: No.

KATIE: Look-and-forget?

GURDJIEFF: No. Titillation ... Here is law. If a person is quick in all things he will be slow in one thing; if slow in all things, quick in one ... Injustice for one person sometimes bear good fruit for many other persons ... Tapeworm is more clever than man.

Woman's heart is placed just below navel. Agree with me, Kanari?

KANARI: No.

"Dreaming idiot," he said during the toasts. "To dream in life is merde, but when know consciously of what is good to dream, then good thing to dream." He said everyone in Hollywood was a Hasnamuss and if he were king he would take them all to the dog pound and make them into soap. For Easter in old Greek and Russian churches there is this prayer: "Essence through imagination—nature presents life; this is truth of all truthfulness." ... "Do something useful or do nothing—don't be American." ... "Do not use the word 'think'; it is property of onanist."

*Friday, May 1**

GURDJIEFF: I can have relation with one atom of active element as with friend, as with man—can command, make do—so now for me is interesting how you are. I make picture.

---

* Katie's Notes.

[He wants an exact description of each small symptom observed. "How is . . ."]

I make go here there, like soldiers. Then when nothing left to do, begin something else. When two opposite soldiers stand same place, nothing left to do, they begin eat each other. This is a law of mechanic life. Soon in you, I make civil war.

When you do a thing, do with whole self, *one thing at a time*. Now I sit here and I eat. For me nothing exist in world except this food, this table. I eat with whole attention. So you must do in everything. When you write letter, do not at same time think what cost laundering of that shirt—when you compute laundering cost, do not think about the letter you must write. Everything has it's time. To be *able* to do *one thing at a time*—this is property of man, not man in quotation marks.

You ask about sleep, you have impulse for sleep with new medicine. Is best not try fight wish for sleep. *Nature knows more than a hundred doctors*. Is all right if you *sleep*—not half sleep, half dream. Sleep with whole self, one thing at a time. Maybe you wish sleep because some accumulator in you is run out—this I give is a general thing and perhaps some special part of you, some special place, have no energy. This can be accumulated in you only when in absolute passive state, in sleep. So you wish sleep.

Tuesday, May 5

He comes in from Rouen, phones from the café at half past seven, "Come at half past eight," and when we arrive he has a big dinner all ready. Since there was no food in the house, therefore for this dinner, "all new, begin from new." In one hour he has bought and prepared:

Hors d'œuvres.
Baked dish, pasta and meat.
Saffron potatoes.
Baked baby lamb.
Soup.
A thin pudding dessert (*best ever tasted*).

"Ekh, ekh . . . so tired . . . last night Rouen not sleep, trains pass. Today long drive. But in one way is good thing be so tired. Can feel now what nonentity is body. Can look through it and see is sheet, can look and find in middle a pearl, the small earned active part—

your I. This gives a happy feeling, is good part of being so tired—to look through and find this pearl—*your earned part.*"

Gurdjieff tells of a prayer which is recited in the Orthodox Christian Church, from Easter until Ascension Day, "*until time when he fly.*" Impossible to translate, he gives exact: "*Essence through imagination, nature presents life, this is truth of old truthness.*" (I have only remembered three lines of it.)

Wednesday, May 6

He gives each of us a bottle of scent, an objective scent which he has composed, makes light all the sorrow of inner world. He speaks about gladness:

"Is two kinds—gladness with reason, gladness without reason. Science explain gladness without reason (only kind we know) psychologically, but is not so. Is chemical thing. Something happen, associations start, change organic functionings. All an automatic flowing, cause result—result is gladness. Feeling of gladness is not anything over which we have any control. Is mathematical sequence, done in us."

Friday, May 7

Gurdjieff expresses a wish for us—Miss Gordon, Solita, and myself with such quiet depth of feeling that I wish to weep, hearing him.

He is talking about his favorite word, a "good word," and how he has said it again and again to us, "sheet, sheet *and* sheet."

"*I wish you be not like sheet*, so first I make you feel like sheet, only from there can one begin. Average normal man have factors. You have none. Americans and English especially. I give exercises to crystallize for factors. Psyche of man is built up on factors. So to have psyche must have factors. Americans have none, are like burro. With my inner world I see a burro. English like sheep, I see a sheep, and French—donkey. For each, with my inner world, I have different relation. Burro, sheep, donkey, is different thing. But I not let them see is different thing. My inner world is *my* world. Is property of man that he never can do what he plan a week ago, an hour ago."

At table he talks, in the mood of being halfway along on our journey. He pictures to us how it will be, our suffering and discomfort.

To Miss Gordon: "Remember about chair? Leave one . . . not yet arrive at next? I pity you. I picture what suffering you will have. I cannot lift you to next chair. I can show way to go, or to right, or to left. Oh, to others you will seem to sit but *how* you sit only your inner self will know. And what suffering, your inner self. I picture to myself how will be for you. I feel sorry."

Sunday, May 24

GURDJIEFF: How you like soup, Sardine?

SARDINE: I think it is very good.

GURDJIEFF: Think—*theenk*—we not use that word. "I think" is property of onanist.

All life is a stage and man is one of two things—is meat (for manure, etc.) or is actor. To learn role is intelligence, to be able to play role is what intelligence mean. (This he says to me when I forget to rise and toast Miss Gordon as "Your Reverence.")

You see, what I tell you do is only joke thing, but it is role I give you to play. If forget for joke thing, how can remember for real thing? You see, I wish you not be meat.

May

About the end of the month, Margaret Anderson and Georgette Leblanc returned to Paris from the Midi and sometimes came to lunch.*

GURDJIEFF: [*speaking to Sardine*] Never I see squirming fish get back to sea—always finish on sand.

MARGARET: Mr. Gurdjieff, you said Louise is combination sardine and wart. What is wart?

GURDJIEFF: Now I put question which will be exercise for your mentation. What is mushroom?

MARGARET: I don't know.

GURDJIEFF: At night you go in field and there is nothing; in morning is big mushroom. When you know what they are, then you will know what is wart.

MARGARET: Then what is she?

GURDJIEFF: She is wart.

MARGARET: Then what is wart?

---

* The following notes (two pages) were made in combination with Katie (Krockodile).

Georgette Leblanc

Margaret Anderson

GURDJIEFF: She is wart.

Later he said, "Devil and angel have more vanity than man. If you are clever, have cunningness, you can make them your slaves. Now Kanari not look on me like cow on barn door, but like burro. Burro have good inside, have clean impartial look. Mouse also have same look in eye—not baby mouse but responsible mouse. Such look you even want to kiss."

Margaret has chosen zigzag for her idiot.

GURDJIEFF: You cannot be zigzag.

MARGARET: But that is my condition now.

GURDJIEFF: Condition? Your condition has nothing to do with inner world. You defile zigzag. Wish go too high. Zigzag is high idiot, goes this way, that way, struggles against merde he knows he is. Is as if you, a deacon, put on archbishop's robes. Idiots best book I wrote. [*To Miss Gordon:*] You superior idiot, have been for years, never change. You are monster.

Saturday, May 30

Alice arrives for dinner in a very nervous state—she has seen an autobus crush a boy on a bicycle.

GURDJIEFF: All things happen around you in life, but you now are obliged to be able to take from each. Save such feelings you have for when something happens to a near one.

ALICE: But the boy had such a beautiful face.

GURDJIEFF: Ah, boy is boy.

ALICE: And I remembered the time I was struck and dragged by an automobile.

GURDJIEFF: That is worse. That is egotism. Egotism for present is dirty thing. Egotism for future is property of real man. Try understand, this very important thing. Miss Gordon, you know what is *lawable*? [*She says something like "increasing tension."*] No. Why you think must be increasing? Can be opposite also, like in music, crescendo, decrescendo. Important thing is that *all together make the total.*

[*Gurdjieff and Krocodile are discussing "genealogy" of crippled Frenchwoman.*]

Under surface with her you will find a shepherd always, no matter where be, how live, how dress, how high in world. (She is a countess.) While for me, I always a "fantasist-scientist."

KROCODILE: A fisherman.

GURDJIEFF: Yes, a fisherman.

KROCODILE: Then you can make good business with her, make a trade, fifty-fifty, fisherman and shepherd.

GURDJIEFF: [laughing] Now this begin flowing in me association. Look at Thin-One (Alice), she not understand how we talk, we talk in images. Have you word in English for talk-in-images? If can find word I can tell a saying. There is old Persian saying, "Such kind of talking, talking-in-images, makes the nightingale full." Can you understand?

KROCODILE: Not quite, but we can get the taste. It has charm.

GURDJIEFF: Yes, is very beautiful.

*Friday, June 5**

Alice and I go to the café to see if he is back from Rouen. He is there with Miss Gordon.

ALICE: Glad to see you back, Mr. Gurdjieff, we just heard on the radio there was no gasoline.

GURDJIEFF: Was none already on road. Nowhere for sale. (No further elucidation of how he got the car to Paris!)

[*I tell him about seeing the Carrousel bridge workers strike last night, how they walked around, fists in air, singing Internationale. He listens attentively.*]

In next forty-eight hours anything can happen. Everything can broke or burn as was in Moscow. Big misunderstanding can be received because of no newspapers—people out in country think something happen here, people here think something happen out there. Suggestibility.

[*We speak about errands.*]

Yes, buy candle. Buy big piece of bread, and water you can find. Then have all that is necessary. I accustom to revolution, for me is simple thing, all life I have had. Bravo Moscow . . . (Using exact same intonation as when he says "Bravo Perrier!")

---

* Katie's Notes.

All Knachtschmidt and Company* lunch. With food shortage threatened, this is what we have:

Hors d'œuvres (platter of fresh greens, Kurdistan cheese, pastourma, fresh cucumber, canned eggplant with stuffing of pimento, and carrot).

Two soups—one "a phenomenon soup."

Special rice made with apricots and raisins, etc.

Roast baby lamb.

Fraises des bois with fresh cream.

Latvian chocolates and Syrian loucoum.

Fruit.

Turkish coffee.

Special individual honey cake.

Armagnac—up to and including squirming idiot toast.

GURDJIEFF: My restaurant is good.

CANARY: You always have customers for such food, even when other restaurants empty.

GURDJIEFF: Only difference my restaurant, here cost many zeros to eat. Food much better, yes. But also cost ten times more here.

[*After a while he looks at me.*]

Why is this a good thing?

[*I think of the two aspects of his restaurant, good food but also ten times more expensive, but cannot formulate answer.*]

GURDJIEFF: Any simple person could answer. *Because he flow from just.*

[*He speaks about money.*]

From first gravity guest on my left (Margaret Anderson) there comes a terrible vibration.

MARGARET: But you know why, Mr. Gurdjieff.

GURDJIEFF: I not know.

MARGARET: But you can imagine.

GURDJIEFF: Excuse, I cannot Imagine. *You* can imagine, but I cannot. I am old man. Thirty years ago I could imagine, even was time I imagine I was God—or your Uncle Sam. [*Sardine is staring at him.*] Look how she look at me. [*Someone says, "Like calf?"*]

GURDJIEFF: No, not like calf—calf always something have in vision—future cow.

[*He rags Miss Gordon.*]

---

* See page 245 for Gurdjieff's explanation of this phrase.

She not believe I know more about her English than Shakespeare. Long, long ago Shakespeare was my pupil. I teach everything, then one day I chick-make. And now history has Shakespeare epoch and nobody know he was mama-and-papa-darling.

[*Canary reminds Gurdjieff that Shakespeare wrote poetry (in a deprecating tone).*]

That only one small part. He write about Onan, you know Onan, the Greek story? We have word from it—onanism, you know onanism?

CANARY: Yes, Mr. Gurdjieff.

GURDJIEFF: [*talking toward Margaret now*] Onan was man who teach doctrine of equal rights. He say, "Now we not need woman anymore. Now can do this thing ourselves, all we need is some soap or oil."

CANARY: Soap?

GURDJIEFF: See Canary now? All thought stop on soap, soap now her center of gravity.

[*Instructs me to explain afterwards. Canary does not wish cream on her fraises.*]

Now you are *joppa*. (Means "ass" in Russian.)

[*Later.*]

GURDJIEFF: [*to compliment Canary for something good she has said*] Now you be not joppa, you be what come from. You know what is?

[*Canary shakes head.*]

GURDJIEFF: [*whispers to her*] Sh——.

CANARY: Oh, now I see the connection.

GURDJIEFF: Connection? How connection?

CANARY: [*quickly*] I mean *relation*.

GURDJIEFF: Yes, of course, relation. Connection—relation . . . difference as between sky and earth. And you . . . a writer . . . my colleague.

[*Later.*]

Life, life—truth, even sometimes I like much material for rejoicings and satisfactions.

Saturday, June 6

Wonderful humor, the strike situation seems to agree. A second great meal, plus this time a plate of Jewish herring. An example of

Gurdjieff's "quality" serving, for each person a certain piece corresponding to her needs. I hold the plates and name them:

GURDJIEFF: Who is?

CROCODILE: Is First Gravity Guest (Margaret), Mr. Gurdjieff.

GURDJIEFF: Ah, First Gravity Guest. You know, she is not tail of donkey, must have best piece, also much rice.

[*I hold the next plate.*]

CROCODILE: Is Sardine-Wart, Second Gravity Guest.

GURDJIEFF: Ah—Sardine—she can swallow ten kilo.

CROCODILE: Next is for Miss Gordon.

GURDJIEFF: Ah-ha. Mees Gordon she like this meat, is not frozen Australian beef, must have two pieces. [*Miss Gordon begs for just one.*] No Mees Gordon, I know your tapeworm, he can swallow two.

CROCODILE: Next plate is Canary, Mr. Gurdjieff.

GURDJIEFF: Canary, she like small piece. Bones also.

CROCODILE: Next plate is for Small One.

GURDJIEFF: Ah, our Small One. Must have possibility grow into Beeg One.

[*He puts much food on Alice's plate and she whispers to him about her sore mouth. "I have pills," we hear him say aloud, all in the flow of his talk. Then my plate.*]

Ah, for Crocodile. She swallow everything except God or the devil.

[*Then his plate.*]

CROCODILE: This for Mr. Gurdjieff.

GURDJIEFF: Ah, Meester Gurdjieff. [*Nodding and putting the lamb's tail on his plate.*] Look he (the tail) come to me all by self, he know is my part.

[*Toast for Louise who is official hopeless idiot, moreover, objective hopeless.*]

Mees, your health also. May all forces from right and left, from up and from down, help you be not kind of hopeless idiot you are.

[*Toast for Alice. Official squirming idiot.*]

Everyone drink all for health of Small One. On her health depend important thing for each one of us. For all group. So I drink, Mees, I hope you be healthy, yes even as cow is healthy, and that you have also health of spirit such as I wish for you.

[*He put two stuffed figs on Alice's plate, then made a long histoire about who put the third fig there. Alice says he did.*]

GURDJIEFF: No, not I. I know me. I would put two but never would I put three.

ALICE: It just came there . . . from your hand.

GURDJIEFF: Yes. He came there, but not from my hand. I *know*. I believe my instinct more than anyone, more than I believe God.

[*Miss Gordon puts up Louise's glass for Armagnac. He scolds and says Louise has drunk too much and Miss Gordon not enough.*]

GURDJIEFF: You see? I tell Mees Gordon about Sardine and she learn more about self than if I tell about her. There is old saying: "You not tell him how *he* is. You tell him about who is under him."

[*He talks about tapeworms, about the expressions on the faces of tapeworms.*]

You see tapeworm?

[*Solita says she has seen one.*]

Then you know how he look. Like this. [*He smiles for us showing supreme satisfaction.*] Tapeworm when satisfied can have such beautiful smile, he look like bird of paradise; but when he want something he make like this. [*He gnashes teeth and growls.*]

SOLITA: Oh, I didn't see an expression like that, Mr. Gurdjieff, I saw only a dead tapeworm . . . in a bottle.

GURDJIEFF: But I know tapeworm with psyche. I speak of such. [*Then he addresses us all.*] Look, Canary see dead tapeworm and now she take part in discussion. That very correspondent with old saying about a student: "He has seen a skeleton and now he talk about life."

Die-like-a-dog—there is a word for this in Russian, one word, a dirty terrible word. It translates exactly, "Go-into-source-for-stench." Try find word for this in your idiot English.

ALICE: I shall walk home. For exercise.

GURDJIEFF: Why you want exercise?

ALICE: To make strength.

GURDJIEFF: Excuse, exercise not make force. When you make body do what not wish do, then that make force. For making do just *one little thing* which *hate* doing, that make more force than whole day of walking.

Note on the "phenomenon" soup:

GURDJIEFF: *Look, look* how Crocodile eat. Not swallow all at once, you notice? Eats slowly. Now I know is good. Soup *must* be good if *Crocodile titillate* with it.

Sunday, June 7

Lunch. A new toast for me: "Let God help you change from subjective round idiot to objective round . . . after which will arrive to you, you will die this life—this American life."

We eat a baked vegetable dish—I find few recognizable greens.

"Three hours after eat this you will experience 'I am'—will have sensing of how is to have 'I am.' "

Alice's new name—"Madame Big Pah."

Solita's new name—"Madame Small Pah."

In speaking of either of them to him, always refer to them as above, but in speaking directly to Solita, can still call her Canary, but speaking to Alice; Solita, myself, and Miss Gordon must call her *darling*.

"Darling is other end of pah." (Pah means in Russian "unfinished," and can also mean "brains-in-behind.")

The sequence of foods—we eat a sweet candy, Gurdjieff then makes us eat orange after the sweet.

"Orange cleans the sticky sweet—this is old knowledge. Man never need toothbrush. Toothbrush very harmful, especially in morning—new enamel that has grown in night is brushed away." Solita says she brushes her teeth four times daily and cleans between. He says, "You yet young, if continue so will soon have no teeth." She says she is not so young and he says, "You wait, you only now begin. You only now have *data for going*."

Before beginning lunch he comes into the room while we are reading Bogachevsky and asks if we can wait a while longer to which we say yes, and he says, "Good, good, continue then read; if read, then tapeworm forget, but if stop reading then *tapeworm make scandale*."

Monday, June 8

"Two kinds people—those with income from some stink source like grandmother, and those with a patron—both are parasites. Workers watch clock, only pretend work when patron is near—cause many patron to go up chimney. Worker kind even worse than income kind. Not fulfill obligation. Also, worker kind always wish be something else. Example—you wash plates, you small man; she cure, she doctor. You wish not wash plates, you wish cure, be like doctor who have two plates of everything because he is bigger man. In Russia small man know big and smaller man depend from him—this is understood automatically because there they work together for common good, only in this way the worker not a parasite.

"Fulfill your obligation with consciousness. If you wash plates, your obligation is to wash plates. If you doctor, obligation is to cure. If you are writer, obligation is to write. Not important what you are, big man or small man, not important what you do—only important how you do it.

"There is a saying, 'Must not put down feet farther than blanket will go.' Some people have blanket only one meter long, they must sleep knees under chin. Mees Gordon, if was objective justice, you would merit blanket only one meter long. Some have smaller blanket. I have need one only handkerchief size, only enough to cover place where tail touches. Crocodile need also only handkerchief size—for cover nose, her sensitive part."*

Tuesday, June 9

Margaret's animal was named during the afternoon at the café. A Tibetan yak, cousin of European cow.

GURDJIEFF: But in your case, you not look on door of new painted barn like cow which concerns itself only with question, "Is that my home, or is it not?" You think like business man about quality of paint, how much cost, if will last, how react in rain—forget self completely.

MARGARET: But Mr. Gurdjieff, cows are placid, I don't wish to be a cow.

GURDJIEFF: Cows not always placid; sometimes yak, this Tibetan cow, go berserk. People run inside house, shut door. Something take the psyche of this cow and entire being is wild—try break through wall—could even kill her children.

[*He fills his glass again, notices Kanari's is empty and Margaret's half full.*]

Here is example of strange thing in nature. Krocodile is small man, should drink small. She (Margaret) is big man and should drink big; but they do just opposite. In my opinion earth-man not have such un-logic. Kanari, one of your seven aspects is fly-mice

---

* End Katie's Notes.

(bat). Even exterior is such for me, can see even when look at your face. You not forgotten I am sculptor, objective sculptor.

KANARI: Oh, dear, bat is squeamish animal.

GURDJIEFF: Bat squeamish? Or man?

KANARI: Man, of course. All mankind hate bat.

GURDJIEFF: Not when I tell what means.

When he named Margaret "Miss Yak," he said, "Has for me Jewish sound," and Sardine laughed, saying, "Could be correspondent," as Margaret always saves things. He then said, "You need not laugh—sometimes when I look at you I see in your face an exact Rebecca. You know story Rebecca?" Kanari says, "At the well," Sardine says, "Water." Miss Gordon doesn't know the story either.

GURDJIEFF: These Old Testament stories can be more important than all the words of Jesus Christ.

KANARI: We don't even know Bible and yet we come here to learn from you.

GURDJIEFF: Yes, you should all have shame. I study Bible when I was twelve years old. Little boy, I sit in corner and with one eye I look from window where other boys play and one day my grandmother see me with attention going out window and she did a thing I never forget to this day. She had long beautiful pipe which she always smoke. This pipe she take and throw at me, not at my head but at shoulder here. I can feel it yet. Pipe all broken and was beautiful pipe. This make terrible impression on me and I understand how much she wish I study Bible. And then I study. I very afraid my grandmother. In village she was the oldest person and had most authority. She had one thousand times more authority than all your kings. She could say to people, "My grandson not study Bible—kill him." And they would kill me.

KANARI: But you don't hate her for it now?

GURDJIEFF: [with great feeling] No, I love her for it.

KANARI: Sometimes second gravity thing seems more important than first gravity thing.

GURDJIEFF: You see that? You understand that?

*Wednesday, June 10**

All of us "Knachtschmidt Company" (naked feet) mustered, plus his brother Dimitri and an Armenian merchant who comes late for lunch.

GURDJIEFF: [*toast to Yakina*] May God help you transformate into some other animal. As you are now, any wolf can take. I pity. I wish esteemed animal sit with me at my table. When I used to hunt for yak, never shot at skull, impossible to kill like that, must aim at heart to kill. Also can kill by aiming at Mary Jane, the soft part.

[*He heaps the Armenian's plate with fruit to take home. A discussion in Armenian language. Dimitri gives him a word.*]

I tell this man to take fruit home to handkerchief. In old Armenian this means for your woman. Man should be such that woman is for him handkerchief. I know four words in Armenian for handkerchief, but brother knows exact old word.

[The *Armenian goes and Gurdjieff excuses himself for such a guest.*]

Sometimes even from such we can learn. You notice, by the way, he very nervous because he not have right collar and tie, wears old suit. For him all world is here and he nervous for clothes. How I hate such jump-up people. Simple man could never be nervous for such thing, only dirty small man like this, only jump-up people.

[*Krocodile says she is accustomed to think of other kinds of people as jump-up—like Park Avenue Americans.*]

Jump-up people can be found in all countries, in every place where is man, in every kind of business. Moreover you can learn just where to scratch him to make him give you his shirt—each kind jump-up have certain place to scratch. I know where is for each country, for each profession, and can make all kinds wish give me his shirt.

[*Margaret says something, using the word "charm."*]

Charm? What is? No, you not tell. I know what is. I know by inner feeling. Is prostitute word. You not use such word. Only man in quotation marks uses such word. When real man hear, he squirm

---

* Still Katie's notes.

inside. Moreover I could tell you hundred just such words—all dirty words, make real man feel dirty when he hears. If you wish be friends with me, you not use such word.

*Thursday, June 11**

Gurdjieff returns from Rouen with much food, "fiancé" chicken for all Knachtschmidt and also for the other dinner party going on simultaneously with ours. He visits back and forth between his two "salles" and Valya carries his brioche back and forth.

This is a terrible night for our automatic brains; there are six of us—Alice, Miss Gordon, Solita, Margaret, Louise, and myself. He talks, then leaves the room to go to other guests and ten minutes later not *one* of us can trace the sequence of his talk—there was a blank space, none of us can remember what happened in it.

Before this sequence-with-blank, he had sat with us, talked with Margaret, asking if she understood something and by the way she answered him . . .

GURDJIEFF: Now I know she not have fat here [*gestures waistband*], or here [*gestures derrière*], but she have fat in brain. I know from how she speak that this is her typicality. Tempo (crescendo) of brain depend from fat in it. For example, now we talk so, in one hour we can talk of Jesus or of Mullah Nassr Eddin; this I know about her.

[*He goes out.*]

MARGARET: Oh, my flashing brain . . .

[*This as I recall is the beginning of the sequence-with-blank. He comes into the room with an unlit cigarette.*]

GURDJIEFF: Light. [*Solita gives. To Miss Gordon:*] You know she (Solita) is sometimes . . .

SOLITA: Kind. I always know you will say that. It's the worst thing you say.

[*Gurdjieff walks to his chair and sits down. Next, he is talking about animals.*]

SOLITA: I thought you were going to say even animals have this . . .

GURDJIEFF: No, not even. All animals.

[*He asks Margaret for a word, she understands what he wants and says, "unconventionality."*]

Yes . . . each animal has its unconventionality.

---

* Katie's Notes.

[Then, about Margaret.]

Look, look, how she look on me. You know Mees Gordon, first time in many year I use this—she look on me like dog on stick.

[Goes out. We begin trying to trace back sequence. Six able-bodied women, six attentive-eyed cats at the rat hole, and not one of us can say how he came to be saying "each animal has its unconventionality." Between Solita's "kind" and that, there is a gap. Gurdjieff returns and finds us in conference. We all tell him how in vain we try to trace back the sequence.]

SOLITA: We can't remember, Mr. Gurdjieff.

GURDJIEFF: Even I can remember.

SOLITA: Will you tell again, so we can remember back?

GURDJIEFF: I not need remember. I know. You not forget . . . I create law of Heptaparaparshinokh. Everything I do, I do according to this sequence. Even in water-closet my function obeys this law. If you hold watch in your hand, you will see that each amount takes a certain time, all according to law. Not necessary strain and spoil organ. Be patient and all will pass, because this thing also take place according to law. This is very important thing I tell. If all merde not go out, then body take back through blood. Health of psyche depends from all going out. First time, second time, third time, each time so much. Then fourth time is twice as long and half as much as first time; fifth time is . . . (can't remember what) and then all stop on sixth time.

[He asks Yakina did she understand something. She says yes—in a life sense.]

GURDJIEFF: Is only way—in life. Everything must go back to as is in life, otherwise is psychopathic. In my opinion among all of you is too much psychopathic.

*["Bless . . . bless" was the way he commanded me to start the toasts today.]**

Friday, June 12

Lunch. Yakina refuses the green onions.

GURDJIEFF: Only jump-up people not eat onion.

YAKINA: Excuse me, but I don't like them.

---

* End Katie's Notes.

GURDJIEFF: You not like with mind. In childhood, idea was fixed in you that only small working people eat.

YAKINA: No, I don't like them.

GURDJIEFF: Not you. Your mind. Nature cannot not like onion. I can prove mathematically that you like, that idea you have is only hypnotic. Your grandfather, grandmother, eat onion and you not eat because you think is not bon ton and only small working people eat.

YAKINA: No, I have no such thoughts about working people.

GURDJIEFF: I don't know about that. About nature I can prove— your mind not. Is another question. Every chord has accord, every accord has chord. In music many notes make accord, but when hear from far, you hear just one note, one chord. Yakina, as she sit here, have part in her from grandfather, grandmother, all past family; but we see only one person, only one note. But I can listen and know who was grandfather, grandmother. In every chord, I hear accord. Even I can know if her father was banker or keeper of house prostitution.

[*Later as he is speaking to Sardine, he sees Yakina staring at him.*]

GURDJIEFF: Why you look on me?

YAKINA: Because I see something in your face, Mr. Gurdjieff. I like to study it.

GURDJIEFF: Excuse, you not see anything my face. For study me, you are too young. Three thousand years in your America, then maybe can study me. Study Sardine. In *her* I make association, I make changes. *Her* psyche you can study, you are not able to do more. Study her where I make changes come.

YAKINA: But I see you do the same thing in four different ways.

GURDJIEFF: Could be one hundred four. But is not the same thing. I never do same thing.

[*Later.*]

Krockodile, Thin-One (Alice) now learned to eat correspondent. You can now swagger.

KANARI: Now she is my colleague.

GURDJIEFF: Excuse, Thin-One could never be your colleague. You could never be like her, or she like you, in any smallest way. All arisings are the same, but after; family, education, background, make different. All come out from one stink place, even me, but then where go? You see now why you could never be her colleague.

[*He lifts glass for toast to Krocodile.*]

Let God help you go Devil through horns of yak. Now you write that down and every morning you read what you have written and in a hundred years you not understand. Mees Gordon, I think now we speak too high philosophy, for them means nothing, only for me is good, I get practice philosophizing. For them it is like putting horse saddle on donkey. In Asia is old saying. Worse to say put horse saddle on mule. Another saying is very correspondent: "Bring executioner who cut off heads into church and let him perform before high altar the special service that only Archbishop can do." Philosophy—you know what mean exact? Logically prove absurdity of absurd.

After roses, roses come thorns. Only then with thorns can man have possibility for happiness. After thorns comes the branching of the river, the two rivers. If not get on river which continues, you go on other which goes down, down—and into water-closet, moreover public water-closet.

[*He graphically describes the contents—lawyers, priests, Americans.*]

I can put everyone in galoshes and [*turning to Yakina*] also all psychopathics. I old hand psychopathics. But I don't know yet how to put in galoshes a shoemaker or carpenter.

Sardine no longer second gravity guest; she is special vow-ding (avowed) parasite.

Saturday, June 13

Lunch. Alice and Katie are not allowed Armagnac because of piqûres.

GURDJIEFF: You must think about the unsatisfaction of Katie and Alice. There is obligation of man for his neighbor. You look and see he has unsatisfaction, and so much you see you must make for yourself, for your inner world. Must make equilibrium.

MISS GORDON: What you make must be subjective thing.

GURDJIEFF: Yes, of course. And so I will make today. I will not lie down after lunch; I will go out without the satisfaction of a rest.

Monday, June 15

GURDJIEFF: My special saint is St. George. He is very expensive saint. He not interested burning candles to him. He wishes suffering, an inner world thing, and only interested when I make some-thing for my inner world. He always knows. This suffering is beyond price.

At lunch we told him we had all been ill from the piqûres. Alice and Katie had cried and considered suicide all day; I had feared loss of memory and my brain had trembled. He said, "Very strong thing, this medicine help your dying, even you can have agony. It makes foundation for this series. Now your body, not your mind, must re-alize its nonentity-ness. There is no word for this feeling that you had." He said to Alice, "Now you not look on me like cow, but like boa constrictor—not like empty snake, but full one. You not have poison, you swallow whole. Like crocodile."

KANARI: Sometimes I feel I look on you like dog on master, wait for you to throw stick or order me to sit up.

GURDJIEFF: No, Kanari, not dog. No dog ever occupies himself with abstract questions.

[*We had to guess how many cabbages in the soup—twenty-five.*]

Funny picture—even camel only eat five cabbages, yet small ca-nary can eat more—when I arrange.

Alice was allowed only one glass of Armagnac, but wished an-other. "Well," he said, pouring a few drops, "we can imagine the glass is smaller." Later she asked again. He said, "No. My weakness is always reconciling conscience with logic. In this case with all the combinations I can make, I cannot with clean conscience give you another drop. I am monster; self I can lose but never principle."

I showed him my mother's picture. He studied it, gave it back to me and said, "Mother is mother."

Tuesday, June 16

Again two "salles" in operation and Gurdjieff is not with us continu-ally as host. Jane returns to his table. After lunch, he comes in with a box of special liquor chocolates.

JANE HEAP: Every day in your house is Christmas.

GURDJIEFF: Excuse, *twice a day in my house is Christmas*, look Mees Gordon, she wish belittle me.

Thursday, June 18

Lunch. We read the entire Skridloff chapter and all of us were deeply moved by the last part, especially the talk of Father Giovanni about understanding, faith, etc.

Last night Gurdjieff told Alice that the last three portraits in his "gallery"—Karpenko, Dr. Ekim Bey, and Skridloff, from which three full books will flow, represent the astral body of man.

Sunday, June 21

GURDJIEFF: Miss Gordon look on me like dog on *buterbrod*. Germans are only ones who have kept this as should be. Many thousands of years necessary for the arising of such expression—was self-created. And now Americans and English with wiseacreing make it bread-*and*-butter which is quite another thing. They have broken what was self-created. Very important thing I tell. For you Americans, it is the same in all things.

All men with quotation marks are the same. By every proof of science, by every test, such man is exact same—same tempo, same vibration. All, even his merde is the same. But men without quotation marks are never the same.

There are many different kinds—seven times seven. I am man without quotation marks.

Ancient science knows that when there is fat in one place, there will be fat in all places. Clever man knows where to look. He look at Mound of Venus. Is lawable that if there is fat there, is fat everywhere. Same for man, woman, and even for middle sex.

Just now we speak about Mary Jane, remind me of ancient manuscript once I read in which try prove God is pederast. Such picture of God they make—surrounded by cherubim and seraphim, which were always boys, all face out and God see always only their back sides. Manuscript say he wish it this way and so he must be pederast.

JANE: Like apes with women?

GURDJIEFF: A little, but that only very small part.

Tonight again he spoke about great bird migrations. Like the story he told of the whole sky darkening. Tonight he was describing an oasis, which was part in sand and part "on continent." This oasis is somewhere between Tibet and China. Birds passing South "from summer house" must stop and rest in this oasis because after it, there is no resting place for a long time. Here one can see every kind of bird—a most beautiful place. If you shoot in air "bird flow down."

Wednesday, June 24[*]

One of our great days. Before lunch he makes an examination of us, for Jane, from which Jane gets something from him, "for luggage." He calls on me to tell Canary exactly how new exercise is done, "as if she had never heard." He gives me his kindness, I don't know exactly how; without it I should not have been able to speak. He carries on when I have finished, he widens the field, shows us new aspects. This is a threefold exercise, every part must be co-eval.

"Man has automatic looking (attention). Every man has a certain amount. This must be put to work, be concentrated. During a certain exercise, contact must be established with the outer world while inner world attention intensifies. This gradually makes clear the difference between the two worlds, will teach you to separate them, not look on things like monkeys, your all going out to the object and identifying with it. Then you will not live in the outer world."

He uses the word "canning" and Katie thinks he said "cunning." He explains: "No, canning. Canning and cunning have same root and in ancient times meant the same thing. I speak of real cunning, not the dirty meaning of the world.

"The highest aim of man is to be cunning. The mag (magus, adept, master) is cunning. The mag is the highest that man can approach to God, because only he can be impartial and fulfill obligation to God. In old times the mag was always made chief because he had cunning. Other mags could do either white or black magic, but the mag who had cunning and canning could do both white and black and was chief of the initiates. Man with real cunning is man without quotation marks. Angel can do only one thing. Devil can do all. Men like that are nearest man can ever get to God, because only then he has impartial justice."

At table, he speaks of sun worshippers. He says, "I can put in galoshes Canary and your President, with *one* question." Then he

---

[*] Katie's notes in combination with Solita.

tells about the ancient sun worshippers and how when Christianity began, these sun worshippers were then called devil worshippers.

"Yet Christians do *not* change the form—*Christians, why not change? Why always look toward sky?* And not only Christians, but every religion since the sun worshippers.

"You not think strange that now the holy day is called Sunday? Half world calls this seventh day, Sunday, and the other half called it by a word meaning Market Day. The day when man does not work, when he gathers together all results of his labors, he meets, he puts out his things, he looks at what he has done."

This was a very emotional lunch. Krocodile tears flowed. When we leave the table, he sits forward. His chin is sunk in his collar, his eyes are looking inward and there is an expression of indescribable sorrow on his face. He has gone away from us. Jane said afterward that she saw a cross behind him then.

Thursday, June 25

Lunch. Solita and Margaret absent, but all the rest of Knachtschmidt are present with Gurdjieff's brother and a fat blonde young girl who speaks Russian. "Look, look," says Gurdjieff, as she comes into the room, "she is just like barrel." The girl speaks a little English, understands more. Gurdjieff is surprised. "How I very surprised because she speak English, I not know she know. Fat—*never you can expect anything from fat*—she must have learned when was thin."

Dr. Bell is the first gravity guest. Since she has no idiot, Gurdjieff proposes her the toast: "May you *do good* all the mornings of your life," and explains at length how if "do good in morning, then all day go well." This time there is apparent to me much more weight in every word of this. The real meaning is far from water-closet business. Everyone of us listened tensely, even Miss Gordon and Dr. Bell.

He tells Dr. Bell about a plate they used to have in old Asia called *"Assiette de Shiva."* In Russian, Shiva is pronounced more like Khiva. Assiette de Shiva had all kinds of roasted mutton, every kind of beef, sometimes goat, but never pork. "Now doctor, you tell which you think is best, your Assiette Anglaise or this Assiette de Shiva I speak about?" Both Miss Gordon and Dr. Bell begin speaking of Shiva, Hindu Goddess of Destruction. "No, no," says Gurdjieff, "*not* India Shiva. Is quite another thing. Shiva I speak of, is a country, near Bokhara, Lake Aral. Is country bigger than your England and is called Shiva, is many thousand years old. A very strong people. Twenty-five years Russia fight before can take. Is from *here* come this Assiette de Shiva . . ."

We have every kind of fruit drink after, with the fruits and candies. Kvass, grape juices, etc. Gurdjieff also drinks each time he pours a tumbler for Dr. Bell and asks if still in England is the custom that host must drink with guests. Miss Gordon says that still they do it, but it's not considered rude of the host not to drink.

GURDJIEFF: But old time host must drink to show not poisoned.

MISS GORDON: Oh, from that point of view, no, we don't do that now in England.

GURDJIEFF: You know why? Because "civilized"—*because life is so cheap now.*

*Tuesday, July 7–Saturday, July 11. Five Days In Vichy.**

Hotel Beaujolais. Winter café—Gambrinus. Summer café—in the park at the farther end near the donkey riding ground.

Alice and I go down on the seventh and do not find him until the next morning in his winter café, the Gambrinus. We have already had one massage.

"I tell you funny thing. Mees Gordon come down today. She have great suffering with her Scotchness when I tell her will be very good for her have massages now. [*A very fat woman goes by, Gurdjieff laughs.*] In Russia, the passing of such a fat one cause betting. [*Long pause.*] You know what bet?"

"No, Mr. Gurdjieff"

"Everybody in café where she go by say, 'What you bet, which she have most, or fat or sheet?' In this case, you know what would be answer?"

"No, Mr. Gurdjieff"

"Sheet, of course, only less in morning."

He tells Alice she must drink Source Hopital, and that there is one special one for me which cleans the throat. He will get the name from a doctor friend.

"I was mineral water doctor at Essentooki, have water there just like Grand Grille here, many more springs there—in Caucasus is great thing."

---

* Katie's Notes.

He tells us that that morning he made piqûre for himself.

"I take half glass of blood and mix with things, beat, and put back. Truth was difficult. Have chairs, many chairs, and mirrors so can see."

We ask how he feels now.

"Now, better; but at first had pains in head, very bad, *even I was afraid for a while.*"

In the Park café—his summer office. There we find him at five in the afternoon. He sits in a white wicker chair, his coat hung over the back, his Panama on the ground beneath. He seems absolutely immobile, presently his cigarette moves to his lips and we see he is watching two twin girls playing in front of him. He has never seemed so divinely at peace. We think we will not disturb him but he sees us and waves.

"We hesitate to come up, Mr. Gurdjieff, because you have a look of such inner world peace, we wish not to disturb."

"Truth, is good place here."

He calls the proprietress, a stout white-haired lady and introduces us. "Friend," he says. Presently Miss Gordon comes.

We are all so happy to see him in such a state of peace. He talks a little, tells how he always had children when he came to Vichy, and so chose this café near where the donkeys could be hired for riding.

"You *can* imagine how was," he says, "four, sometimes five small children come to me, run around, make cry . . ." His smile wishes they were all back around him again. The trees are so beautiful, great lime trees above, in blossom.

MISS GORDON: I cannot believe, Mr. Gurdjieff, that we sit here with you like this. I think about that chapter—"Reflexes of Truth"—how great a man was being met for the first time, how difficult to see him. And now here we sit.

GURDJIEFF: Yes, all is different since accident. Then I die, in truth, all die. Everything began then from new. I was born that year, 1924. I am now twelve years old boy, not yet responsible age. I can remember how I was then—all thought, feeling. I was heavy, too heavy. Now everything is mixed with light.

He is speaking about mineral springs, Vichy and Vittell, and about the idiot Russian dukes who bequeathed to the French government great sums for the building of bath-houses and had streets named after them and maybe the building. "Such idiots," he says.

GURDJIEFF: Once all French mineral springs were, for Russians, places of prostitution. I remember that if American or English pass by, he was pointed out with finger. Twenty years ago never see English in such place. What I say? Twenty years? When I say twenty years, always means much longer. Twenty years now mean nothing to me. Now with my inner world I am unable recognize twenty years.

[*To Alice:*]

How feel? I bet you never before, even as child, feel so well.

ALICE: True, never before in life. As a child, I was very serious.

GURDJIEFF: Was only turkey serious. Now if with new soil you are serious, this can be real thing.

A dinner with two Russian men and a twelve year old girl. Gurdjieff speaks in Russian most of the time with his men friends. Toward the end of dinner he plays his rub-down-the-face game with the little girl, and when he reverses the gesture and catches her nose, he says, "Lucky it is not her nose (pointing to me)."

Then he says, "Crocodile, I have three formulations for such nose you have. Two are not bon ton, I cannot tell. One I can tell. Question is, why God make such nose? Because once there was a poor man, he have nothing; no horse, no wagon, no plow—only he have wife with such nose like yours. And he take her, put her feet under his arm, face down on earth, and so he walk through field, face dragging, making deep furrow. For such purpose God create nose like yours."

We have one lunch; Miss Gordon, Alice, and myself, when he is in the mood for wonderful talk. We drink to Canary's health at this luncheon, one of the most rare occasions when he drinks the health of an absentee.

The chicken is not very good.

GURDJIEFF: Theen One, what you think this can be, buffalo or chicken?

ALICE: More like buffalo, Mr. Gurdjieff.

[*This starts him talking about buffalo.*]

GURDJIEFF: In Asia is many buffalo, work very hard.

[*I tell about the American buffalo.*]

GURDJIEFF: Buffalo is everywhere on earth.

ALICE: In Egypt too, water buffalo.

GURDJIEFF: Yes, and up that river there is great big animal, instead of two horn like buffalo, have one from nose like this [*we tell him the name, rhinoceros*] and you know this animal is only animal crocodile is afraid of. Are many such animal, how you call, and many crocodile up that river; many times I see him take horn and make so . . . rip crocodile in two.

He tells us how he found there was a Russian doctor in St. Germain des Fosses, how he sought him out, finally found him, and now he has assistance when he makes injections on himself. He begins this story by saying suddenly, "Strange how career of man depend from situation. Then the story about finding this Russian doctor who many years ago studied with him in the same medical school, in Russia.

GURDJIEFF: Many year ago he have nearly written across forehead would be foremost doctor. Now I find have five children and wife who once was pretty, is now fat, and now all he think about is bread—how get for five. Is small man now, big in that small town but before me he have shame. And you all are now like him. Now as I look at you (we are drinking Hopeless toast) the word "hopeless" come with difficulty. Now you all have possibility, is written across forehead of each. All now depend from situation.

[*Some dish, the salad, is very good and we comment.*]

Whenever you travel with me and have any good thing, always you must thank Madame Hartmann. All the year she travel with me, everywhere she go in kitchen and tell just how must be for Mr. Gurdjieff—have much suffering then; but now, even after all these years, whenever I go place where she was with me, they always remember . . . so well she tell. She never think of self, but always of me. I give example, something I not know about, one of my people tell. You know how woman carry always small valise—once someone of my people see she have in this bag a box hemorrhoid medicine, because *five year* before that, just after accident, *once* I have hemorrhoid . . . and Madame Hartmann always remember that and for five year she carry, just in case, if I ever have again, she can give to me. That is why she is first friend of my inner life, such thought she had for me.

[*Miss Gordon is very touched by this long story. He sees this and says to me:*]

You know when Miss Gordon was born, small devils, not big ones, but still devils—stand around and prepare her in totality for me. From her, not from your Rockefeller, my future depend. Small devils make, arrange her whole life, not for her, but for me.

[*This way of thanking Miss Gordon is too much for her. She is weeping. Gurdjieff nods toward her, not looking, and says:*]

You know, if she were not drunk, she would cry now.

[*For dessert there is a perfect melon Gurdjieff has brought with him from Paris. He says it came from Beluchistan, first flown to Constantinople, then to Berlin, then to Paris.*]

From all over world such things come to the rue Labie.

MISS GORDON: And when you eat you think of friends all over the world.

GURDJIEFF: No. When I eat I think not of friend who send. I self-remember. I have impulse which gives self-knowledge with conscious satisfaction—impulse self-valuation. Because I am such that such things come to me.

We go once for a promenade in the hills. Gurdjieff gets to the top of a mountain ridge and hunts a valley to descend.

"There is dark place, must be something interesting there."

The pines look so black in the hill folds and we descend a wild ravine where a small brook runs.

"We will follow him, he will grow as he go down to meet big river. Ach, Mees Gordon, what place for picnic."

Magenta fox-gloves eight feet tall hang from the embankment, a smell of pines and our brook winding over stones and Gurdjieff says, "Ach, Mees Gordon, such water I like to drink," and he slows down a little, thinking about the brook. I get suddenly boy scout and say, "But I can get for you to drink, Mr. Gurdjieff, I have cup here."

"No, no, I speak only in general."

A back spring breaks with a crack, the spring under Miss Gordon. Gurdjieff teases, "She eat too much while in Vichy, now will cost her much money," and Miss Gordon and I say we can walk the twelve kilometers back, but Gurdjieff arranges Alice in the back, over the broken spring, and us in front with him.

He nudges me: "Every stick have two end, now for once is ideal that Theen One is light, for this moment she perfectly correspond to place where must go, and if this not were so, then we would have difficulty . . ."*

Monday, July 13

Café de la Paix. Alice and Katie remind him they are sailing soon.

GURDJIEFF: I will fix in you what I have made already so it will not be lost. I will give you a program for living so you can know how to live in inner life. You must remember when you feel bad you must not lose yourself with mind. Some days you feel bad, then with swing of pendulum, you feel good. On your worst day, prepare for best day. This is the law. What is important is that you never lose self. Let mind be big sister to take care of little sister who is now in the house. Your nature is the little sister.

[*Same day. Lunch, rue Labie.*]

GURDJIEFF: Yakina cannot understand as much as Kanari because she has fat behind. And when she makes merde, yak kills all small animals. Can you imagine what would be if yak could fly?

[*He had said before, "Funny picture how yak tries to be nightingale."*]

When Kanari makes, not serious thing—even on head could only be wetness. Yes, it would be terrible if yak had wings. [*To Yakina:*] You like? [*Yakina does not reply.*] Think what picture that makes. You like such picture?

YAKINA: Like is not big enough word. No, I *not* like, Mr. Gurdjieff.

GURDJIEFF: But you understand more than usual?

YAKINA: Yes.

GURDJIEFF: Then you must like. This is first time in life you ever heard such, never any other place can you hear what you now heard. So you must like.

[*Later.*]

MARGARET: But esteemed animal, Mr. Gurdjieff, how can yak transformate into esteemed animal worthy to sit at your table.

GURDJIEFF: You notice pig I *never* eat; but I like eat yak meat. [*This doesn't clear it for Margaret. Pointing to Crocodile:*] Another example, crocodile meat I not like, never could eat, but crocodile I like. Is sometimes esteemed animal—crocodile I can send ahead of me to

---

* End of Katie's notes.

swallow enemy, crocodile can be useful to me but never I wish eat, never I can be friend with. Now you understand?

[*His toast to Louise-Sardine:*]

May both sources help you to make something for you that is your own. Even if only small thing.

[*Later.*]

Sardine, you have small brain. Kanari have big brain, for such animal, a very big brain. And is cunning brain. Sometimes is as clever as dog.

[*On Gurdjieff's left is the French woman, "Toll One" and next to her is Louise, then Crocodile. Louise's stomach sings loudly.*]

LOUISE: Oh my tapeworm.

GURDJIEFF: Crocodile, I notice you put attention on a certain thing, so I ask you a question, something I wish know—*in whom proceed, was that one from me or two from me?*

CROCODILE: Was two from you, Mr. Gurdjieff.

[*Gurdjieff takes his iodine and asks if we notice how he knows without looking exactly how much to take up in the dropper.*]

GURDJIEFF: And all done with great speed, without looking, aftomatically. I learn when I study chimie (chemistry). I could [*he makes scoop motion*] take up three hundred and forty-five drops in the hand like this—and you would count after and find exact.

Tuesday, July 14

Alice gets a new toast.

GURDJIEFF: Let God help you transformate into ordinary idiot which is very high. Next after unique, when sequence begins again.

ALICE: I hope I fulfill your wishing.

GURDJIEFF: Not hope. In my opinion hope is an evil thing and the reason man is merde, why he is nearly not man any longer. Man must use what he have. [*Says someone in England is dirty dog.*] Dirty dog is terrible anathema. Highest title in hell is dirty dog.

[*Yakina asks him to play for us.*]

I would have played had you not asked me. In order to command me, you must have three zeros. But I not play on such command. I am my own host—but you are slave to anyone.

[*Alice says she will go dance in the streets for Bastille Day.*]

Yes, dancing can be good thing for education. Go watch faces— you will see faces of stingy donkey—will see your future there. You must see and hate, hate so much you will have big wishing not to be such. Yes, go dance in street, can be educating thing.

Wednesday, July 15

GURDJIEFF: Today I constate one thing about Sardine-Wart. Before she was dead—only reason not stink was that one small part still alive. Today I see other parts begin resurrect and I begin to take interest. She is still hopeless but another kind. Now is for us newly arrived baby. I nervous and angry now because in my kitchen sit three parasites who destroy the good of nature. They swallow pieces which I need for tonight and I have not possibility for buying more. They drink my blood.

KANARI: Dangerous parasites if they drink your blood.

GURDJIEFF: No, blood can be cheap thing compared what I tell. You speak of blood, not even know from what blood proceed. They do worse than take my blood, worse than if take three liters, because for me to be angry or nervous costs more than three liters of my blood. [*Kanari has seized upon "from what blood proceed" and longs to ask.*] Kanari, I see that some impulse proceed in you. Now she look on me like dog on stick, not dare speak.

KANARI: Yes, I will speak, because the words you use just now, "impulse proceed," might be telepathy. I wondered if blood proceeds from a different impulse other than organs.

GURDJIEFF: Blood is only result—not important. There is many another thing in man.

[*Then he speaks of active elements.*]

KANARI: Can active elements change bones? Since I have come to you, even the bones in my hands are changed. Everyone has noticed I no longer have the same hands.

GURDJIEFF: Yes, of course. Can change even tail in man. Active element makes everything. Even the kind of breath you have depend from active elements . . . Now my tapeworm sing—not Marseillaise or Internationale. He would only sing God Save King, never would he be communist—only monarchist or republican. Tapeworm of man is lazy and spoiled. He not have, like man, possibility of denying himself or wishing to suffer and make sacrifice for future.

[*Later.*]

Forty-five francs I can get with bonbon. Four hundred and fifty francs I can get with my smile. Four thousand five hundred I can get with my cunning. But forty-five thousand, what I hope to get tonight, I must sell part of myself—not whole self, but a part.

Thursday, July 16

The "naming of the plates" during serving.

CROCODILE: So and so is for so and so—is for my darling.

GURDJIEFF: Ah, *your* darling. If is your darling then must also be our darling because your relations with her are objective.

Friday July 17

Lunch.

GURDJIEFF: [*to Yakina*] Which you wish help you now? God or devil? Devil this time? Ah, then will have roses, roses—for millions of years, until so hate smell of roses would rather have merde to smell. Now I wish drink alone this toast with Thin-One, because tomorrow we talk. Not one drop for you, Kanari, you are representative of art and not understand commercial thing. Even if you gave all, it would mean nothing, because it is your nature not to understand such values. But when she and I talk tomorrow, only she will understand, because she have factors for this and much data. When I need money, you representing art give all, give nine thousand francs and think it is great thing because it is all. But she knows it is only merde and small thing, not even to speak about. For example, remember how I tell about man who take home food for dog? A commercent person never do this, but representative art would take, even if he had no dog, he would say he had, and take for his own breakfast.

[*At compassionate toast (Kanari's) he looked at Yakina and said:*]

GURDJIEFF: Now you formulate. Let devil help . . . [*Yakina hesitates.*] Tell, tell. You must tell your good wishing for Kanari's health.

YAKINA: But I already said it—in my mind.

GURDJIEFF: Is cheap thing in your mind. Many things can happen in your mind that we not know about. You must make effort. Show your wishing with your whole presence, with *you* in it.

YAKINA: May devil help—

GURDJIEFF: Too late now.

YAKINA: Better late than never.

GURDJIEFF: Now you are two times cheap.

[After lunch and the music, Gurdjieff speaks about man doing the impossible, and cites a saying.]

GURDJIEFF: A man cannot jump over his "eggs." (Which Solita hears as "legs.") *[He tells us this is a most difficult thing to do and once he saw a man practice for it.]* Must always practice in water, because when you fall, you always fall on your back, and this can hurt if not over water. But you must actualize this *not* over water but on land.

When he leaves the room we speak together, getting a picture of a man trying to jump higher than his organs, which means he must start his jump from his back, keeping his feet always above his organs and Miss Gordon explains that this can mean a man practising to achieve the *nearly* impossible—and over water, she thinks means "wishing"—water being symbolic for that. Afterwards Gurdjieff teases Solita about not knowing the word "testicles" given to him in place of "eggs."

SOLITA: I did not think Crocodile was right; I think you meant other thing.

GURDJIEFF: Crocodile was right, moreover many times is right, you know why? Because is crocodile.

Saturday, July 18

Alice and Katie take money to him at the café.

KATIE: Here is one pair of group who have strange property—one has cunning, the other canning, and when they work together they have good result.

GURDJIEFF: You speak in joke but what you say is good thing. Both cunning and canning are necessary in all things. This is why there are two magics. Black magic is cunning—often also is cunning and canness—you understand the difference? Black magic is ideal for being. Cunning and can-ness is like conscious and unconscious, or like two words used in Bible for meaning two kinds of evil, voluntary and involuntary sin. You, Krocodile, have cunning; I see possibility for developing big thing. And Thin-One have very great canning possibility. What you have now you think is big thing, but compared to how you can be, is like baby made but not born.

Tuesday, July 21

Luncheon. "Toll One" and "Child" are also there with all Knachtschmidt. Child gives the toasts, and forgets no one's health. (Prompted by our various suggestions!)

Gurdjieff has made a special dish—courgette with many spices, baked in meat sauce. It is a whole meal. When finished, he tells the child in French, "Quoi vous mangez n'est pas plat, c'est musique."

Jokingly during the meal he speaks of Yakina's eating capacity, says she can swallow more because have two stomachs. Then seriously to us all:

"You know cow have two stomach? Also sheep. Also camel, only in camel is not stomach, is more like storehouse. In cow, the food in first stomach is all prepared, so when pass into second stomach can begin immediately digest. One stomach for keep food, one for digest. Food pass one stomach to the other only when is place for it, when *ready*. Nature so fix because cow must give much milk, necessary eat all the time. And cow, when lie down and chew (cud) she is eating, you notice she never sleep when do. When chewing, she is eating—this chewing she do when food pass from one stomach to other, to make pass, to start juices in mouth."

Wednesday, July 22

GURDJIEFF: Time has come when must do inner work as well as outer. Also exercise I need, so have made plan to make certain kind of massage for a friend who is sick, made such plan down to smallest detail. Today I make this stomach massage truly with almost end of my force—should not do but must do, is part of my task. Now I tell one most important thing, one lawable thing. If something you must do—some work or task—you must plan ahead of time, you can never do at the time, but if make exact plan before you must do, then is as if have aim and all prepares for this. Now each day, wish or not wish, I will make this massage because plan was made, special combination with friend who now expect it each day. This I not do for him, but for myself, for my physical exercise necessary with the inner exercise I now do.

Toll One and the child are with us for lunch and as before, the child gives the toast. Gurdjieff now addresses the mother as "Mere," "Mere" do this, do that. Explain to child so-and-so, "Mere."

GURDJIEFF: [*speaking to us about child*] Now I know one thing is necessary—she must learn speak English. If she will be my secretary, must speak English, is better for my ear.

CANARY: We all will speak English to her, to help her.

GURDJIEFF: Excuse, not can help; she must first know three thousand words—learn automatically, then can be help, speaking and hearing spoken.

He does the hand-down-the-profile trick with the little girl saying, "See, how easy it go," then his hand goes upward unexpectedly, catching the nose, throwing head back and he says, "But *why* is this, you tell me, why not go easily, why?" He laughs and tells us his teacher in Greek first did this trick on his little friend and Gurdjieff went home and thought and thought, why such a thing could be. He characterizes thus his Greek teacher for us: "He love children, his life was in children."

[*Kanari's toast.*]

GURDJIEFF: Let God help, only in this case, let devil not take. Devil like people who drink. You drink, only cannot drink. You therefore not correspondent for devil. A slave drinks more than he can. The master drink *what* he can. Not be slave.

[*Later. Kanari is staring at him after some great formulation (unfortunately forgotten).*]

Look! What state she be in. There is old expression for describing such state. With one eye on heaven and one eye on earth and in place between exchange opinion. How is up there, down here, what can be, what will be. But when tired, she not look on sky or earth, but look on merde.

KANARI: [*utters a cry of protest*] Oh, no!

GURDJIEFF: In general I tell. Is such law. This expression from centrum come.

He tells us his plans for the child, how he hopes in six months she will be "head of my home" and we will all have to be so-so-so with her. Then he looks at us, speaking in English (which Mere does not understand) and says, "Only difficulty, must educate mother also. Also must buy for her if buy for child, and you know, she is big.

Never twice in life you see such thing come down street. In all thing is exceptional. Even bed. I can not buy ordinary bed, but musted order special bed for her. If sleep in ordinary bed then next day she cannot do what must do."

A pause. Then he says to us in another voice, "But you know, she have one factor which make life not so ter-ree-ble." He looks at the child then he says, "All mine are big now, no more small ones left. Grown big—all spoiled—was many, fifteen eh Mees Gordon?"

Thursday, July 23

Dinner. He is telling us about "the best deacon" at his table, a Russian in Priory days, who made a great ceremony about each toast.

GURDJIEFF: There are many details you not know. For Patriarch, for example, he would rise, cross arms so (across breast, fingers touching shoulders) and bow.

CANARY: That is very esteemed.

GURDJIEFF: No, not very. Are many gestures much higher. That (crossed arms) mean degree of slavishness—you are slave to whom you make this.

CANARY: They do it in Church.

GURDJIEFF: Only before God should you be slave. But now do it everywhere, your representative of art defile such holy thing. There they not know is part of great hierarchy that was known in centrum seven thousand years ago.

[*He has made a special dish, our courgettes of yesterday spiced and baked, served with potatoes. He wishes Crocodile's opinion.*]

CROCODILE: Is for archangel, Mr. Gurdjieff.

GURDJIEFF: Archangel, yes, can be. But you know when he have? When he make this . . .

[*He sticks out his tongue and does the boot-licking sign.*]

CANARY: Even archangels, Mr. Gurdjieff?

GURDJIEFF: Y-e-s, Mees. Are many kind archangel; high, low, they also have hierarchy. [*He points to Crocodile, still overcome by the picture.*] Look, she not understand. You tell, Canary. [*To Crocodile:*] Once I ask you tell Canary, but now she must explain to you. You know why—because she is specialist such science, all sciences very high understanding, and you know why is specialist—because she have assistant who help, and for such reciprocal companion, she could have one like Yakina for example. [*To Margaret:*] You understand, Mees? You not offend?

MARGARET: I not only understand but I am offended.

[*Gurdjieff jokes about her being offended, then goes back to Alice still with the pudding-motif.*]

GURDJIEFF: No, in truth I compose this dish for Our Darling, for crystallizate in her data for remembering, so that when far from here, in other world, America *can* be other world, she remember how she eat here, and this make her come back sooner. For her I compose this dish because she not so much in my centrum as you all and I wish make, so I compose special thing for making quickly—I am cunning.

[*Alice's toast comes.*]

GURDJIEFF: Ah, squirming ... [*to Alice*] Now I ask you whenever you have glass Armagnac in your hand, on boat, on train, in your other world—think of your idioticity, then you think about what I just now tell.

He is speaking about the terrible situation he is in today. Sixteen thousand francs worth of medicines held up at the border and his car taken away from him by the huissier—the sheriff. Formerly he "went chimney" for great sums of money, now the same thing, but for small sums.

GURDJIEFF: Five times I millionaire, five times I go chimney. Not millionaire because grandmother give, I make myself millionaire. Is nothing for me lose all, always before I come down on feet. Before was such situation for six hundred thousand francs, now can be same thing for six thousand—three zero yesterday, one zero today.

MISS GORDON: You'll never forget that time, Mr. Gurdjieff.

[*Referring to the six hundred thousand franc time.*]

GURDJIEFF: Excuse I never forget *this* time. Then was *out me*—general life thing, but now is *in me*—subjective thing. Is why I will never forget this time.

Friday, July 24

Lunch. There is a special baked eggplant dish. Yakina wonders aloud what it is and Sardine emphatically pronounces it "aubergine" (eggplant).

GURDJIEFF: Who tell aubergine? Sardine, you speak of only one thing. You not see in this the one thousand fly wings I put. Wing of fly is most important part, all rest of fly I throw away. Practically I will tell you what wings mean—with wings can go many places and I, night time, in dream with wing can fly. Yet you not see. First necessary see all, then speak aloud. *And* aubergine.

[*Canary's toast.*]

GURDJIEFF: Now I constate one thing, very astonish. From today Canary not compassionate. Now already is new kind idiot. What is, I will not tell yet, next time ceremony will say. So I, as deacon say: "And yours also—meanwhile." [*Miss Gordon says it ought to be more "as you were in past."*] No, meanwhile is exact—[*He drinks to Canary's compassionate-meanwhile . . . next comes Alice's "idioticity." Gurdjieff turns to Margaret.*] You can enter into my situation—soon will not have Our Darling next to me. Will perhaps sit next one who stench, and I will always remember how Our Darling was. You know how is? Is for me Indifferent Source, you understand? Indifferent not make different, not stink, not give high pleasure. Never cacophonic, never sonophonic but always for me equilibrating. Her I see my best part of every day, my best time, I take habit—now soon will not see for three month. Is long time.

[*We have all eaten watermelon until we burst. Still three pieces remain on the plate. Gurdjieff urges us to eat, and we all refuse.*]

You know what call such pieces? Everywhere in world is called *shaming pieces,* because everyone wish take and he have shame and not take and always is *best* pieces.

[*A little later.*]

Is another expression, even better than this: "I wish from all my neighbor shaming pieces have every day."

[*He speaks of how well we fare at his table.*]

If bust, then bust with music. Though not have pay for coffee in Café de la Paix, I always have for table. And moreover have things not even your Rockefeller can buy. In café I make manipulation but always have for table. This very characteristic, original, and strange.

[*He plays a divine music we have never heard before. Afterwards—*]

Is Greek music. When gods on Mount Olympus drink "doosiko" and eat small salted fish, such music they have—three choruses.

CROCODILE: [*fresh from Pogassian reading*] Maybe this is what Pogassian heard when he drank doosiko with English sailors.

GURDJIEFF: Pogassian was small for this kind of thing.

[He continues talking about the gods and Olympus.]

GURDJIEFF: Original mountain where live gods not in Greece—is in Turkey where is Green Temple. [*Crocodile reminds him of the Green Mosque at Broussa.*] Yes, just near Broussa is mountain, is small convenient mountain, easy to get up, which prove Greek god was not idiot. Olympus could not go—very high. Is also another mountain very difficult—Mount Ararat—this stand alone, only one little mountain to north, then nothing for hundreds kilometers. Only very few times can man breathe from top. Is like Everest where your English spend much money for climbing and never man set foot on top. But maybe Russians, now they try with such thing for going down in sea (diving apparatus), maybe they succeed. We see.

Before lunch in the café where Alice and I go for instructions, we find him in the toils of a "terreeble" situation and he tells us how many small things go together and make suddenly one "beeg" thing which can now be disaster and how he struggles and manipulates. He goes out for a moment to the pharmacy and when he returns he says, "New law I just now discover—where struggle is, there fly 'birn' elephant. (Where struggle is, there flies give birth to elephants.) I had around me flies—now I have business with elephants."

Saturday, July 25

At the café.

GURDJIEFF: How with you, Krocodile?

KATIE: Much trouble the last two days with concentration for the exercise. My inner world state has been chaos.

GURDJIEFF: That interests me to hear. Long ago I tell you I must first decrystalize factors for fantasia—all factors from past life. Then would begin crystalize new ones. The results you imagined from exercises were self-suggested and when you tell me how you concentrate, I smile inside and say, "Let be." Now you see what terrible thing is self-suggestion—it makes red see white, white see black, church see divan. You now go through the dying I tell about—maybe you can now see the merde and nothingness you are. Now you have cleaned and repaired apartment, but it is empty, you still have no furniture. You see yourself now without effect of Kundabuffer. One side is a terrible thing for you, other side is cause for objective gladness.

KATIE: And after all these months of work!

GURDJIEFF: It is not so easy, what we wish do.

[*Later, at lunch.*]

GURDJIEFF: This dish today is not horse meat. The French eat horse meat because they have centime-ness. All my life I have prayed I would not have to eat horse meat. The French understand only centimes. If you tell them you pay one or two francs for something, this means nothing to them; you must say you pay eighty or fifty centimes. Then they are interested, this begins to be big thing. There is a word in Russian which is very correspondent, a word for measure, about this long (a yard). This is divided into sixty versts, and each verst into four parts.

The name for one of these parts is a word for expressing this centime-ness. In Russia you say just this word for a man and it is as if you wrote a whole book about him. This already gives valuum his smallness.

[*Later.*]

Half the world is Christian, yet steals old Jewish God. Like the Germans, all people begin now to hate Jews. Yet they carry old Jewish God in heart.

Sunday, July 26*

[*Crocodile's toast.*]

GURDJIEFF: Your whole future depend from this: that she come back manifesting outwardly, that is satisfied you are good for her little sister.

[*Theen's toast.*]

May God give you in life, one more Sunday like this.

A reading of Ekim Bey. The boyhood friend who pursued the same aim and this gave rise to an inner world intimacy—as if they were "arisings-of-a-homogenous-causality"—the feeling of brotherly love.

I remember this phrase at table when he is telling Solita that always she will have such feeling for Alice, whether hate or love, nothing in her family love can equal, because they have pursued common aim together—and also "from same barrel." I give the ho-

---

* Katie's notes for this meeting.

mogeneous-causality phrase (just read and luckily remembered) and he says, "Svoloch, what memory she have!" but is pleased.

The lunch is relatively quiet, he has guests in the bedroom-salon and must occasionally go and drink toasts with them.

Tuesday, July 28

Lunch. While we are reading about his experience in the artillery-field with Karpenko, he is roaring in his bedroom in Russian, rage to split the walls. Then he comes in with us, asks us if we noticed what he said, and we say we heard the voice but not the words.

"You notice was scandal-voice. Man is such svoloch—first time you give to him, he prostrates himself; fifth time, he sues you for not giving enough. All ordinary man is such. I am old man now, never in all life I find one who is not such." And tells about the friend he was raving at, "with inside I feel sorry—but must make exterior so."

He warns us we must remember this trait of ordinary man and tells us (the explanation of it) will be the preface for something important he will explain to us.

At table he tells us the beans in the soup will have for us the property of castor oil, and presently Canary is asking him if castor-oil beans grow in Egypt.

GURDJIEFF: Everywhere now it grows. Not only Egypt but everywhere. Even in your South America.

[*Near Buenos Aires he knows about a Russian who grows castor-oil beans now and is making big business.*]

CANARY: Is it true, Mr. Gurdjieff, that you can make a poison from castor-oil beans?

GURDJIEFF: Yes, of course. Can make poison from all things. Even from you can make a poison. I tell practically how—first, boil for a while, then marinate—from such process can make poison from you.

CANARY: In that way, saying everything, you spoil us.

[*A little later he laughs to himself, then to Canary—*]

Look, even they all take habit expecting you will be put in galoshes. Even they know with such question where you will go. Only difference each time is how you go—this time go head first, next time feet first, but always you go. There is saying for such property you have, "Concerning praying she with conference in water-closet will begin, concerning sheeting she with conference at table will begin."

He is asking who will be his secretary when Miss Gordon is away and asks Canary if she is going on vacation. When he learns she can be his secretary, he says to the rest of us, "See how convenient. Now you all can send to Canary what checks you wish send for me."

CANARY: And hope send check for secretary too.

GURDJIEFF: Now you spoil all. You not wait for data be fixed. Only after one data be fixed, then you can speak of another. (Now again Canary is in galoshes.) But one side is good—she make pratique. Is good have pratique, then go in and come out easy—never stay long in, never long out. Now when Yakina will go in galoshes, she will stay for ever.

CANARY: She never asks question here, Mr. Gurdjieff, but at home she is mouse-valiant.

YAKINA: I wish take risk, Mr. Gurdjieff, I wish ask question.

[*Gurdjieff gives the permission.*]

We wish to know what is the interior animal of Crocodile.

GURDJIEFF: Is baby. Interior is baby. Naïve ...

[*Someone says Crocodile now has a colleague in Jane Heap.*]

No, is not same thing. Mees Geep have baby much older—Crocodile two and a half year. For her being baby inside, I not blame entirely, partly I blame Our Darling and for this I make so ... [*he makes the prod-goad gesture*] Our Darling always wish be mother and this very strong in her. There is a saying, "If call self mushroom, then in mushroom basket must go."

[*We mention the pepper in potatoes.*]

GURDJIEFF: [*answering Yakina's question as to whether pepper is good for one, etc.*] Twice month is necessary eat pepper for disinfecting. Your doctor say not eat but each year I eat in pepper weight of one of your doctor. But not this black pepper which England now make grow everywhere and which is not real pepper. I eat the red pepper. This goes not in the blood, it goes all through the mucous-membrane linings and tomorrow morning, if put attention, will notice how it burn. [*Alice mentions red pepper among our Indians.*] Yes, just this one place is the *real* pepper eaten, always your red Americans, the real Americans, have this pratique. And I tell you one thing you have never notice there; when Indian come down from mountain with load of red pepper he grow, he sell his pepper and when go back up mountain, *he carry stone, never he wish go back easy.* Such thing you not notice, but I see. Next time, you look.

[*Later, again galoshes, Gurdjieff is warning Canary.*]

Will come one day when Yakina go in galoshes and if you there already, she come on top of you and push so deep never you can get out, can you picture? Canary under a yak will be pushed down into the deep place where is worst stink.

YAKINA: And what is my interior animal, Mr. Gurdjieff?

[*He does not reply because he has already given it—tapeworm— and Yakina has forgotten.*]

Wednesday, July 29

Before lunch we talk about frogs, the subject arising from his naming of a certain dish (his sturgeon and chopped egg baked dish) which sounds like "gorjunksakhr," reminding him of Miss Gordon, and which means in reality sardine-wart. Then we talk about frogs and warts and he tells how certain toads, from a liquid coming from their mouths, make on the hand that touches them, hundreds of warts but just on the hand. Certain other frogs make this same juice from the pores. He is interested to learn that even in America we have this understanding about the arising of warts, that as children we were warned not to touch frogs. "Everywhere in world is such understanding."

Then he tells us how he has eaten *everything,* but frog he *hate*— never can swallow such thing. Is perhaps only thing he hates. Sea fish, anything that comes from the sea has for him a *stink*, but now he eats a few sea fish, sometimes. But frog-meat, *never.* Eel also he never touches. In his family they sometimes ate it, all except his father who would never touch it. We speak of the many kinds of frogs and he says he knows hundreds. "Also one kind in tree sing like bird. One important thing come from frog nobody know about which can cure a 'four-year-illness' in twenty-four hours."

GURDJIEFF: This melon we have for dessert has all kitchen garden in it. Miss Gordon, explain, you understand kitchen garden from Prieuré.

[*She speaks of vegetables and the perfume of flowers.*]

No, not flowers. Kitchen garden is useful for man. But never have I flowers growing in kitchen garden. Flower is dirty thing, is the poison of the earth, is masturbator thing. You know why created? For helping Kundabuffer. In old science it had evil reputation, it was material for black magic. Flowers not grow lawable.

KANARI: [*whispers to Yakina*] There go our flowers.

GURDJIEFF: What you tell?

KANARI: I said I had instinct that soon flowers would be taken away.

GURDJIEFF: Sometimes you have good instinct.

ALICE: And roses, even roses? The Bible often speaks of roses.

GURDJIEFF: For certain things roses are good—but must be in combination. Roses in the Bible are always mentioned with thorns. There is an old saying: "You can understand and love me only when you love—have a passion for—my thorns. Then only I am your slave." In old poetry, not your poetry but religious poetry, there is a very beautiful song that the nightingale sings to the rose: "Even though I hate your dirtiness, I must love you and sing to you."

Thursday, July 30

Lunch. This is a great day, our day of "destiny-aim" and private instructions. There is a soup for Miss Gordon which makes "property of capacity."

GURDJIEFF: [*regarding Kanari*] Look, she have oily face, she wishes I fill glass. [*Kanari refuses.*] Come, drink, drink. It will relieve my aching left corn if you will drink.

KANARI: No, even for corn I will not drink. For what purpose was my suffering last week if today I drink more than necessary?

GURDJIEFF: Come, come, give glass.

[*She refuses, he takes her hand.*]

I wish you to be able to drink like ordinary man. Drink like man who not like to drink. Wish or not wish, drink as those who drink around you, drink for company and not be slave.

[*He sees Yakina smiling and turns to her.*]

You spoil with smile what I make just now with Kanari. In truth you have not data to be friend for anyone. Now I would never choose you for friend. A moment before, a moment later, would not have been so bad, but at exact moment you smile, is as if you had said, "Ha, ha, ha." [*To Kanari:*] You must never have exceptional-ness for drinking.

MISS GORDON: I regret what you said about flowers, Mr. Gurdjieff. I am very fond of flowers and you once said I could be manure for flowers and I felt glad I could help them.

KANARI: And you said I could be manure for lettuce, even lettuce.

GURDJIEFF: Not even lettuce. Lettuce is good thing. Even *might* make manure for lettuce. Even is important word. And Yakina—she might make manure for betterave (beet)—big, round, too much have.

MISS GORDON: Too much sugar.

GURDJIEFF: Too much there is of everything. *By the way*, is sugar. [*To Alice, for her toast (squirming).*] May God give you strength to understand what I told before lunch and may you well go and well come. I hope only in memory you will suffer for my food in America, but that all other parts of you will wish for the other food at my table. Let the food you eat here stay in memory only, but the other kinds of food carry with you.

[*Square idiot toast.*]

GURDJIEFF: Not often we drink Crocodile's health, every day we drink Miss Gordon's, so often we do it automatically, but square is far along, and when we drink we put attention on it. Though she not have it every day, when she have, she have quality wishing.

Let God help, Devil take . . . or Devil help, God take.

[*We come to round. Yakina says perhaps she can be candidate for round.*]

Candidate? How be candidate? Maybe already for a long time you have been round . . . [*pause to digest this surprise, then he goes on*] but you are not round. You are the idiot one after zigzag, farther along than round. Idiot de naissance.

ALICE: Is my animal really boa constrictor? (Her interior animal is tapeworm.)

GURDJIEFF: Yes. It was easy for me to put serpent in her because she already had by heredity a capacity for great swallowing. Now what suffering she will have. Because I put the serpent in her, she will always wish to swallow. And sometimes there will be nothing to swallow and so she will doubly suffer.

*Friday, July 31**

Goaded by the others and by my own curiosity as well, I asked him for the only "portrait" we have not read—Prince Nijeradze, mentioned in the Ekim Bey chapter as one of the portraits in this se-

---

* Katie's Notes.

quence. In his room he tells me it is not here. At table he tells the others:

GURDJIEFF: Do you know what she asked me? She ask for chapter Nijeradze and she not even have checkbook, not even possibility of checkbook. [*To me:*] You know, for reading this chapter, necessary many zeros. You are too young, too poor. This is a big thing—for translation of this chapter alone I spend more money than for all others together—so important it is, I wish it be exact. Already it is translated into twenty-eight languages, each translation I verify word by word. If you wish know, there is even copy on your continent America, one in Persia, and one in Germany. None in your England Mees Gordon, and so far none in France. Maybe will be in French since I remain here, will see, later. And for such thing she ask and she cannot even write be-gind on check.

[*He tells us how Monday will be a sad day for Nicholai, he will go for a certain teaching in mechanics, but such kind of teaching as is known nowhere else on earth. He tells Miss Gordon about the teacher whom apparently she knows.*]

One atom of this boy worth the whole of ten men of any of your English or Americans, such mentation he have—never I see such on earth. Greater he is than your king, your king never could be such as he is and he could never be king of such small thing as England. When he will be king, will be objective sense. I have prepare. When I die you will not know about him at first. For two years after my death everywhere on earth will be subjective revolution. [*To Margaret:*] Now you say you hate yourself, you love yourself, but only with outside; after you will say with inside. Such thing will happen when I die. All man must die early, lately, and moreover man now have special time, cannot live beyond. I also. (And in subjective revolution he will not take part, he will only take part in governor's revolution, afterwards.)

[*He re-fills our Armagnac glasses, talking all the while with the Russian man, Black, who is at the table; and after the re-filling, he looks at the level in each glass—exact.*]

GURDJIEFF: You notice how even, my "just" is part of my aftomatisme? [*"And you not even look, Mr. Gurdjieff," someone says.*] Of course, not even look.

[*Turns to Margaret and asks if she understood what he said.*]

MARGARET: I understood perfectly.

GURDJIEFF: I am glad. Sometimes even Englishmen forget their English when I speak.

[*The soup comes—a super-borsch.*]

I will tell you one thing. In this pause, if you will work how I tell yesterday, if you will not be lazy, idle, you can have such soup every day for the rest of your life—*and everything correspondent with it.* There is more than you know of food at my table.

[*An aside to Solita, clarifying a difficulty in her mentation which he has perceived.*]

Stick to be stick must have two ends, to be part of stick is nothing, there are million million atoms in a stick. Fly must be . . . no, not elephant—tiger. Such cunning he must have.

Eat, eat. Enjoy possibilities scale of tasting. He see fly but not see elephant. Behind fly can hide only flea or body crab—something you can chick-make (destroy). But behind elephant can be tiger, and you know what is tiger. You can't chick-make him, but he can you.

[*After the melon is served he notices three sprigs of estragon beside Louise's plate and asks Canary to hand them to him. We all think he wishes to eat greens. He holds up the estragon—*]

Such an amount of fresh green costs five francs and she defiles. Such is lack of education of American people. Such thing and you defile. You sheet on my labor, can you understand this? In your home you can leave what not can eat but when you are guest among people with different taste, different understanding, different checkbook, you must *take only what you can destroy.* You must *know* for you how much this is and only so much take.

LOUISE: I tried to put back on plate, Mr. Gurdjieff, but Valya took it away too fast.

GURDJIEFF: In this case Valya is servant; he not supposed to have to think about such thing, this is not his work, it is for *you* to know, and take only what you can destroy. Such is understanding among all educate people. You must know about this.

[*He has been telling Miss Gordon something presumably unwelcome and she looks at him steadily.*]

You know how Mees Gordon look on me? This very complicate explanation. First must tell how in old Armenian there are three words for sheet; liquid, medium, and hard. If you know what mean, you know. And now I tell Mees Gordon look on me like liquid sheet on castor oil.

[*Later in the salon after music, he lets Alice know that he notices she is sitting on and on while a hundred small last-minute tasks wait to be done, and this is how he says it:*]

Look at Theen One, how she sit. Last day here she wish do many things and she is thinking of all the cinemas and music halls she must see so she can tell at home how is in Paris; she wish satisfaction of being able to tell what goes on in theatre, in opera, in cinema, and music hall, but at same time she knows here she is in centrum where is quintessence, and she know *only from quintessence can there be something for the future.*

Also, she think about hat. And by the way Mees, that hat you wear with veil make arise in me such feeling of deuil* that no matter what was color, I see black. You know long ago I was in modes; I make suggestion for the new mode, was specialist, I know about such thing. Never such hat as that one will be worn, or here in Europe or in your America. Man will buy but second day will beat self for having bought such hat.

Saturday, August 1

In the café, Alice and I are having one of our "last conferences." We tell him we feel "strange," we have just come from Margaret's porto party for us and could not talk of anything but him and the work and that all else seemed foolish and light.

GURDJIEFF: Yes, it is so. You will feel strange. As you are now, you are out of one chair and you have not yet the data for sitting in the next chair. All that you will do will seem like a pouring from the empty into the void, all meetings with people, etc. Later when you have the data, you will go back and do this same thing and it will mean something to you.

[*He sees our several hat boxes. I say, "Monkey business." (He hears the expression for the first time and likes it.)*]

GURDJIEFF: Monkey business—so have I monkey business, but more than you. One monkey business is monkey business. Two monkey business is donkey business. Three monkey business is tiger business. I have tiger business.

[*He tells us he sees a few people around in the café, waiting to speak with him.*]

---

* Bereavement.

85

GURDJIEFF: Now I see one or two jackals, you know what is jackal?

ALICE: Like a wolf.

GURDJIEFF: No, wolf is honor. He come, he take directly. You can see him coming and can take measure, but jackal, you never know from where he comes or which way will jump—he is false.

And now you must know a most important thing about man— man cannot stay long in one subjective state. Subjective state from a thousand things depends, you can never know the subjective state of another. It is typicality of man that no two subjective states can be same, they are like thumb whorls, each different. When you see her (Alice) in some subjective state, you not try understand what cause this, even she cannot know. If she is angry with you, you say, "She is not mad with me, her state is mad with me." *Never reply with interior. Never revenge association have.*

Monday, August 2

Gare Saint-Lazare. He is there waiting for us in his "station office" with the extra bottle of KRK for me, and a shopping bag with two huge watermelons and two Persian melons—"special," for us to eat on the train. He has separate "subjective talks," first with Alice, then with me.

GURDJIEFF: [*to me*] Keep the fire burning. One thing you must know, nervousness has a momentum. Mind cannot stop nervousness, but it must go until momentum finish. Important remember this; when you see our darling nervous, let be, soon will pass.

To see us off—his tail—Solita, Miss Gordon, Louise, Margaret, Georgette, and Monique.

As the train pulls out our whole Knachtschmidt is on the quai under our Third Class window. He stands alone, apart, and he never takes his eyes from us. There is such a look of sorrow in his eyes. As the train moves, he raises his hand, palm towards us, raising and lowering three times for me in blessing, three times for Alice in blessing. I didn't see anyone else in the group at that last moment, only his palm raising up three times and his eyes deep and sad and forgiving us already . . .*

[*Lunch.*]

GEORGETTE: This soup is strong.

---

* End Katie's Notes.

GURDJIEFF: Every good thing is strong—it must be so. Now, Sardine not help as must with putting plate—she is only good for dog business, shaming business. Eh, eh. We all have shaming business.

[*Later he spoke of people who were either hot or cold in a disapproving tone. Kanari asked about what Jesus had said, why he liked hot or cold but not lukewarm, and Miss Gordon spoke up.*]

MISS GORDON: But you have said, "Go the whole hog."

GURDJIEFF: That is not for people like you—you cannot go the whole hog.

No Date

GURDJIEFF: Kanari is picnic director. All information you must ask her.

KANARI: [*aside to Yakina*] I never thought I'd get to be picnic director.

GURDJIEFF: What that you tell—"Get to be?"

KANARI: It's an American expression for become—I never thought to become expert for picnic.

GURDJIEFF: When once initiated for one thing, is like chain—one link flows to another—then whole chain flows. *Garder* should mean "*savoir employer*" . . . Tapeworm angry when hungry; also can be angry when full. Man too is like that—he is two kinds of angry—when empty and when full. One kind I chick-make like louse; other necessary make suffer first, then chick-make.

[*Later.*]

How is your friend, Kanari, the Frenchwoman?

[*I said she was very interested.*]

Interested! That is small word. I raise from carcass and she use word like interested for such thing.

GURDJIEFF: Kanari, advice yours give. Shall I invite Miss Gordon coffee drink? You my secretary, especially in this case.

KANARI: You make things very difficult for me. She is my mother superior and I'm afraid of her stick.

GURDJIEFF: Not difficult. Miss Gordon, will you drink coffee? [*She assents.*] You see, *not* difficult. Reminds me of one saying, "If had stick right kind, could move world." What call such stick?

KANARI: Lever—like Archimedes.

GURDJIEFF: Oyoy, hear what Kanari tell. She know Greek mythology, what educated person.

KANARI: But every child is taught mythology in school.

GURDJIEFF: Then why not they know? Nothing ever know or understand of such thing. Mythology have great meaning. So instead of teaching something Americans can use, they teach something they cannot understand. So later in life they have nothing useful, nor this thing either.

[*Yakina has said her shell was cracked at last.*]

GURDJIEFF: You must know your self-love before you can kill it.

[*Yakina says she knows it now.*]

And your vanity?

YAKINA: Nearly the same, are they not?

GURDJIEFF: Is sister. Still not enough to know them. Must now have something independent.

[*Later.*]

Truth, I tired. Must at all times make effort to move. Then sit—sleepy. Struggle and relief . . . at such time I can observe how psyche of man is independent thing.

[*Later.*]

Is one thousand kinds sour.

JANE HEAP: [*he has been talking of king*] I forget sometimes to stand up when they play God Save the King. I forget there is a king in England.

GURDJIEFF: Must remember there is king and stand up. This is organization, and you must respect it. Outward you must do. Man has two worlds. Outside he must ceremony make like others. But inner world is yours—all man has is his inner world, his independent place. There you can tell your king is merde and be sorry you have such king. This proves to me you read Ashiata Shiemash like American newspaper article and you not understood what you read. [*To Georgette:*] Pity you not understand.

GEORGETTE: [*fondly*] Yakina will explain later.

GURDJIEFF: *She* explain? How could she understand? Perhaps three months after—never she understand till three months. Now look—she angry.

[*Concerning wolf and sheep (in us) confided to our care.*]

GURDJIEFF: Wolf satisfied? No, full.

KANARI: Is the difference between satisfied and full a psychic difference?

GURDJIEFF: No, objective. Only such a condition is a guaranty for wholeness of sheep. Life must always be such—and every day. Not only outer life but chiefly inner life. If so live your life, you will be intelligent. Can only be intelligent when self-sufficient—enough for all in yourself.

KANARI: Then I must be intelligent, for every day I spend in this struggle. But even when sheep is safe, wolf is always looking around—so I'm not intelligent.

GURDJIEFF: No. Only candidate for.

KANARI: I remember what you said—always fix your eyes on the point beyond—and take that direction.

GURDJIEFF: Yes, but necessary take account every day of even this, or else that direction will become only a point fixed in mind—a habit of thinking.

[*Gabo carries in a baby pig for Gurdjieff's inspection.*]

KANARI: Even looks pitiful like human baby.

GURDJIEFF: No. Animal baby has possibilities give active element. Human baby I not like. Only possibility of giving merde.

[*Later.*]

Now I hope I have not offended your Scotchness, Miss Gordon.

MISS GORDON: No, can't any more offend my Scotchness.

GURDJIEFF: But you I can offend—angry make.

MISS GORDON: Yes, can angry make.

GURDJIEFF: Of course. From same source is Scotchness and offended-ness. Same root have in psyche. You, Kanari, more than another, understand when I tell allegorically. You have smell.

[*The word "lousy" comes up.*]

American use this word and not even know what is louse. Louse already is something. He is king of parasites. All others are afraid of him; he is tiger among parasites. You see under microscope? He has a fat face—even like that last photograph of me. Same face have.

[*Later.*]

Seven kinds of merde have men. My merde has nothing active; is honor merde because all I use of my food. No animal or bacteria can use. Even can be poison for certain microbe.

(To me he said when he heard I was going to the Hospital de St. Louis to study, "Nerves are pipes—like those for electricity and radio. Remember this when you study. For earning money your articles, only four hours must work if intelligent—only donkey work eight hours. But study is different—forty-four hours a day study, because is bank for future.")

[*Later.*]

As cell is in body, you are cell for planet; planet is cell for large system. You are louse of planet and planet is louse for universe. All feeds on bigger organism.

One Summer Day Lunch

[*Miss Gordon, Kanari, One Frenchman, One Russian.*]
GURDJIEFF: [*to Russian*] How your interior?
RUSSIAN: [*patting stomach*] Very full.
GURDJIEFF: No, that is not your interior. That is your merde.
RUSSIAN: Oh, perhaps you meant my heart?
GURDJIEFF: No, that also very dirty.
RUSSIAN: My soul?
GURDJIEFF: No. He who masturbates can never have a soul.
RUSSIAN: Then what is my interior?
GURDJIEFF: Man's interior is his psyche. About this I asked.
(This was in French.)

Another Dateless Day That Summer

Miss Gordon and I are alone with him at lunch. We eat in silence. Then he says, "Good, eh? Miss Gordon not even wish speak."

KANARI: When I remember how we all used to wish to not take the time here to eat but only to ask you high philosophical questions, I wonder why you didn't kill us.

GURDJIEFF: Because is such stench country for police business.

Tuesday, August 18

An old Russian who lived at Pont de l'Arche with his tiny old wife has just died and Gurdjieff is very upset. Last night he loaded his car with food and flowers and took me to Rouen with Valya and Dimitri. We visited the little house and afterward had dinner at eleven—tripe and Armagnac.

Later, I had coffee alone with him and he talked till half past two. He said, "I am sometimes God and sometimes I have ten thousand devils." He seemed very upset, and for the first time, talked on and on, manifesting out loud like anybody else.

Up the next morning at six, and to the Doctor's for coffee. On the way back to the little house, we passed the village pall bearers pushing a wagon by hand. No horse. The village friends were already standing in line at seven o'clock. The Rasputin-type priest Mr. Gurdjieff had engaged to watch and pray for three days, led the procession, dressed in lavender robes, swinging a censor, his long greasy locks falling down his back. Then the women, Mr. Gurdjieff, Dimitri, Valya, Nicholai, and I, followed. It was a long way to the village cemetery.

Afterward, back in the house, Gurdjieff talked all the time to "Babuska," how fine to have such important priest and all best people of the village, such flowers and such dishes he had brought! To cheer her, he called for luncheon at half past nine and made her drink Armagnac and Vodka. Needless to say, he paid for everything.

End Of August. A Trip To Vichy.

We started at one o'clock from the Café de la Paix in his car with our luggage, a sack of watermelons, and Gabo and Valya in the back seat. At Fontainebleau we stopped at Dimitri's house for lunch. There we left Gabo and took on his brother and Nicholai. Although we stopped on the road four times, we made Vichy before ten o'clock—less than five hours. While he rushed through the stormy night, I worked the windshield wipers, found the roads and Esso signs, and lighted his cigarettes. We did the roads through the woods at a hundred and fifteen kilometers per hour, and went through the towns at ninety. At Vichy there were no rooms at his Beaujolais, so we stayed at the curb while Dimitri gloomily went to look for rooms.

After visiting eighteen of Vichy's five thousand hotels, he found us shelter and we had dinner at eleven. Gurdjieff had caught cold in his left arm and it maddened him for four days. Also he was poisoned by the food at our first luncheon place, Russian, and was ill for two days. The drama of rendezvous began on the second day. He told us all where to meet him and every time no meeting could take place. He would either have said the wrong name, the wrong hour, his watch had stopped—anything.

Then those who had met would be sent to search for the missing, and thus, hours passed. Or he would walk by a table where I was sitting reading while I waited, not see me, and tell me later I had not been there. "Even I look on each face." The dinner procession was headed by him, very grumpy, me entranced, Valya carrying watermelons in newspapers, Nicholai with Armagnac in newspaper,

Dimitri in the rear with indigestion, muttering, "Jamais un peu de repos." Sunday was unfortunate for meetings, especially the one in the park. He had told me to meet him in the café by the river and I waited for two hours before the boys found me and led me to the café in the middle of the park. He said, "But there *is* water—can see if stand up." Monday was bath again, then at noon we drove seventy kilometers to have a picnic. The base was watermelon and Armagnac only, so he stopped on the road many times for other provisions. At Clermont-Ferrand we picked up a Russian nurse and her little boy and they sat on the three men's laps in the back seat. The heat was intense but all the windows were kept closed because of his arm and cough. We looked for an ideal place for a picnic for an hour. After passing real paradises, he finally chose a steep hill where we could not keep our balance, sat on pointed rocks and held the food to keep it from rolling downhill. The men tore the chicken apart with their hands and wiped their hands on their trousers. There was one glass for all. In ten minutes the picnic was over and we went on to a lake. Dimitri said, "Just think, to eat a piece of bread we must come seventy kilometers and spend a thousand francs." In the car I was talking to seventeen-year-old Nicholai and Gurdjieff was angry. "Mees, you not see all the places I pass because you talk." "I talk to Nicholai about his future." "You had better think about your own future, Mees." He said to look at the mountain before us. "Only now you can see, after eating. Never can man see anything when he is hungry—only a bit here, a bit there."

We drove another hour to look at a lake for ten minutes. On the way back to Vichy the mother had to stop the car because the child was sick from Armagnac and watermelon. The moon came up about nine and he stopped the car to look and walk about. He pointed to the moon. I said, "You say in your book it is bad for us." "Not for everybody—for some it is very good." I asked what Germany is as an animal—American burro, French donkey, England sheep. He said "Jackal." . . . "I am not God. I am only man. The only difference between me and other men is that I know more." . . . "Eat, eat, Canary." "I cannot eat like a tiger Mr. Gurdjieff." (Meaning him, of course.) "Then eat like sparrow. You know that for canary, sparrow can be tiger."

On the terrace of the café in Vichy he said, "Now sitting here reminds me of nine years ago when I was writing the chapter on Good and Evil. I wish know name I call, what that man name please? . . . Made on Atlantis." I said, "Man's name was Makari and he made a tablet in two pieces." "But what was name I call this tablet? Not memory you have. There was name. I made from two names I see on those two shops opposite here. Please you call waiter, ask what name had shop nine years ago." The waiter said, "Dé d'Argent." (Silver Thimble.) Gurdjieff's face fell. The waiter returned to say he was mistaken, it had been the "Boule d'Argent." "Aha! Now I remember. Name of stones was Boulemarchano and you sit in galosh. You only remember liquid, Mees."

Thursday, October 8

I saw Gurdjieff at noon in the café. I told him that the momentum of nervousness from life-business had destroyed my concentration for being work (Janet's illness, especially). He said, "Every stick has two ends. Your remorse of conscience prepares you for the next work which will be very difficult. The more uneasy and nervous you are now, the better for you later. Your wishing for being has been more or less theoretical, you must have more real wishing."

He summoned me at nine o'clock tonight for dinner and I asked, "Also Sardine?" "Late come." As we went in the door I said to her, "I've had enough of these all-Russian meals. I'll tempt my fate in English tonight and ask questions."

I began with the first Armagnac: "Please, what is Kodansky joppa?" He said there are three kinds of joppa (derrière) idiots—all arch for the toast: Kodansky, Morse (walrus like Mees Geep), and Jerryhund (he makes an impolite noise). Kodansky is herring kind. Holland people are herring like English are sheep. Holland is name representing man's sex organ and as such is known all over world. Now, Mees, try to see properties of Holland nation in herring. Look in eye—*not fish, but herring*. And also they eat such fish which increase their properties. Smell like fish also. People think God made them. Not so. Just such sex organ, not God. God has more to do than such unimportant business. While man's organ is representing Holland, woman also have country for representing, but I not tell which."

Then a joke I couldn't understand. I said, "If Crocodile were here, she would explain." He said, "Not this time. And you not ask me. In such case, wise man not continue."

He said, quite suddenly and unconnectedly, "If you work well for next six months, you can have great wish—even your dream. All depend from your today—from your present (not past or future). You can go to Tibet." "Literal Tibet?" "Yes." So he even knows our dreams!

I told him all about Kathryn and Alice, how good they had been, how they have worked and obeyed with honor. He smiled that smile and seemed happy that all, after all, is not *merde* in the world. My toast has not yet been changed. Still compassionate—without the meanwhile. I have been the "deacon" but he won't let me pass the plates much. Poor Valya has fasted nearly forty days now.

After dinner:

"Kanari, come with me now for promenade in taxi."

"Where?"

"Oh, low place, I tired."

"I think not, Mr. Gurdjieff."

"Trouble with you, Kanari, you always look for high thing. Must have both in life."

"Have had low thing, am late for high thing."

"Oh, go, go home then. Devil with you."

Friday, October 30. My Birthday.

"This day of your birning." He is very angry about Edward's abdication and says can't believe even such degenerate son of such degenerate father and cousin of degenerate Tsar would do such thing. Even though degenerate, has something royal in his blood, an heredity, which could not permit.

In the evening he invited me alone; birthday cake, caviar, clean table cloth. My toast came so unexpectedly soon, while I was eating, that I tried to swallow quickly.

He said, "Never defile Armagnac."

"But I haven't yet drunk—I'm waiting to swallow."

"No, you waiting only for me to drink."

"Not true—yes, both true."

"Always in galoshes at your toast."

"Perhaps I am candidate for round?"

"What is round but candidate for square? What is square but candidate for round?"

Later he said, "Your name mean 'alone,' already I know it, existed in Egypt. I know all names from there. One man there was called Holy Merde, and from name he swaggered—because meaning was, he had fulfilled such transformation with honor, used all active elements according to law. There was ceremony in Egypt for name's day, not for borning day. Day of physical birth is only of domestic interest. Real day was day you were given some great person's name."

I spoke of sign I was born under—scorpion. He said, "Well, not so bad as falanga, not always die when bite. I remember I used to put scorpion and falanga together in bottle and watch struggle. Except once, always falanga win." About Americans. "They not yet spoiled. Nice burros. Future is donkey, yet at same time might be something else. Not yet crystallized into turkey who have no future. Now this is your day. You may have what you like—only, of course, not question."

The Russian woman who was serving us was laughing at everything, even when he scolded her. He said, "Such empty thing she is—perhaps better she laugh. Even merde can smell sweet. Now I go Café de la Paix. Before I lived with somebody—woman—now I live alone. Live with angel would mean nothing to me—because I live with devils." I said, "And I live with someone who is always angry." "Always angry, always laugh, always with lovingness, not make different. All is empty thing."

Saturday, October 31

He telephoned, "Come destroy hors d'œuvres." At lunch he said his seven-year task which had become nine years' work would end on November sixth. Had it not been for the death of Orage, he would have finished two years ago. "Only a sheep, only an Englishman, would have died just then. Any other man, man who was real man, would have waited to die." Sardine said she hoped Roosevelt would be elected US President in a few days.

GURDJIEFF: No, better the other. No matter how bad is other, better than Roosevelt who has something in spine that make him not complete man. By his illness, he lose one or two parts of the seven that make his "mind." So better any other whole man.

Tuesday, November 3

Gabo told me he had said to Gurdjieff that his stomach was mounting too much, he was eating too much fat. Gurdjieff gave him a look of scorn and said, "Since when egg tell something to chicken?" He spoke to Miss Gordon about a mistake he had made and said, "Even God make mistake—one big mistake he made."

MISS GORDON: But I thought you said He had arranged everything with Heropass?

GURDJIEFF: All—but not one thing. He made umbrella when he should have made enema. So now he idiot like everyone else and sit in galosh.

Thursday, November 5

Dinner after a silent lunch. Miss Gordon, Yakina who has not come for three months, Sardine, Kanari, EW.

Mr. Gurdjieff gave Yakina one quick look and said only, "Already late. Sit." At toast for squirming idiot he said, "Yakina, official arch, but now also squirming. Like when take fish from water and put on earth. For this I have formulation. Two chairs. You never can sit in same chair as when first come here, but you have possibility of next chair. Is now or never. I am not Scotch about money like Miss Gordon, but about time I am very Scotch—stingy. You understand? You are merde, all what you do, think, everything. Physical and mentation. God is one point, merde is other point, and between is gradations, involution and evolution. Even sometimes God can be merde."

[*Later.*]

GURDJIEFF: There are seven aspects of hopeless—dirty hopeless, harmful hopeless, stink hopeless. (He did not give the others.)

KANARI: Seven aspects subjective, but objective only one?

GURDJIEFF: No, is also seven. Everything is seven. Which of arch idiots is worse, do you think?

KANARI: Jerryhund?

GURDJIEFF: No, morse (walrus). Yakina, do you know which is morse?

YAKINA: Yes, like Miss Heap.

GURDJIEFF: Yes. Morse, this walrus sit, look around. In him are all idiots, like in man. Everything like man he have, even brain. And so

96

it goes, down to tail part. All parts in him idiot, all idiots in him—except of course, unique.

[*Later.*]

I tell you everything with conscience clean like Kaiser Wilhelm. If get caught, never paper is guilty, only fly.

[*After lunch Yakina explains to Gurdjieff that the reason she has not come is because she must finish her book.*]

GURDJIEFF: Such merde your book, all you write. I pity you. You are turkey. Now if too late, you cannot come to me any more than you can kiss your own elbow.

Wednesday, November 11

Alice and Katie return from America. He showed some strange fruit, one color, many shades.

GURDJIEFF: Once I painted picture with this one color alone—yes, once I was sick man for art.

[*Later.*]

Man is like melon. Exterior all the same have, but how is interior, that is another question.

[*Later.*]

Caricature is always mathematically exact, is quintessence of line, anywhere can recognize subject. Is art. Is seven kinds, like in everything else. Take example Kanari. From one side is exact caricature of grandmother, from another side is quite different, is comic like cartoon. Is monster, like all contemporary humanity. She is cartoon.

*Monday, November 16**

We speak of changes in each one of us, Sardine is notably taller . . .

GURDJIEFF: [*to me*] You also I make change.

CROCODILE: Not outwardly maybe.

GURDJIEFF: Yes. I always make picture when I meet a person for first time. I always imagine him without clothes, naked, this make easy for me recognize the next time. For her (me) you know what picture make? You remember how was? Her gesture she make so— formless. [*He illustrates.*] The picture I make: In some countries they

---

* Katie's Notes.

have skin, for carry water, for milk, even I see for butter; but also, use such skin for carry away merde from water-closet and this the man do at night, when there is moon. This skin filled with merde is heavy, man get tired. So he put down, beside road, in moonlight—and you know how such a skin act when put down; almost like living thing, take positions with arms, with legs, move a little, settle down . . . put head on it and chapeau and could be man. Kaki Toolook, such was my picturing for her.

(The special skin used to carry off manure (human) in the moonlight is called in Russian, Kaki Toolook.)

Tuesday, November 17

GURDJIEFF: Do your exercises consciously, mechanically, and chemically.

[*We speak of miracles.*]

Old Jews believe Jesus Christ fed many people with six, seven fishes; you remember how many was, but *how* was filled, the people that not tell. Another example, they believe He turn water into wine, but *who* get drunk on such wine, that they not say. And once more, they believe He walk on water, but *how deep was water*, they not speak about that.

Thursday, November 26. Thanksgiving.

Turkey at his house with a dressing made of chestnuts and sturgeon. This is the first dinner gathering for Knachtschmidt since the pause. "It is because this is your holy-day, your toorkey day." For himself, for his own diet, he has made "egoist thing," a sturgeon soup. We must eat this with him, only *after* turkey. When it comes, he speaks of sturgeon.

GURDJIEFF: Is tiger of the sea, all fish are afraid. When he pass, not even need go near a fish, he can cut it up and later return and eat. This is because of the sturgeon's scales.

Gurdjieff has a scale brought out of the refuse for us to see. As big as an oyster shell, nearly same shape. Solita and I later take it home, polish it, and reveal it's beautiful form.

Kanari refuses a second candy and explains she is afraid will make big (around waist).

GURDJIEFF: Ah, she afraid. Now I tell secret, always I wish see her real type, so I make big. In Russian there is expression for such size stomach, they say a man has three . . . what porter wears. Aprons. Yes, man have three aprons. Once I see in bath, great rich man come, three big aprons, have two men each side, lift each fold for washing underneath. Necessary two men for lifting *one* apron, you *can* imagine how big was.

[*As he goes out of the dining room he looks back with a twinkle.*]

For Kanari three aprons will make moral also. (Poor Kanari.)

Friday, November 27

We go to finish the turkey. The day before, to "make partition" between main course and the dessert, to "tromp down," he had given us each one wild fruit—the small tomato-like fruit in a papery pod. Alice remembers these from childhood, so I tell him now she had a subjective night and this starts him talking about them.

GURDJIEFF: Truly is very strange and original thing. Is God thing. Hang from under three small leaves, very beautiful, and is of such color—there is no word. Like that I write about in book (seven hundred shades of grey were once perceptible to the human eye, in Babylonian epoch). You cannot know what color it was when you look at this, this is dead color, but when alive, is *so* beautiful . . . many many year ago I see for first time, and such impression it make, even now I could make that color."

[*Kanari exclaims.*]

Yes Mees, then I was sick man, for art.

[*Once, he tells us, he painted a whole picture with this one color alone.*]

This fruit has one most original property, nothing else on earth have such. Sometimes the tissue-like pod opens up like flower, with the orange fruit its center. Opens up, not for sun, not for rain, but when air is pressing down in certain way, *this* he like and again and again it will do this for atmospheric pressure until it dies.

[*Louise eyes the candy, wants another, but does not take.*]

GURDJIEFF: Take.

LOUISE: I not wish, Mr. Gurdjieff.

GURDJIEFF: You *do* wish. I see how you look. Your tapeworm wish. You not good man in relation your tapeworm.

[*Talking about bath, how he goes regularly on Saturday.*]

If you wish, even one picture I can tell . . . and he gives us story about the little girl who sits up at bath, behind cashier desk, awaiting Mr. Bon Bon, how even when he is late, she sits there fighting sleep because she knows will be given bon bon. For her, this chief aim of life is.

Even bear fly—yes, is such expression in Russia, old Russia. Always you hear from old peasant who come down from mountain. Very great meaning have. Even bear fly, can be such thing. You can imagine bear up on top mountain, he step over where think still is mountain and is cliff, and down he go. You are standing below. What you see? You see bear fly—he come not like dead body, but so and so. [*Illustrates arms out clutching, every effort tense.*] He not fall, he *fly*. Maybe is last fly, but meanwhile he fly.

Saturday, December 5. Day Of The Chaplets.

GURDJIEFF: In Old Armenian exact meaning of word for this (the black substance) is *night*. Every language have different word—meaning. But in old time was known as Inanimate Helper.

[*Scene at parting.*]

KANARI: Thank you Mr. Gurdjieff.

GURDJIEFF: For what?

KANARI: For . . . more work.

GURDJIEFF: Look, look how she lie, she mean for more Armagnac!

Sunday, December 6

All-fish lunch and melon. There are two kinds of melon, looking the same, on the plate. One is infinitely better tasting than the other and we remark.

GURDJIEFF: Yes, of course. You know, is like man, all melon same exterior have, but what is interior, that is another question. Man is man; Mr. Roosevelt have two legs and two arms, like Madame Crocodile—but interior he is paralyze. So with melon, all have same exterior, same couleur but this one now we eat come from warm place, even more south than your South America, where emanation from sun more strong. Long ago, after accident, such plan was made, every month from some place, melon is sent me. But *that* melon—where is grown, how grown! Yet nobody know because all same exterior have. Only *I* know.

[*Kanari doesn't need prunes.*]

KANARI: I can assure you Mr. Gurdjieff I not need.

GURDJIEFF: Assure? How can assure you not need? You wish invite me in water-closet with you?

[*He thinks she said "show" instead of "assure." When explained, he catches her again.*]

Aha, you say assure, but is same thing, philological question is—assure-ing and showing all from same word come. You can only *assure* what you can show; what not can show, not can assure.

Tuesday, December 8

Dinner menu like old times.

Smoked herring hors d'œuvres.

Then baked fish-pâté dish.

Then soup—fish consommé.

Russian meat cutlet—"officer cutlet" as known in Russia, as opposed to "soldier cutlet" which is five parts black bread to one part meat.

Melon—two kinds.

Candy—new kind—the raspberry "sausage."

[*About the baked fish dish.*]

GURDJIEFF: You have eaten more than ten men need, so much there is of . . . what is that word, that new word, you make fashion word of? Vitamine. Yes, you make fashion-word of vitamine, as if new-thing is; calor is old Greek word, calorie now you tell. Was time when every educate man know such thing about food. You make fashion word of vitamine but I, when boy already begin learn about such. Melon—you know Mees Gordon, this come from place which belong England, but they not know about this there; they not see. They see only English pound, whiskey, and English frozen meat. But you know, every month the Viceroy there tell, "Prepare one melon for Mr. Gurdjieff, and even if they have to steal from other, they prepare. But I am small man, not king, subjectively speaking. But objectively . . . this is for objective business.

Your king, you know what should do? Three men should kidnap him, take him away, kill him, so that even his stink not remain on earth, such dirty thing he is. Is stink idiot, the nineteenth, harmful, the worst kind. If he were eight years old, I could feel pity. But after eight he should be prepared. He not prepare, not take from around him what was correspondent for him—not prepare himself to be king. Was onanist. Even I prepare. When I was small boy I see that around me all people was animal. I see and I know that for me that must not be. And I was son of poor man. Even bread not have.

[*Kanari tells him that Mrs. Simpson has offered to give up the king.*]

She lie. She not wish now to give up, to free from bad situation. She now have inside her state of "All or nothing." Before she had cunning, now she have appetite. She wish now only big thing.

[*He questions Miss Gordon about the word "cartoon" he learned last night for his mentation meaning a comic drawing, Miss Gordon says cartoon means caricature.*]

No, cartoon is only one kind caricature. For example [*he goes to the market-place painting pinned on his wall, Lutte des Mages*] here is Mr. Hartmann, this is caricature; caricature is exact, mathematically exact, is quintessence of line, anywhere you can him recognize; but at same time something about this is comic. This is art.

Is seven kinds caricature, like everything. Example, there is Kanari; from one side is exact like grandmother, but from other side is something quite different; is monster like all temporary (contemporary) man. She is cartoon.

Friday, December 10

Now the king has left, the radio speech says not for a long time will he return. He is like a man without a country, I say.

GURDJIEFF: This case, he is my colleague. Children toy is good thing but when you see responsible man play with such, you feel shame for him. This is what your king do.

[*Alice sympathizes with Queen Mary who has seen her first born fail, etc.*]

No, not pity. She is exceptional, not ordinary person. Early she took habit of vanity. All her humaneness went into ego. She has pride for class, only people who represent something can be important for her. Already she turns to this next son. He is more nonentity than brother, therefore safer for country. Kind he is, for example, if he wish kiss your hand, he will between arising of wish and expressing it, forget a thousand times what he wished and when he speaks he will not say, "I wish kiss your hand," but "I wish break your ribs." This is good formulation for nonentity. Now his brother who was king, I could cure in two days of his disease. If I had to choose between being like him, King of England or eating plate of merde, I would choose plate. For his subjective sickness he would make a million people suffer. Miss Gordon, you not have objective reason about your king, such idiot you are, though our patriarch. Why I talk with you, I not know. Until your king, the dirtiest thing I know to say is dirty dog psyche. Now I know even dirtier and I can kiss hand of dirty dog because king is dirtier.

[*Gurdjieff speaks of his own "cure" which now is half done, now half of his inner world is free, now he begins to feel like a man with mustache. For us, he makes a picture of his state.*]

Now in me is very curious, very original state. Now in one room is old man and baby, and *both have equal rights*. Can you imagine such situation? Both have equal rights. Baby, for example, like fresh air, wish open window; old man not like, not wish, can even be harmful for him. Now you see, even this rum grog I order, this for baby is not corresponding thing, but for old man is very good. Very original situation. Yes, also is terreeble.

Saturday, December 11

Countess de Messey and her friend join Knachtschmidt and Company for dinner. After a wonderful dinner he plays a new music, then he asks Miss Gordon:

GURDJIEFF: Which you like best, dinner or music (to have fulling wholeness)?

MISS GORDON: Is different thing.

GURDJIEFF: No, is all same thing. Different octave but from same scale composed. I hope some day you will understand the unity of the law of Heptaparaparshinokh—everywhere the same.

[*Later.*]

Man never can have will. Only "I am." But not forget and say automatically. If thus always remember yourself, you can have force to move object across room.

[*Later, talking about the king again.*]

Man has million times more time than he needs. King was spoiled.

[*Miss Gordon says no, his family never spoiled him.*]

Yes. Is even law, so must be. First born is always spoiled. Even with animals is law. But truth would be impossible he be king. Once, when I live in Grand Hotel, I look out window early morning, three or four o'clock, down boulevards, and I see your king there with two

103

these girls who sell flowers. He have arm around each and is having very good time, they also. Such thing for him make data for life. Moreover, good thing for your parliament that he not be king. He have just enough initiative to upset plan made by your parliament. Idea arise in him, something he wish do for people. Independently such arising could be, and could be just enough to spoil all plan parliament. His brother have no initiative, also no data for life, so he for parliament and people will be better king.

[*Someone says, "Our five senses."*]

GURDJIEFF: Five senses? How you tell—senses? Firstly, is not sense. Secondly, you have more than five. Sense means sensation. You have not word in English for what I mean—feeling-with-sensation. Kanari, what would be word?

KANARI: I don't know.

GURDJIEFF: But try—say what word you think.

KANARI: Would "contact" have your meaning?

GURDJIEFF: No. With eyes I see you and you see me. But unless I wish, you not have contact with me. Svoloch language, your English.

Tuesday, December 15

KANARI: Now once we come to my toast and I not in galoshes, Mr. Gurdjieff.

GURDJIEFF: You chronically in galoshes.

[*As he leaves us, he says he has had only one half of him massaged, masseur now waits to do other side.*]

If not do, then I be lopsided. [*He wilts on one side.*] Lopside, you know, have one end. Is not like stick which have two ends. If man is lopsided, then everything he receives lopsided. If on bad side, then all receives bad; if on good side, then this is not harmful thing. Is why man can sometimes be happy.

Thursday, December 17

Dinner. The melons are served and Gurdjieff points to pieces at the bottom of the pile.

GURDJIEFF: Look now he sit down, at lunch only I cut, but so delicate thing is.

[*This begins the sit down, stand up talk.*]

Sit down, where can you sit but down? Stand up, how else can you stand? In forty-five languages I know no such idiotisme as you have in your English. This is why I say only, sit. People who not know, think I uneducate man, I not take time to tell, only now I tell.

[*We tell how as children we were told by parents to sit up, meaning not to loll, etc.*]

GURDJIEFF: No. Sit up. Up not correct word. Is other word, exact. Sit *right*. For each this mean sit as you were taught to sit for such and such occasion when such and such person present.

[*Alice's green Chinese bone pin lies on table. Gurdjieff picks it up and looks closely.*]

You know what they take from? This exact form have—pipe smoke opium. Everywhere in Orient, Turkestan, Asia, they carry when go far from home, not wish smoke public pipe. Man, woman, everyone carry, like brush (tooth), each his own. This (the pin) exact form have, only must have hole here and here; here put opium, here light, here suck.

In China, in earth, they find special kind glue (he means clay)—very, very strong; from this they make pipes, never can broke. Such hard thing is.

[*When we precise what kind of glue can come from earth, we learn he meant clay and we say we did not think he meant the glue which comes from fish and animal hooves, etc.*]

Also from man comes this glue. Three things man can make; glue from brain and feet, soap from fat around middle part, and manure from all parts.

[*Later.*]

Function is the process of transforming from one scale to another.

MISS GORDON: Oh, I always wanted a definition of function, I did not know it was as simple as that.

GURDJIEFF: Yes, this is what function mean, exact from old Greek word come.

Saturday, December 19

Lunch (Canaryless). He has Michele, the seventeen-year-old specially trained girl there for us to see. She speaks only French. Gurdjieff asks Miss Gordon, in English, what she thinks of this girl.

MISS GORDON: I think very nice, Mr. Gurdjieff, I have a good feeling about her.

GURDJIEFF: [*to Alice*] She tell like English. Now Mees Gordon, I wish you listen while I ask Thin One.

ALICE: I see a big change from this morning in the café, Mr. Gurdjieff. Already something happens to her. Now I see more deeply, one thing she has is not good, I cannot say what it is, I always look at hands. (Michele's stumpy thumbs!) I think you can make of her what you wish, she is clever.

GURDJIEFF: You think can be educated by me?

ALICE: Yes, in worldliness.

GURDJIEFF: Truth, you are good. [*He turns to me.*] She (Alice) unconscious education have. She not have education from book, but somewhere unconsciously she take from life. Truth, when I ask you, I kill two rabbits. Now I see much. Miss Gordon, you, in relation Thin One, are joppa.

[*He tells how he tried to educate Tall One and child.*]

In beginning was good, she put attention on small thing and I not have to tell. If I have to tell how to do, I can do myself. But soon dirt begin come, everywhere I look is dirt, even apartment smell. Also, for other things not good. Now this one I prepare special. *I must have someone.* I have right, Mees Gordon. I must have someone think about small thing around house. Before when was no one, was very difficult for me—*I assurance that quiet night, quiet morning, never can have.* Always some idiot thing to do. I get up, inside feel good, then I see dirt and for me, inside, all is spoiled. All is lost, all, all. Terrible thing. No soap.

[*He sits with us after giving us piqûres.*]

Now I hungry, but for you, best not yet eat, so I also will not eat. I see around me objective just, and when man sees such, he must sacrifice his subjective. This is one aspect of religious morality—what religion teaches. Religion is morality. Morality in English is for you big word, in Russian we have two words; one means morality, ordinary, such as we speak of now—other also means morality but more strong. It means opposite of shameless. Objective shame. This man must have.

*Tuesday, December 22**

We look at the lighted tree. We look at hand blocked handker-chiefs. We look at thirty-five boxes, one of which will be named for Knachtschmidt. There is roast turkey, a pig's head, and special her-ring; "from England come, but is Jewish, from Russia." Miss Gor-don's health is drunk.

GURDJIEFF: Your health, also health of all Jewish who create such thing. You not part Jew, but all Jew because you are Scotch. Scotch is all Jew. You know, every race in every country seven kind of people have—Tartar, English, French, etc.—but Jew have forty-nine kind in each country. A legomonism exists that tells; until last age, no cleaner people exist than Jew. Never they mix. If marry outside, then all children from such mixing must die—such law was. Clean people, very special.

[*Kanari says Bible called them God's chosen people.*]

God not interest such business. Always among many idiots, one super-idiot exists, he more idiot than ordinary, therefore he is super center of gravity. In this case Moses was such. He was center of grav-ity of Jewish people and *he* make them chosen, not God.

[*Miss Gordon says something about Great Britain.*]

GURDJIEFF: Great Britain, how you call—you know *why* call great? This they take from time when Bretagne was important, then in England go many more people, so they call it Great Bretagne. But from Franco originally come; here was center of gravity. Now today Germany do same thing. Have corresponding names.

[*Miss Gordon asks what names.*]

That I not tell. You could sell for thousand francs. I tell only quin-tessence, main fact; I know all begin from two people, from Greeks and Romans. Your historians make other thing, for me only this exist; Greek, Roman, and from these, two streams sheet flow and many strange things happen these two streams on the way.

MISS GORDON: Always you tell two original people, Mr. Gurdjieff. Never you speak about people from the north. Yet all Northern Eu-rope is mixed with these people. Scandinavian.

GURDJIEFF: Scandinavian? I not know such name. I know only Samoyede. But this was not important people, at time of Greek and

---

* Katie's notes combined with mine.

Roman was only second gravity people. Later they come, they mix. Samoyede, you have such title?

CROCODILE: Yes, we have Samoyede.

GURDJIEFF: Samoyede, you know what mean exact? This mean *self-eating.*

[*Miss Gordon talks about people from the north and Normans in France who are clearly a northern people, etc.*]

From the north how *you* tell. For me, all is mixture. From same source come materials. Only is different how they are mixed. They make of these northern countries you speak about—a cocktail. Imagine I have seven different cocktail here before me. All taste different, even look different. Here is one you call "yellow cocktail." But only I know sheet when stay long hermetically sealed turns yellow, dark, and more dark yellow.

Study peoples, see how they flow from two main sources, how they mix, how they divide. Even the English people divide, many thousand kind there are. Even are the kind that eat margarine and the kind that eats oleomargarine, both artificial butters, each with separate stink. Even British people divide selves by what stink they have.

[*Miss Gordon agrees, perhaps too willingly.*]

Mees Gordon, you are English. English never see such thing can be for him; always he see for someone else. English not have sensing on earth for entering into situation of others.

[*Special potatoes, curried, spiced, running with butter are brought in.*]

GURDJIEFF: Miss Gordon, I think never in England you see such potato.

MISS GORDON: [*falling into the trap*] Never—and cooked in so much butter!

GURDJIEFF: Look, already she begin to be worried concerning how much cost butter. You know, for such potatoes like this, must be boiled in butter. But still not clean. You know, potato difficult to make clean, so first butter must be poured off, then again must be boiled in butter. But still not clean.

MISS GORDON: Then three times boiled.

GURDJIEFF: Yes, three times boiled in butter.

MISS GORDON: I knew there must be three.

GURDJIEFF: Excuse, there is fourth time in this preparation. Fourth time potato is baked in butter.

MISS GORDON: Oh. Now must go to seven?

GURDJIEFF: Of course. Or three or seven. This case, seven.*

[*Yakina takes one of his cigarettes.*]

Ah, now I see you have satisfaction. You know, is law—so much satisfaction have, so much dissatisfaction must have. Everything exact valuum have. The rule is add one zero. If your satisfaction cost fifty francs, you pay me five hundred; if one hundred, you pay me one thousand. You pay in money, of course; here on earth is only money for paying. If not pay me in money, you must later pay me in coal. This expression very ancient understanding have. In hell, of course, is coal for fire. But *how* you pay. It takes for each person so many kilos coal a day for roasting him; ten kilos you and you, twenty for me, for example. So if you pay me in coal, this means that each day you must take from under me so many pieces of coal and put under you. So if enough you pay, then I can be very comfortable. But your situation—you can picture how will be?

Wednesday, December 23

He enters from the kitchen with a suckling pig, holding it like a baby, "See what sympathetic expression it have."

GURDJIEFF: [*toast*] Sardine, hopeless, yes, you are hopeless. May devil help arise in you hope. Look, she not like devil. Angel, then. Now my obligation with her finish. Now all depend from her, from her surroundings, who she be with. Moreover, if she continue eating how now eat, she will look like second cousin of what we now eat. Also for all of you I tell. Now fat can hinder work. For beginning was necessary have fat, now must take off and make all hard, compact.

ALICE: [*looking at the wonderful melon*] I like melon because it is sweet.

GURDJIEFF: Sweet you must not like, you must use.

ALICE: I use for energy, Mr. Gurdjieff.

GURDJIEFF: Excuse, you not use for energy, you use because you like.

ALICE: No, I don't like sweet.

---

* One day after Miss Gordon had died, I reminded Mr. Gurdjieff how he had tortured Miss Gordon about the butter he used on those baked potatoes. He smiled and said gently, "Even she believed me."

GURDJIEFF: No, you not like—you are slave to one thing I notice about who like sweet—always in atmosphere around him is bitter; saliva also bitter, even emanations.

[*Kanari, as usual, staring at him in admiration.*]

You like how I tell? You like my mentation?

KANARI: Anybody would like, Mr. Gurdjieff—such objective mentation.

GURDJIEFF: Not anybody, only American. Always you say anybody. To you it seems wonderful, but not my fault America not have habit such mentation. Moreover, I tell in objective sense I not complete objective mentation have. I not yet complete initiate. There are many thousands complete men on earth; not in world, but on earth. I still have far to go.

Thursday, December 24

At the café.

GURDJIEFF: Difficult tell taxi where go—only know three names— Étoile, Opéra, Montmartre. When in my car, can go directly where wish, find smallest street.

KROCODILE: Like an Indian in America, he can find his way through forests.

GURDJIEFF: Not so much for forest am I. I specialist for sand. Never can I get lost in desert. Travel in desert depend from secrets—two— which pass from father to son, a legomonism. One I tell. Always big ridges on dunes lie a certain way, according to winds. Before you start, look how lie these dunes, judge about angles, how you must cross, they never change for small storm, only big can make different. Very important know this, because once you are fifty meters from starting place, there is no right, no left.

[*That night at dinner we help him arrange the presents under the tree and pack forty boxes of fruit.*]

GURDJIEFF: Yakina, look your glass. You are yak, yet you not drink even one quarter what Kanari drink. You are big animal, must do big, all you do. Kanari drink four times more, yet think how many canaries would take to make one yak.

YAKINA: I have so much to say, I cannot talk.

GURDJIEFF: Not necessary talk. Only have shame.

[*Kanari evidently should not have had four times Yakina's Armagnac, for she is manifesting and is in galoshes as usual for her toast.*]

KANARI: Galoshes again, Mr. Gurdjieff. It's almost like a law.

GURDJIEFF: Is not *like* law. You know, it takes seven years for creating science idiotisme with great knowledge of typicality, polarity. Everything about each is known. I write many books about each. So for you is typicality that you always be in galoshes—your profession is. Look, they not even laugh any more.

KANARI: Chronically in galoshes, once you said. Chronic, like disease.

GURDJIEFF: Not only like disease. Chronic have two meanings; in Greek there are two words, sound nearly alike, chronos means concerning time and other chronos means keeping. When I told you chronically in galoshes, I mean you are keeping you in galoshes. Many newspaper named Chronicle—not concern time, but keeping you au courant.

[*Later.*]

Now I see arise around me three lice, fat like canary.

[*None of us follows his meaning here. Presently Alice wonders aloud, "I wonder why does lice bite?" And we laugh at her grammar.*]

GURDJIEFF: [*not realizing why we laugh*] This is not idiot question. Why is always where reason is. Why is for what not is known but at same time exists.

[*We come to the melon course, he offers Alice a certain piece which is sweet but not the squeamish sweet we spoke about yesterday. I remind him how he says "bitter in atmosphere."*]

Not just in atmosphere. He emanate bitter. All what come from him is bitter; saliva, sheet, emanation—all the same. For you this word sheet make shock; but it is relative word. For me when I tell, it is nothing, so long and so much I know about it. And you know, is not always bad thing. Sometimes it can have more vivifyingness than roses. Sheet sometimes more esteemed can be than your teacher.

KANARI: If it is that kind.

GURDJIEFF: Always I tell *if*.

Christmas Morning

I go early at 8:30 a.m. to his house to see if he needs a chauffeur. He has been up since six and is the quintessence of wide-awake. He invites me for breakfast at the café. He takes some cheese in his pocket. In the café he orders butter for me, "You being American take habit for butter and in truth is very good thing with this cheese. Not order for me only because I not have such habit."

GURDJIEFF: [*eats in silence, says to Krocodile*] Now we can service nature. You know this is what food is for—for servicing nature. Truth we are slave, such poor slave. Nature not give this food, all life man must work to earn it and when he eat, it is not for him. Nature give only one thing, only air. For the rest, man must spend life working. And that Old Idiot what create such, he swagger now, imagine, for having created such absurdity.

I give no indication that I have ever heard of the second food, or how to use it. He goes on. He tells about the comic pictures Mr. de Salzmann made—God and Gurdjieff. Gurdjieff is visiting heaven, not dead, but in spirit. God is in a chair, has work around him, even typists, and has in hand a compass for making circles. When God hears who is coming in, he hides his compass, puts it under himself, sitting on it. This picture has a very comic aspect, for him, he laughs like a small boy when telling it to me. "Too bad many details I forget."

[*Alice comes in and speaks of Dionne quintuplets, how scientists wish to study them.*]

How can study when scientists themselves come from same barrel, same nonentity is. With five from same birth, nothing to study, no individuality can be there. If people understood what this really means, they would cry. Man now begin to breed like mouse. In old times, even twins was rare thing. Soon five will not be notable, people will speak of six, then seven. Nobody see what this means, that quantity destroys quality.

[*Alice notices he looks well.*]

Yes, I am well. Well—how relative is this word. It not take count of terrible struggle of functions. In me was war, real war. Sometimes even head could not remain independent—falls so . . . [*Gestures sleeping exhaustion with his head.*]

Christmas dinner at Gurdjieff's house. All Knachtschmidt are there including Georgette and Margaret. Before we go in for dinner I make Alice show him the lump on her knee, the result of her fall. He looks closely, moves it, seems amused.

GURDJIEFF: Now you unhappy you have such thing, now I know you never will have in throat. Also, from this, many another thing I know you never will have. You be glad for this.

[*Much later at table he refers again to this lump.*]

Theen One not hungry, I notice she take long time select what pieces she will eat. [*To Alice:*] You should eat like mother, mother with seven month baby. All of you must know that she will be first to give birth to a being—this will be an *abstract being,* whether he be angel or devil we not know. There already on her he begin rise (on her knee). [*Then to me:*] Why you see such thing and not tell? You now should be happy. In my book I will write about this first "birning" and you will be written about like Mary Magdalene because first you see. Only after, I see.

[*Solita goes in galoshes when she refers aloud to the real Mary Magdalene and what she saw in Jesus. Gurdjieff rages.*]

But I not tell what see. Only analogically I speak. Always you far go. Moreover what could she see, this Muggy Muddalene you speak about? She see nothing, she only prostitute.

Georgette asks if the melon came from North Africa and Gurdjieff roars that *never* he eat anything French, all French food is for him like soupe à l'oignon as is all French mentation; all English are like frozen meat. He struggles to find French equivalent of frozen meat. Congelé, glacé . . . we spend a long time on this philological question and he roars about the French language saying it has no words, never he can find word, seven hundred and eighteen words he *knows* it not have.

GURDJIEFF: *I god languages.* Only not for such idiot thing as this that anyone can learn. I speak scientific, very simple I speak. Why learn idiot words good only for idiot talk? I not have time.

MISS GORDON: What a picture of God that is, speaking only scientifically, but every word exactly understood, every word known like a leaf on a tree going back to a main root.

GURDJIEFF: Yes, is so.

KANARI: But for such idiot word, you not need know Mr. Gurdjieff, such nose you have.

GURDJIEFF: This can be so, only nose is no good in alien country, good only where in general land is familiar. Imagine yourself in Oriental country, not one word have for you association. But there is always language of the smile. Anywhere on earth you can get what you wish with smile—wheat for horse, water, bread—because this smile exactly correspond with what other man feels.

Wednesday, December 30

GURDJIEFF: This is most important day for you. In twenty-four hours from now when you have assimilated this medicine, you will be responsible for all your acts, conscious and unconscious. You take position of responsibility. A record is not kept for each soul, as people believe, but only for responsible souls. There is a law of sinning and you are now subject to this law. If not fulfill all your obligations, you will pay. For every satisfaction, so much dissatis-faction—the Angel Gabriel's books must balance.*

---

* End Katie's Notes.

1937

Friday, January 1

GURDJIEFF: Around your body is electrical envelope. On quality, quantity, of this material depend if people like or dislike you. Once I had this so strong I could push ship across ocean—and back again.

A scale will always involute back to its beginning '*do*' unless you continue through to '*do*' of next scale. Nothing remains half way. This is law. But once you have reached next '*do*,' the scale you have gone up is always yours and you can never lose what you have made. If you have gone up scale while transforming your apartment, even if you have no furniture or roof, you have always your doghouse, where you are safe. There are seven times seven scales and formulation for forty-nine is "You-in-yourself."

Now this morning Sardine come disturb me in café. She think because I sit and look out window that nothing I do. But under such lazy exterior is such concentration that no man is capable of. Million things I must think about. There is saying, "Measure a thousand times before you cut cloth." Another saying, "Before you give teaspoon medicine to your neighbor, test a barrel of it. This is what I do when I sit alone."

KANARI: Mr. Gurdjieff, you are spoiling us.

GURDJIEFF: Spoil? How can spoil what already is spoiled?

*Saturday, January 2**

Dinner—the Rope four. He comes into the salle in time to hear my last word of titillation, "January."

GURDJIEFF: January, what January?

[*Alice tells him that January the sixth is my birthday.*]

Ah, January six. Then is not tall of donkey day if is your birthday.

[*I say, Epiphany, according to Catholic calendar.*]

GURDJIEFF: No that can not be. Epiphany mean when many people come together for be baptized. Must be mistake somewhere.

That day was when Jesus was baptized. In Armenian and some other countries, always birthday and baptism day are same day; Jesus was not baptized until twelve days after birth, and because of this you can make a joke in Armenia which is big insult, always make angry. You say, Jesus must have been a premature baby, they were afraid to baptize the day of birth, had to wait twelve days until he be strong enough and not die. This make Armenian very angry. But in many countries, Armenia also, *Jesus is not the hero, but John the Baptist.* From legomonism I know that he it was who was nurse to Jesus for first twelve years, in Essene Brotherhood; after this first twelve years, then in this company the responsibility to another give. This is the story how I know from legomonism.

[*At table he speaks of the melon.*]

Always best at the end of its season. Soon no more will be; already now, in place from where come, they dry this melon, they cut in slices and dry in sun. This they must do, because only this melon grow there, nothing else for food. Except one kind of chestnut, but not called chestnut, called pig nut. It is a three-sided nut and one curiosity about this nut; if eat too much of, it make drunk. Even the bread they make from the flour of this nut, makes you drunk. People eat, and afterwards must sleep, because they are drunk. Those who know about this of course not eat.

[*He offers to drive us as far as Café de la Paix. We reach Concorde and say, "Please can you let us get off here, it's shorter than from the café."*]

If already is shorter than from café, then I will make more short.

[*He drives us to the hotel door.*]

Friday, January 8

He returns from three days taking the baths at Vichy. He is tired, but cooks a milk lamb for us, the Rope four. We do not talk of work done in his absence. He seems to be in something; he looks at each one of us, with terrible penetration, then leaves us saying only to Alice, "Then, if you did not identify with it (your cheek carbuncle) this can be worth more than first prize in the Lottery which is three million francs. And to me, at table, "Crocodile, what is the matter, you eat badly tonight?" And to Kanari, "She will eat sweet. Crocodile, I bet you she will eat one of those sweet, already I see water in corner of mouth."

He is so tired at table. He says he has gone several days without teeth, and now tonight, with them, there is suffering. He would not even eat from fingers of godmother, and is too tired even to drink tears of godmother. A moment later he says, "What is it you drink? (He has forgotten the word "tears.") We tell him and he says, "How my memory is bad for such idiot thing, only one moment ago I say this word and now when wish say again, I forgot. But can remember a page of writing, such specific have my memory, even where on page come a certain thought, even I can remember mistakes in printing—exact where on page they come. For such thing I have memory, but not for small life thing. Of course this will pass."

He excuses himself early from table after Alice has rebound his finger with the new Bandtex, discarding the old grease soaked bandage. He says, "You excuse me, Mees Gordon, now I go rest. I need such; if stayed away any longer, then could be dangerous for me. I will take ninety percent risk, even will take ninety-nine percent risk, but never will I take hundred percent risk."

"Even sometimes you take hundred percent risk, Mr. Gurdjieff," said Miss Gordon.

"No, *never* I take."

But he smiles as he goes out the door—almost a grin.

Tuesday, January 12

This is the anniversary of my total abstinence from cigarettes. He speaks of man's "dogs."

GURDJIEFF: This for you makes source for force. But at same time any man can *not smoke*. You must smoke. Only not take habit. You not wish do what any man can do?

KROCODILE: I remember your grandmother.

GURDJIEFF: Smoke then.

[*We speak of dogs and Alice says a fine big car is one of hers.*]

No this only artificial. Man even artificial dog can have, such is man. Man have few dogs. Smoking is one, alcohol another.

[*He has made a dish which as he says, "make melody in mouth." Have no place for the sweets.*]

Eat, eat, Mees Gordon, still remain sweets.

MISS GORDON: Ah, but your hospitality is so great.

GURDJIEFF: Truth, my hospitality so big it is my idiocy. The Jews not have this hospitality—they think it idiotic. Jews of all countries never have friend. Each family stay apart. They not spend money for hospitality because they always see cost of small thing, never big thing. This is one of the aspects of humanity-ness. Not humanity, for word humanity only gives address, while humanity-ness shows a property of humanity. [*To Kanari, agog with appreciation.*] You like? I not know good your English, I only translate my thought.

Sunday, January 17

The dish he has made is called *Salanka.*

GURDJIEFF: This is dish of Ghengis Khan. Also he like trout, that spotted trout from one river in Tibet. And this he have fresh every day. He have organization, even one hundred thousand people from Tibet to wherever he is, in Caucasus for example, and this trout in buckets they pass. One man twenty-five kilometers go, very fast, then next man, and so on. Such Emperor, such influence he have. You know, sometimes history show that one man could take almost all world. Ghengis Khan was such. Ten your Napoleons he could in pocket put. Alexander of Macedonia took much, even today in many places they keep souvenir of him, almost like holy thing.

[*Later.*]

Brach (brock)—to chick-make with inner self but outwardly to treat as brother. A brach person is like damaged good; can be sold, but at a loss, never bring profit to the shop owner. So a brach person never can he be of use to the man who produced him, ninety-five out of every hundred are "brach." You must think of yourself as if you are sitting in prison.

[*Later.*]

Full is fool.

[*Later.*]

Job never complained. He even pick up worm that fell from boil and put back.

[*Later.*]

Nothing takes habit so quickly as man, not even pig. With man, once or twice makes habit.

Saturday, January 30

GURDJIEFF: The French can do nothing when hungry. English a little better. Americans can forget and work on—especially if they get paid a little more money.

The rose is king of flowers. Always in Eastern literature is put with nightingale. Rose is loving—loving rose. And besides loving, rose can have many another emotion which idiot English have no name for. Yes, even nature can feel loving—like woman.

The French have no friendship for anybody. Americans have too much—a disease with them. Even in their house they have special room named for strangers. But in some countries is real friendship, such that if I have one shirt only, I am obliged to give half of it to my friend.

Miss Gordon, I am empty.

MISS GORDON: Yes, you must be hungry after bath.

GURDJIEFF: Not that kind empty. Never is man that kind of empty I speak about, even if not eat for long time, is always full of merde. I tell another kind.

Who from paradise go out, goes out automatically. But to go out from hell must have individuality and cunning. Destroy factors in you of faith, hope, and love in your old understanding and make new factors with your new understanding. Know yourself, then mankind, then the planet which is only another organism like man, only higher. I say stingy like Scotch for American and English understanding. For Russians I tell Stingy like Americans. You see, I make réclame* for America.

KROCKODILE: But only in Russian.

[*He laughed.*]

KANARI: She is taking your advice and becoming light.

GURDJIEFF: Not light enough or often enough.

KANARI: Stingy like Scotch, stingy like Americans—then where is truth?

GURDJIEFF: In this case, truth is in logic. Man never sees truth in his own subjectivity, only in other nations. Stinginess, Jewishness in all man is, in each according to his subjectiveness and his heredity. All mankind is merde, all different kind of merde, like I

---

* Advertisement

tell about that time when I sit in certain field and see about me all kinds, shapes, and smells, each different but all the same, merde.

Friday, February 5

Lunch.

GURDJIEFF: Trout, he very spoiled fish. Not can live in any river but only where water move fast over stones and difficult places, only then can be happy. Also you notice one thing; never any sauce will mix with him, only butter, fresh butter. This alone mix with what he have specific under skin.

Saturday, February 6

The Riviera trip. Cannes, Hotel Splendide, dinner.

GURDJIEFF: Yakina, you must be happy here near mountain. Yak have one specific, very original. Is heavy animal, too much have inside, yet always go where is most difficult, like goat. Choose to go where is stones, where no other animal would wish go, except goat who is light and for which going is natural. But yak will turn from smooth path and choose steep high place with stones. Also another very original thing have.

KROCKODILE: [*hopefully*] Mama-papa business?

GURDJIEFF: No. Merde business. Then yak very original movement make, not like any other animal. If you could watch you could learn much about the human psyche. Look, Krocodile wonder about mama-papa business. This also she makes very different. But here you would not understand about Yakina, for she is too far from you.

[*Dinner. He drinks for the first time in many days.*]

Look, I am already drunk, yet take only small amount. But all in body wait to take. I even assimilate more than is.

Sunday, February 7

In two cars we go to Èze Moyenne-Corniche for lunch. Hors d'œuvres, trout, baby lamb, and Vieux Armagnac. First we must climb up to old town (and believe me he sits below watching that we do it) all except the frozen Kanari.

GURDJIEFF: What you need—Armagnac and pepper.

[*Lunch. Alice says she feels her face is red, also says Kanari.*]

One thing interest much, how she can know without mirror that face is red. But what interest most is how Kanari feel face red (we look, she is not red). You know, only two places on body blood go to make red. Or face, or Mary Jane. So now question I put . . .

[*Alice serves the last small roast potatoes, saying to Kanari, "You must eat, this is bijou."*]

Bijou, Kanari will not eat because she is bijou. You know what is bijou? Bijou is adjutant for maquereau. Adjutant you know, always near colonel and always, one day, he become colonel, because wish colonel be. So bijou one day will be maquereau.

[*Alice is full of retorts (also Armagnac!) and this brings about his observation that today she must have put on the right stocking.*]

Such belief there is, if put on right stocking, then all day be right for you.

ALICE: Yes I know about that, Negroes in south tell.

GURDJIEFF: But only one side they tell, lopside. Example, they do not know that if you born odd month, first, third, fifth, then always it must be left; if even, then must be right first.

This is conjury, you know what is conjury?

KANARI: It means "with swearing"; con, with; jure, to swear with will. But we use only in sense of magic.

GURDJIEFF: No, conjury is not magic. Is real English word, real English meaning have. Wish, not wish, conjury you must believe because all life consist from conjury. For example, what I do today can be good for me, because I do it, but for Mees Gordon would not be good, would be opposite, because is objective conjury and parallel with this is scientific knowledge.

[*About trout he speaks and I remind him of yesterday's formulation—trout is spoiled. Trout then is like knachtschmidt—spoiled.*]

No, *not* like. Trout cost something!

[*He takes us down from high moments with a reminder about time. Points to one of the patron's girls who once he held on his knee as a baby, now she sits at table with sweetheart.*]

Grow up, too important now to sit on Gurdjieff's knee. But I would not wish her to sit there now. When was small, I liked to smell, was sweet; but if now she would sit, I would not wish even her smell, she would stink, stink ——. Such thing has Heropass made of her in so short time. [*Then toward Kanari.*] And you too are not now what was, one year ago, ten year ago. Today are not what was yesterday, and tomorrow will not be what you are today. Time take from you, will make stink —— of all, such is life. The Heropass.

We drive back to Cannes through alleyways of Nice avoiding the carnival we came out to see. At Cannes there is a terrible sick stooped old lady in Hotel Splendide, with her daughter, English.

GURDJIEFF: Look, Mees Gordon, you know what is? (Meaning the old one.) Is squeezed aubergine.

ALICE: That must be her daughter.

GURDJIEFF: Yes, from same kitchen garden is; only is squeezed potato, frozen potato.

[*He has a formulation for all the riviera people—paint and then, with ceremony, throw in sea.*]

Like old automobile you paint and make exterior like new, but still is only good for throwing in the sea. But with ceremony, big ceremony. Such people here is, "pant and throw in sea."

[*He sits in his Cannes café. We talk about cunning and he gives us a formulation:*]

Naked for combination is cunning.

[*He hears music. He says always at important moments in his life there is music (some decision to make).*]

Long time music center of gravity was, writing was by the way.

[*He remembers "Pianina" he once heard up in the mountains behind us, at St. Vallier.*]

So fine and clear were the notes in the mountains. Is different thing, music high up. There the vibration is more fat.

We go on a "picnic" away from the mimosa and sunlight up into the snows and we open cans of sardines, anchovies, tuna—fish oil dripping on our hands and only snow to wash in! And he is in his element sitting over cold food on a patch of snow, on a forty-five degree slant, with jagged snow peaks circling us and if he could only have his hand organ up there, and play to us (from a snow peak still higher above us) we would know something about the "Deevine!"

Tea at Nice. Alice goes to the lavabo.

ALICE: [*returning*] They are dancing on there Mr. Gurdjieff.

[*We sit on the terrasse.*]

GURDJIEFF: Everywhere they dance, but you know what is? Is practice for passion. This is how I see with my special eye. They masturbate publicly, you can see in faces. Some can even no longer masturbate, on their face you see "please, memory, please . . ." They hoping for association which will take them back to time when they had such thing. Never can I look on dancing, only when both are young, but this you never see. Or old woman with young man, or old man with young woman.

Tuesday, February 9. Monte Carlo.

He takes his whole "tail," and we sit in the deluxe café opposite the casino first.

GURDJIEFF: One custom I have always in Monte Carlo. To all the children I give money and they must play all in the casino. If win, then half they give to me. So now . . .

He gives one hundred francs to each of those deemed children— Margaret, Solita, Dimitrivanich, and me. We have a wild half-hour gambling. Solita more than doubles her hundred, I come back with a hundred and fifty, and Margaret and his brother are cleaned out. We divide with him our winnings.

A "boorjoui" lunch in the swell casino café restaurant. I want to remember Gurdjieff picking up a trout skull and sucking out its eyes in that place!

We take the "La Turbie" road home, Gurdjieff gets stuck in a blind alley, tears off fender paint and knocks two pebbles from a Frenchman's entrance and pays and gives candy which they leave scornfully on their wall where he places it. Curses, yelling, a Buick penned in a space for a Rosengart . . . But he gets out, with "help."

The two-car return via St. Raphael, with Vichy (!) spoken of as the night's stop; rain and rain, cars lost. Alice and I get to Lyons at 11:00 p.m. and rush out at 5:00 a.m. for Vichy thinking he might be there with his brother and Miss Gordon in the car but he isn't and there is a telephone call at noon—he will be there by two o'clock. At three-thirty I am in the street looking up toward the gare and I see a high square car come *nosing* down the street; nosing in at each corner curb as if to smell if this is the hotel and finally he arrives. His car is packed with boxes of food, both old (from Paris to Riviera) and new (the St. Raphael wine, red and white) and Dimitri is in the back. He "comes up" like a white worm when the back porch boards are lifted. The boxes slide away, the mimosa parts and his haggard white beardy face appears. "Oh, jee swee mort!"

There are the Vichy tail people at a dinner table for twelve people and we have trout again. Gurdjieff tells a "fresh trout" story about the Tiflis fish merchants famous for humor—to know if a trout is fresh you smell behind the ear, just as you smell a chicken in the Mary Jane.

Monte Carlo Addenda

"Who from paradise go out, he go automatically; who from hell go out, he go where he wish, he individuality have. Try this small philosophy understand."

Sunday February 28–Monday, March 1. The Rouen Weekend.

"Knowing tapeworm is more than knowing god."

Tuesday, March 2. Paris.

Krocodile helped peel a bushel of potatoes. He squeezed them, hot, in his hands, added four pounds of butter, then a quart of brown liquid, eighteen spices cooked together, grated boiled eggs, and a bowl of chopped onions. This is the dish the king of the caravans eat—caravanpashi—"You can imagine how is, eaten in oasis, with cold water from well."

GURDJIEFF: Look, Thin One not like. Not according to her American gout.

KROCKODILE: [*aside*] True both ways.

GURDJIEFF: How you mean, both ways? Another meaning have this word?

KROCKODILE: Slang word, goo, means something without taste or substance, nothing in it you can recognize.

GURDJIEFF: Good word. Even in Bible is. You know how begin— "In beginning there was—*goo.*" People also can be such.

Wednesday, March 3

He comes from the kitchen suddenly into the salle.

GURDJIEFF: You know Mees Gordon, there is one country called Kafiristan where people one strange custom have, always they begin dinner with the sweet; then roast, then soup, then hors d'œuvres.

Many thousand years a civilized people live here; is high in mountain, those mountain that shut off India. These people very strong.
Even I see here two hundred *English people* who are slave, they
work like donkey, with my own eye I see. Many traveler try go this
country, even they try make of it what they made of Tibet, but these
Kafiri own (control) all the mountain passes and only let pass who
they wish pass. Afghanistan, Armenia, Russia, put many thousand
man in those mountains, try to pass through, but Kafiri with one
stone can kill many thousands because every stone they know. Also
they shoot with gun—in one hundred shots they never miss one—
can write your name on tree at distance. Yet they are honest people,
once say will let pass, you can count on them, only you must pay
high. But not money. Money they not wish. You must buy your way
with one of three things; women, guns, or horses. Only these they
like. And always these people stay in own country, they are satisfied, not wish go any other place. This is good country—mountains,
high places. So now . . . we will begin our dinner like them, with
sweet. (A sweet macaroni dish.) Come, come, *eat. This is kind of
people we wish be.*

[*At dinner he speaks about English travelers.*]

English travelers go a thousand kilometers to see a place, if two
friends say it is beautiful. But on the way for a thousand kilometers
they see nothing, not look, sleep or read newspaper. If ask them
about a mountain or lake, they cannot reply.

[*Yakina laughs.*]

But also American thing is, though they see more. Now you, Yakina, for example, you not notice one thing that change my face.

[*He twirls his mustache which is again turning black at it's roots.*]

You not see one change?

YAKINA: I see nothing, except your mustache turns up.

GURDJIEFF: No. You have months looked on me, always you look
on my eyes and not see anything else. Yet this is crying thing on my
face.

[*Someone tells her.*]

YAKINA: I never see color, only line.

GURDJIEFF: Excuse, man must not look on one part—is onanist
thing you make to see eyes or nose only. Must total see. Man must
have normal vision.

YAKINA: I am not interested in mustaches. I look on a face as I do
on sculpture.

GURDJIEFF: Sculpture. Now you have offended me with this word. I am objective sculptor. I see *all*—even all of you, I see—even your navel. Crying thing on my face. Good expression, eh? Even your Shakespeare could not write such. He was pederast. Between every line (his poetry) I can smell pederastisme. Such dirty life he had, not like what he write.

KANARI: You not like or you mean his life did not correspond with what he wrote?

GURDJIEFF: No, not correspond.

[*He leaves the room but Yakina wishes to argue on.*]

ALICE: [*calls out*] Mr. Gurdjieff, Yakina here is still very excited and wishes to ask a question.

[*He waits at the door.*]

YAKINA: Mr. Gurdjieff, you know that a change in color is not so essential as a change in line!

GURDJIEFF: Yes, Mees, I agree that your American art books is written so. But still I am changed man. You know why? A week ago I had not time to waste in discussion with you. But now [*twisting mustache*] I have auspicious exterior and suspicious interior, so I must do everything corresponding, even titillate with you.

Thursday, March 4

Lunch. We have (among other things) boiled chicken.

GURDJIEFF: You know what kind cheeken is?

THEEN: Is not fiancée, Mr. Gurdjieff?

GURDJIEFF: Is fiancée. Never satisfaction had. Specially they make so . . . once each day with such chicken they put in another (rooster) for make play, but never they let do. When wish make mama-papa business, they take off.

MISS GORDON: Why torment so?

GURDJIEFF: There is also something else I remember. In Russia is one fish. [*He gives the name to Dr. Stjernvall.*] Even doctor not know name this fish. Every day they take this fish from water and *beat him*. Then put back. Many many times they do this. This make liver large—the liver very expensive is. Only rich people can eat.

KROCODILE: Anger makes the liver big?

GURDJIEFF: Yes, somehow is so. And such liver it is, have active element, like what this chicken have.

MISS GORDON: One would have to be sure that only a deserving person ate such food, after such cruelty.

[*Then he tells us about the bouillon which came from the six chickens he has.*]

GURDJIEFF: Best part is in bouillon and this we will eat tonight if we can liquidate the Banque de France we all have pressing on us.

[*We decide we can.*]

KANARI: Mr. Gurdjieff, may I also tell Yakina? She thinks she is in galoshes because of last night.

GURDJIEFF: She remember?

KANARI: Oh yes, she knows she was impudent.

GURDJIEFF: Not *was* impudent. She *is* such. One Russian expression there is, you tell her this.

[*He gives it in Russian, the Dr. translates.*]

DR. STJERNVALL: *A hunchback can't be made straight even in the tomb.*

(Yakina wished me to state in these notes that she had no idea of being "impudent," that she had too much respect for Mr. Gurdjieff to be impudent.)*

Friday, March 5

Georgette's French friend, "Bedouin" is there; twenty-one, BA, MA, PhD Sorbonne etc. Gurdjieff knows where the corn is. At table:

GURDJIEFF: Mees Gordon, you know I have long memory, but *what* memory—every detail for forty years and now I bet you I know, or her uncle, or cousin, or father—somewhere I meet, even if forty years back, I remember. You *know* from where come—from Araby (pronounced Aravie).

[*Then he tells Yvonne that Solita is half canary, half Jew, and that next to her sits one who is half crocodile and half Jew, this is how he reads our genealogical trees. She of exotic descent looks at us poor mongrels.*]

KROCODILE: You must be afraid, finding yourself next to a crocodile.

---

* "Much perturbed by this completely false, and certainly unauthorized, report of my reaction. I said I realized I had been stupid; I could never feel (let alone know, realize) that I had been impudent. Everyone knew my reverence for Gurdjieff. I could never even imagine I could have been impudent to him. Such was my 'idiocy' in those days . . . and ever after I suppose."   MCA (Yakina)

YVONNE: Afraid? Moi? I *never* have fear.

[*She takes another drink when there has been no toast announced. Candidate for Armagnac is what she was called, so will be it.*]

GURDJIEFF: Aravie, I could even prove, such science there is. I can resurrect by smell instinct of nation from which she come.

[*Now she warms up on another toast, Gurdjieff watches.*]

You not feel strange here?

YVONNE: When I heard that musique I felt myself promenading among the pyramids, une musique sacrée. [*We think she is kidding, but she isn't, she goes on.*] Vous êtes la demeure de ma vie antérieure.

GURDJIEFF: Tell, Kanari, what say.

KANARI: Just can't translate, it's embarrassing.

[*He howls at another one of us.*]

KROCODILE: She says you are the living place of her past life.

[*She turns on me and says, not past life, previous life. And she goes on about man falling out of space into the death of life. She does what Margaret named "the smoke spiral" to illustrate the arising of man. French has no expression adequate for this but she has gesture. We come to coffee.*]

GURDJIEFF: Coffee from Aravie.

YVONNE: Coffee of my country.

GURDJIEFF: No, of your essence. [*He watches what he has made for us to watch.*] Look, soon she will take passeport.

KANARI: For going.

GURDJIEFF: No, not for going. [*To Alice:*] Big difference is between going and coming.

Later, (but we don't know about this) she gets the fire and water test (fire in the breast, water on the knee) and fails of course; but we knew we wouldn't be seeing her again.

Tuesday, March 9

Lola is there for lunch—big headache, no appetite. Gurdjieff babies her along until he turns on her with rage for shock. It's about the platter of fresh greens. We have all commented on estragon at that season, fresh, young.

GURDJIEFF: [*to Lola*] Not even president, your, can eat, but I can eat. Next month I this not will eat. You not know why? Because then everybody can eat this thing, in all market you can buy. *I eat only rare thing,* what nobody can find; when everybody eat, I not eat, there will be other thing. [*Then to us:*] Too bad she not understand.

KROCODILE: She not know your grandmother, Mr. Gurdjieff.

GURDJIEFF: True, true.

[*This is the day when Alice receives her new title: "Lady Cellarer of the Royal Household of Gurdjieff"—because she takes care of the Armagnac bottle.*]

Only when my labor you eat well, then am I satisfied.

[*Momentum—inertia—Kanari tells at table how Gurdjieff put her in galoshes about these two. She did not know they were the same thing with only the difference of time. I tell her I knew, Theen One and I had talked just the other night about this (from some star book).*]

KROCODILE: Momentum, an object sent off moving in a given direction cannot initiate change of direction from within itself—there must be a shock from outside. This is how I understand momentum.

GURDJIEFF: Since you interest take, one formulation I will tell for you: "Momentum is when your going not depend from you." Inertia: For instance, Theen One drink my coffee from inertia. Many month she drink it my house, she take habit, but she not *like* coffee. She drink from inertia.

Another day, we are speaking as usual about eating till we bust.

KROCODILE: I'm glad your piano is not here yet, Mr. Gurdjieff, because then would spoil piano also.

GURDJIEFF: This is true. You know, when I bust, whole house go down, all wall, all floor, everything. But when crocodile bust, all block destroy.

[*Margaret looks mystified because we are talking (and laughing) about busting, pianos, houses and blocks destroyed, and when someone clears it for her, she laughs.*]

Why you laugh? You have skin ten times thicker than crocodile. If I wish shoot with gun, bullet not go through . . .

[*This is the day Margaret's arch toast is, "May you transformate into elephant."*]

Now tapeworm . . . he try voice!

Wednesday, March 10

There is a soup—chicken, apricots, white grapes etc.

GURDJIEFF: Fast soup. (We're in mi-carême* I think.)

KROCODILE: This is feast soup, Mr. Gurdjieff.

GURDJIEFF: No, is fast—only *how prepare* make feast soup.

[*There is baby mutton.*]

Bravo England. England two good thing have, mutton and pound sterling. All rest is dirty thing. I remember how everything smell of margarine; in street, in house, people, everything. But English, they not smell, they have in bones. Germans invent this (margarine) but they not use so much now.

[*Alice tells him about the material in a collection she saw with "God Save the King" woven in an all-over pattern. The plan is clear to Gurdjieff; someone here, with English connection, plans to put England in galoshes for pounds (house of Molyneux!) he will take patent on this design, sell high, make all England buy, and England must because they are so partial for their king.*]

English are such, they cannot look on king with impartiality. Such sheep are. Only if Englishman lie alone, awake, at night, can he sometimes see. But moment he is with one friend, he partial. But *we* can now say, not "God Save the King," but "God Keep King," we not see him. Other king was will-less but him you could look at; this one must not even be seen. Good conference, Theen One? What English people would think if could hear?

ALICE: Would have to mentate for a long time, Mr. Gurdjieff.

GURDJIEFF: They not have time mentate, too much time they take to digest Australian frozen meat or margarine.†

Thursday, March 11

GURDJIEFF: Man can develop taste as he can hearing for music, knowing every note that makes up total harmony. Even he can develop so that he can take doses of poison that would kill other people. Kanari, perhaps you see such in theatre?

KANARI: No, but I have read. People say Rasputin was such. (I'd been waiting for months to ask about this.)

GURDJIEFF: No, he was idiot, merde, nothing he could do, nothing know.

---

* Mid-Lent.

† End Katie's notes.

Friday, March 12

Alice drinks a small glass of kraut juice during the hors d'œuvres course (as he *once* taught her).

GURDJIEFF: Not must drink before, drink after, otherwise you spoil appetite. Americans ignorant about food, not *one* thing they know, not even simplest medical knowledge they have. Only one small thing they do shows this—drinking glass of water before meals. Body work twenty-four hours to make liquids necessary to digest food but before eating, they drink water which sucks out all these special liquids; dissolves them and they go off and when food comes, nothing there is for it to mix with, nothing for transformate; they eat only to make merde. Not only this they do but also they eat butter. Butter coats the stomach lining and all the insides, and what must pass through the walls cannot pass—they even eat chocolate before eating. Chocolate coats inside and takes away all feeling of hunger, this is only for travelers, mountain climbers, etc., to eat only when they *wish* this effect when not can have food. This is why soldiers ate chocolate during war. But Americans eat before meals, such uneducate people they are.

[*An iodine toast.*]

"Let devil help devil take."

Saturday, March 13

He tells the priest something. The priest watches with eyes popping, mouth pursed, tossing back his curls. We know something is happening—

GURDJIEFF: Just now I tell priest God is old man, only I use old Russian formulation for old man. You know this thing used in old days for make writing dry—sand. This is how we tell old man—sand run out and he cannot stop it, moreover, any devil can take. This I tell him. He not even angry.

[*On the fruit dish is the same old monster orange we've been seeing for many days—bright dark orange with rough pebbled skin.*]

KROCODILE: Ah, there is the patriarch still.

[*Gurdjieff hears and looks amused.*]

GURDJIEFF: Now you put in me curiosity.

[*He goes out of the room to his storehouse, returning presently with another monster; a little older and darker, the original patriarch. He shows it to us without a word.*]

You must be careful about such thing you see in my house. Remember my storehouse have communication with Karatas.

Tuesday, March 16

GURDJIEFF: Mees Gordon, pity you not know valuum of rice. On earth thousand kind is, but you not know. This is Persian, special.

MISS GORDON: I know how good it is, Mr. Gurdjieff.

GURDJIEFF: Not how good. Rice you praise only for how soft is, yet at same time each grain you can count.

[*When the fruit comes to table, Kanari touches an apple admiring it's color.*]

Look how she interest take in exterior like all representatives art. For exterior she make imagination, fantasie. She even so far go she opposite sex make when present self. Such formulation there is. [*To Miss Gordon, asking if she took her iodine:*] You had, Mees Gordon?

MISS GORDON: Yes, I have.

GURDJIEFF: I not ask if have, I know you have in pocket, I ask if take.

[*We begin discussion about our idiot language, how you must say, have you had, yes I have etc.*]

KANARI: We would say among ourselves, "Did you take your iodine?"

GURDJIEFF: No, excuse. This you speak with intonation. Your intonation tell all. Your manipulation make understand, not your word. But I not know your intonation, I strange your language. For me only word exist. Exact word.

MISS GORDON: Language changes with the times, Mr. Gurdjieff, we grow careless.

GURDJIEFF: Excuse, *life make language change, only life*. But now man go ahead and make change before ready go. For example, English have mentation shepherd, somewhere they learn Greek, so now when they speak even with fisherman they understand only fifty-fifty. Normal man never try change language. Only life can do this.

[*As we go out the door, Alice says, "Now we go to our labors Mr. Gurdjieff."*]

GURDJIEFF: *Only one measure there is for labor—oof* (money). Labor without oof is onanism.

Wednesday, March 17

Three of us get new toasts.

[*Compassionate toast.*]

GURDJIEFF: My dear Kanari, may God help you transformate into crow, not so much dirt have crow, which if it is small, quality have. After you are crow, we will see.

[*Squirming toast. To Alice:*]

May God, the devil, and all the people of Karatas help you be not squirming that you not be in future what you are today.

[*Square toast.*]

Krokodile, God help you transformate into elephant.

ALICE: Ah, longer legs will have.

GURDJIEFF: Not only legs, other thing they have long also.

[*Speaking to Miss Gordon, he brackets English-Scotch together as one word and Kanari admires how cleverly he does this. She did not expect his thought about two separate peoples would go in such a sequence.*]

But why astonish? All same is. You know how I call in book that island . . .

KANARI: Albion, from Latin alba, meaning white. Roman name became white chalk cliffs.

GURDJIEFF: But excuse, in book I not spell same. One letter I change and you not see. Even many pages before, I prepare for this when I speak of Khorassan goat, Karabach ass, and people of Albion. But you not see.

KANARI: Middle part I cannot remember.

GURDJIEFF: Middle part not important. Only beginning and end important. Middle part is only bridge. Beginning preparation make. From beginning flow middle, and end flow from beginning. Bridge not interest. Only interest for turkey. *I hate turkey. I write for crow or for peacock.*

*Saturday, March 20. Vichy.**

The patron of Hotel Mondiale served boiled eel.

GURDJIEFF: Why you serve such thing? This is not fish, is serpent, is merde. Normal man not eat such thing. For him is like oyster. Only idiot or German eat such. For us is merde, like oyster.

We all send out our eel untouched. The patron's situation is too awful to go into.

The great exoteric platter of fruit is brought in for dessert. The Vichy Russians look at all the strange fruits, and Gurdjieff divides grapefruit, mango, and avocado and watches them eat for the first time. Their marvel over the strange fruit leaves them naked, so after it is over, he calls the garçon, and proceeds to feed him pieces of unknown fruits—and now the Russians are clothed again in scorn for the garçon, and amusement at his marvel over the fruits which they just five minutes before had also tasted for the first time.

We see the garçon run out and presently return with twelve pieces of store pastry for our sweet. Each one mentally selects what he will eat. Gurdjieff glowers. Then he says, "If you wish good thing next time, don't touch this now." So the plate of pastry goes out untouched.

Sunday, March 21

The morning of Palm Sunday in Café Gambrinus.

GURDJIEFF: We will plan promenade, since Sunday is.

KROCODILE: And special Sunday—Palm Sunday.

[Gurdjieff remembers Easter is near and speaks of fasts.]

GURDJIEFF: We were in Nice beginning of Easter, must be forty days ago. Easter fast have fifty days.

MISS GORDON: Always forty days Mr. Gurdjieff, Bible tells how Jesus fasted forty days.

GURDJIEFF: Excuse, English Bible made for old maid. I not know your Bible, from older source I know. Before Christmas is forty, then two more fasts in the year, one for planting, one for taking (harvest). This is custom among men through the ages. I know from custom, not from your English Bible.

---

* Katie's notes.

[*He invited them to his room for coffee in fifteen minutes. They were three minutes late and Krocodile said it was her fault.*]

GURDJIEFF: Not to one I speak, small or large, all from same barrel, same stink. Now coffee is cold.

KROCODILE: But it is good, not cold, just right.

GURDJIEFF: This is how *you* like. This you must not tell among many. For you is good but what is your good is spoiled for another. You must enter situation of other—see what it is and put word in your mouth to correspond. Even polite bon ton book tell this.

Monday, March 22

After an enormous lunch.

GURDJIEFF: Now how will be about dinner?

[*Miss Gordon says she could eat nothing.*]

This answer for present is English property. Tapeworm always answer for present. Man with mind must answer for future; must see how *will* be, not what *is*.

[*At dinner he looks in the mirror at a blonde hussy behind him.*]

That blonde, you know how is? Is liquid. Every part is liquid. Even there is formulation for such. Her woman-ness is same as after twenty-five glass tea.

[*After two Armagnacs, he recalls some name or some place which others have been trying to remember for him.*]

You see how I remember? After two Armagnac, memory is thin—thin in quotation mark.

MISS GORDON: Fine, perhaps you mean?

ALICE: Precious.

GURDJIEFF: Precious—exact word is—under pressure. Same root have. Precious and pressure.

[*I speak of diamonds, our most precious stones made under great pressure.*]

GURDJIEFF: Yes, you see?

[*Coffee later in his room. We speak of his hospitality, the coffee, and the mountain of fruit.*]

Hospitality, yes. Man not have, in him is atrophied. Hospitality is now only cunningness. Organically man not have. As for example, in that place, Turkestan. There still exists humanity-ness. From heart. Friend there is when two people buy something together, one sell his part and make money, and this he divide with other, fifty-fifty. Two times he do this and friendship is established for always.

[*We tell him about the men with "language of smile" who came aboard our boat in Constantinople, bound for Mecca—teapot in hand, umbrella in the other—how we knew instantly something different had come aboard. From Kirghiz steppes they came.*]

GURDJIEFF: Kirghiz, yes, also such people they are. Moreover, they go to Mecca, prove that they are holy men. Simple people with heart. Those places are centrum of humanity-ness.

ALICE: China and Japan also?

GURDJIEFF: No. China already merde is—also Japan. Already spoiled. They in process of change from crow, not yet is peacock.

Often as boy I go to holy places, but was psychopathic then and different thing received it. Later I see Etchmiadzin, holy place in Armenia, like Jerusalem. Last time I go I remember how different it was; all changed. People, faces, all. All go so fast now, not have time assimilate. In last fifty years, customs of thousand years go. *What take long time come, long time stay; short time come, quickly pass.* Now even small boy there read newspaper, you can imagine what idea he receives.

[*We talk of going to these places.*]

GURDJIEFF: Wait two, three year Mees Gordon, then can go by airplane.

ALICE: Then will see nothing, I wish to go by train.

GURDJIEFF: Even in train, nothing will see. Must go on foot. Once in Russia I lived liked gypsy. I had horse, donkey, tent, friends. I make twenty or thirty kilometers one day, then stop, rest two days. Only such travel is real. Then you see how everything is—if each place has three or two stones. Go this way from Paris to Turkestan and will complete education have. Moreover, if you stay a long time with such people, you will gradually become like them, like real man. To astonish you, I will tell I once go three hundred kilometers on goat—special goat, special training; over the Pamirs to Kashmir. Donkey also good for difficult places. Donkey special psyche has. If he not wish go, he will die first. You can beat, you can kill, if he not wish, not will do. But if you understand psyche and are friend with, then he will take from you all heaviness and go until he dies. Oh, many friends have I among donkeys.

[*He puts his last fifty francs in his coin purse explaining it will make grow more money. It is a culture.*]

What make grow yogurt?

[*He won't understand culture, the nearest we can come to it is yeast.*]

Yeast, yes, this can be. Make bread rise. Also [*this in perfect seriousness seemingly*] this is from where you get name for this holiday—Easter. In reality it come from *Yeaster*. Christ rise this day. Yeast he musted had, like bread. Same root. Yeast. Yeaster. (Easter was Anglo Saxon for Goddess of Spring.)

Tuesday, March 23

At the last lunch he sends candy over to a little girl who receives it with a jump of joy and rubs her feet together.

GURDJIEFF: Look she make play with candy as if is poupee. You know, Russian word for navel is "poop" and French, for doll, "poupee." From same root come. I could for half-hour with this word "poop" make very dirty thing, and then for half-hour make clean with "poupee." But she must not know this relation because she already spoiled is. Such children must not play with doll because dirty thing they receive from it.

[*The last night—he is talking and working on Miss Gordon's sock. He gives Alice something by the way—a candy, a fruit.*]

GURDJIEFF: But Theen One not interest, already her sock empty is.

KROCODILE: Barefoot, we call that, we even have a famous poem about a "Barefoot Boy."

GURDJIEFF: Just this word I seek for long time—always *this* I wish to find for book. Exact corresponds with Russian.

[*"Barefoot," he says, over and over. As we rise from table, the garçon thanks him using the Russian word for Prince. Gurdjieff does not understand, so the garçon shows him the word Prince he has written on a paper, specially hunted out of some dictionary that day.*]

No, this not important. *Any barefoot can be a prince.*

Thursday, March 25. Paris.

An unknown fruit for lunch.

GURDJIEFF: [*to Jane Heap*] Such thing Mees Geep not from planet earth. This is food for man, real man, not man in quotation marks. Nature hate man in quotation marks, you know, for "man" nature not give such thing. Cookies—also for real man is, if you such, you can have all the time. Here is quintessence of all good that exists.

[*To Alice:*]

Your health. Soon you must change from squirming which is idiot I not like at my table. Always something dirty have. Squirming is only passing state for man. Is state like fish out of sea, man must not long stay or he die and be obliged to be born again. (This is the only time I ever heard Mr. Gurdjieff say anything that could be referred to Ouspensky's specialty, Eternal Recurrence.) Man can stay squirming two or three months, but not for a year.

Friday, March 26

We have small tinned lamb tongues from Tibet, from Lhasa, and he tells us how he used to have to butter his whole body, then cover with rubber underdrawers (made in Germany) then over all that about six inches thickness of fur garments—and even then he was cold in Tibet.

GURDJIEFF: Only part of body have satisfaction was face under hood, warmed by breath. Such cold you never can imagine. Also, such smell from "booter" after many week!

[*One other very cold place he stayed for a whole winter was in the Pamirs.*]

There live under snow—have houses under snow and even tunnel connecting each house like streets and so cold was, that when you lit fire, the solid snow ceiling melted just an instant, then froze over immediately.

[*This night we also drink Dalai Lama's tea—he hovers over the pot and pours out the small cups himself, measuring sugar first, telling us how to drink.*]

Too bad I not have time make Tibetan tea with butter—boiled, and small amount of flour of roasted wheat—such a drink have *all*.

[*However, this tea we drink is sublime, and we say so.*]

You see, not such idiot there in Tibet. There you can find everything, if you know how; Tibet direct communication with Karatas has.

[*He tells us of the wood they burned in their Pamir under-snow houses.*]

There was one black wood and one white.

KROCODILE: Birch, what our Indians use for canoes, the "skin" of the birch—birchbark.

[*He goes to look up the word in his Russian dictionary because he's not sure birch is in Europe, certainly not in England where Miss Gordon claims to have seen it. He finds birch is right and tells us how they made shoes from the "skin" of it. Again he talks of quintuplets and multiple births.*]

GURDJIEFF: Imagine what kind of children will be when all must divide what should be for only one. These births are in nature's plan—quantity instead of quality. Nature obeys command from above.

Tuesday, March 30

Jane, Miss Gordon, Sardine, Krokodile, and Theen. I stayed in the steam baths—I did not go to lunch with the others and he was very angry.

*The first half of the lunch is eaten in silence. Alice as Cellaress refills my glass. Gurdjieff thinks I am drinking false until I tell him that I begin from new, then he looks at the other glasses not as full as mine. Miss Gordon hid hers, he finds, and turns to Alice—

GURDJIEFF: Theen One, your obligation you not fulfill. You not see all around you, only ones near like me, Miss Geep, Krokodile. This is small obligation I give you but you not fulfill. If not can do this, then all you do will be false—even hat. *You must feel your subjects around you, you for them must be king.* King with all his objects; house, people, checkbook even. Yet even all this is cheap thing beside real man. One man without quotation marks is worth all your kings with all their objects.

[*Alice weeps, not having heard quite all, and looks away.*]

GURDJIEFF: [*to her averted face*] Why you look on Sardine? Look on Mees Gordon, she much higher is.

[*He wants to be gentle now that he has made her cry and tries to pull her back when she leaves the table for a moment. She returns powdered and cooled. I stand beside the soup pot. He bangs his ladle into it, splashing but drawing up each time same amount of solid and liquid, exact. After I am seated, he says—*]

---

* Katie's Notes.

Krokodile, you notice my justness. *Never I give more or less than necessary.* But they not see, they not take what I give for what is.

KROKODILE: [*I understand he is talking about Alice*] It is good food, Mr. Gurdjieff. This must make good for them no matter how assimilate.

GURDJIEFF: Ah, that is another question. (But later when he shakes me by the back of the neck I think it's because I understood Alice through the soup analogy.)

[*We have compassionate toast before soup.*]

GURDJIEFF: Compassionate not here. She in bath. She exterior dirt has made clean, but never interior dirt will she make clean, such dirtiness this is. Never if go every day to bath, never if use ten kilo soap, will she make clean, such interior dirtiness have. Still she in dirty surroundings stay.

[*We begin the soup.*]

GURDJIEFF: Krokodile, who not eat . . .

KROKODILE: Perishes like dog.

GURDJIEFF: Yes, and like dirty dog. Two kind of dog there is, you know, dirty dog and dirty dog. You understand Mees Gordon what difference is? Dirty dog and dirty dog.

[*Squirming toast.*]

I wish with all my presence, with my real soul, you soon transformate from squirming to some other idiot. Let all devils help you.

[*Square toast.*]

May you be useful in near future, my service, for all humanity.

This has been a terrible and grave luncheon, and he in some kind of pitying hidden rage—about us, I feel sure—and his disappointment. All the time I felt tears and Jane said afterwards, "Today he is sorrowing with Our Common Father. It's because of us, what we have done, we haven't been able to take enough of what he gives, we've failed him somewhere.

Thursday, April 8

The beginning of new exercises with piqûres.

GURDJIEFF: I hope with all my heart that there will rise in all of you feeling of humanity. American and especially English people cannot feel for even one person except self, so spoiled he is, so degenerate. Even your Negroes not so spoiled, he has twice times more feeling for humanity than you Americans who hate him. Negro I like, I can be friend with, they understand tones and gestures.

Friday, April 9

[*Krocodile forgets and skips Kanari's toast.*]

GURDJIEFF: For fifteen minutes she make plan about what next come, then with great swagger she tell wrong. The terribleness of it is that man—real man—must remember, if not himself, then what he does in relation to his surroundings. Man must always prepare for what he do and necessary that he at all times think about what he do.

How many you eat, Miss Gordon?

MISS GORDON: Several.

GURDJIEFF: But I not give you several. I give you not more than five.

MISS GORDON: I ate three and three is several.

GURDJIEFF: Kanari, what do you say?

KANARI: I say three is not several—must be seven, eight, nine.

GURDJIEFF: One is one, two is two and three is three and so on to ten. After one hundred can be many. After two hundred, too many.

[*Alice suggests yogurt to Lolo, who says, "No thanks," and makes a don't-like shrug. A little later, when there seems no connection, Gurdjieff says*—]

Now I remember one old Persian saying. Something Theen One do make me remember. From where could donkey learn taste of ananas (pineapple)? Then eat this, madame.

LOLO: That is not in my régime, do you not remember?

GURDJIEFF: How can I remember? For you to remember. You are only one and here in this room I think only of eating, not you as individual. In other room I think of régime things and in salon of music. In each room I am a different man.

[*Gurdjieff has made mint tea especially for Lolo who cannot take coffee today. She drinks to the last drop, obviously appreciative. To Lolo:*]

C'est pas mauvais, Madame?

LOLO: [*to be witty*] Oui, c'est mauvais, très mauvais.

GURDJIEFF: [*to us*] Look how she is not gentille. I ask, like domestique, "Is it good Madame?" And she reply, "It is shit." She call result my labor such word.

141

[*The burst of horror from Lolo sends him on: "Oui, Monsieur, c'est merde."*]

GURDJIEFF: [*to Lolo about the fruit*] Madame, eat, mangez.

LOLO: I can't.

GURDJIEFF: Eat, eat, [*he puts fruit on her plate*] you see even how I beg you eat. You know, in Persia, how they ask you to eat? This I will tell is quite bon ton there. They say, "Madame, eat, eat, this cost only shit." Such understanding they have, no one stop on this word, with shock, like English, French. Even if what they wish give cost a million, they say cost only shit. Very bon ton there, this word. Always they use, for everything.

[*He sees me staring (with joy) and says to Kanari—*]

Look how Krokodile look at me. We discuss grammatical question, Krokodile.

KROCODILE: Grammatical in quotation marks.

GURDJIEFF: Excuse, this time is only grammatical question. This is exception. All other times what you hear was in quotation marks, as your understanding received it. This time not. This is first time you are worthy to hear grammatical question discussed.

[*He tips and half spills his coffee and says immediately, of Alice:*]

Look, she make black magic, she do this, not I. She is . . .

[*"Witch," we say.*]

Yes, witch, she is witch.

[*"We even say be-witched, Mr. Gurdjieff when someone make black magic against you."*]

Yes, this exact is. She witch-ness have. You can see it in her nose. Always you must look on nose to know about witch-ness. Also, Sardine have, only not so much as Theen One. First at this table for witch-ness is Theen One; second, Sardine. [*He turns toward Alice.*] Any man when see such face, he immediate association have for witch-ness, all he remember from child comes to him by association. [*He makes a stooped magician gesture.*] Only she not have garmony, because too much one thing she have. Six parts her are empty, one part have too much, this is why her witch-ness not have garmony.

Saturday, April 10

[*He catches Alice watering her Armagnac. He sees her blush.*]

GURDJIEFF: Look, now she begin have one property of Mees Gordon. [*But he doesn't scold, he says with disarming tenderness—*] Mees, if you put in three drops of this (soy sauce) then you will have real Armagnac. [*Alice puts in four drops.*] Now is *too* old (for color of old Armagnac he means).

[*Next toast.*]

ALICE: [*drinks and looks at Gurdjieff*] Is not improved, Mr. Gurdjieff.

GURDJIEFF: No, but (the) water is.

[*He tells something to Lolo and says he hopes she is not offended. Kanari translates for Lolo, using fâchée for offended.*]

GURDJIEFF: No, this is not the word. *Fâchée* is opposite of *gentille.*

KANARI: Froissée or blessée for more strong.

GURDJIEFF: No, the word is dessalée. (One of his super-shock French words which we don't know.)

[*Lolo holds her head and tries to think what it is.*]

GURDJIEFF: Look, now she try know, but this will take long time, because she have thick skin, like crocodile.

MISS GORDON: [*lovingly*] Not *our* Krocodile. (Katie is her pet.)

GURDJIEFF: All is same—all breathing creatures are from the same family, like man. All breathe same air from same planet. All make water-closet business in morning and papa-mama business at night. English, American, French, all have thick skin like crocodile. What go in, go slowly. Crocodile skin never could be skin like cow. Never could be cow, like this French woman here, but could be camel. Like all creatures that breathe, even he takes measure, like man with pill, because he need cleaning.

KANARI: You said that even God needs enema.

GURDJIEFF: Yes, but has umbrella. You know what is umbrella and what is enema. Two ends same stick. This is why I tell always enema-umbrella. You can imagine when need enema, but only have umbrella to put in behind. Then when press button (spring), umbrella open inside.

KANARI: For six months we tried to think what umbrella could mean.

GURDJIEFF: Now you see, simple thing is. Everyone know umbrella—when rain, put up. Such system I put inside. Man even will take in him this thing, because wish exist. Simple thing is what I tell, and you philosophize six months.

[*Alice says, " No meat" in her soup, she has not room.*]

GURDJIEFF: Excuse, many year ago I prove that you are not pig. Pig can take only so much, then must bust. But man have caoutchouc stomach, he can take till one side go in one room, one side in another room, and only then will he bust. *Such possibility man have.*

[*Krokodile exclaims, seeing for the first time a deeper sense. Miss Gordon laughs.*]

GURDJIEFF: [*to Krokodile*] See, she think is joke thing I tell.

KROKODILE: Even for me is first time I see what this means Mr. Gurdjieff.

GURDJIEFF: First time, yet every day I tell same thing, why man is not pig.

[*After the next course he asks Miss Gordon how is her tapeworm.*]

MISS GORDON: Too full even for singing, Mr. Gurdjieff.

GURDJIEFF: Truth, now he cannot sing because such fullness is here, but he know that such a fullness means satisfaction in one half hour, when all go down. Though cannot sing, he knows this is the beginning of satisfaction.

ALICE: Tapeworm knows more than God.

GURDJIEFF: Excuse, tapeworm know more than man, not God. God is very far—him you can never touch. Tapeworm you can touch. He is in you. He know more than man because very thin (fine, sensitive) his mentation is.

KANARI: Even have imagination.

GURDJIEFF: Of course. Also have more sense of reality than man. Moreover, if you know tapeworm *scientifically* you can go up. Him you have possibility of knowing. Him you can touch. If know him, you can go up (scale) scientifically. Even has his psyche like man.

[*Square idiot toast (Krokodile), and he explains carré idiot to Lolo.*]

Round idiot is idiot from all sides, square go this way (he squares the air) here, here, here, and here he make stop, not all times idiot.

[*He notices Alice did not finish her glass on Krokodile's toast and chides her thus:*]

Look, you not drink all, and moreover for your friend. Now one thing I know about you and Krokodile, you unconscious animosity must have, one for the other. Even with such Scotch drink you not finish. Scotch, not Jewish. You know, Scotch is concerning material thing. Scotchness is organic thing, Jewishness is psychological thing. Scotch I hate physically but Jewish I hate more because he psychic dirt have—self-love, vanity, pride. Except for this, I like Jewish, I like for friend. Only he is dirty in objective sense, because he has had possibility for knowing. Scotch not dirty in objective sense, he is not guilty. Jewish born with possibility for knowing so he is guilty.

KROKODILE: Now we understand!

GURDJIEFF: Of course—such separation I must make for my mentation. This is why I always tell, or Scotch or Jewish, two quite different things these are. This is why Scotchness have stink and Jewishness have stench.

Insert

At the beginning of lunch, Kanari with chicken grease on her hands, gets up to go and wash and says to Mr. Gurdjieff, "Excuse, Please."

GURDJIEFF: [*after she is out of room*] Always I excuse, for every thing man do I excuse [*I see a look of unimaginable gentleness on his face, then he adds:*] I am always bon ton. Always I excuse.

MISS GORDON: [*who perhaps saw same look*] But with arrière-pensée, Mr. Gurdjieff.

KROKODILE: Behind-thought.

GURDJIEFF: No, better unter-thought (under-thought). This is not begind but unter. Tell Kanari when she come in. [*Kanari returns.*] While out we find new word, "Under-thought." This is good phrase? From this you can write whole article. I excuse but not tell my under-thought. [*He goes on, telling how polite he is.*] My politeness was born before me. [*Hearing such a phrase from himself he stops with astonishment like ours.*] Good phrase I tell! How could such thing tell in article?

KROKODILE: Would have to steal, exact, Mr. Gurdjieff.

GURDJIEFF: Truth, must be exact. One word changed and would spoil.

[*Later, after another philological brawl, he laughs and says—*]
Look what interest everybody take in one word.

KROKODILE: Always I notice people fight about philological question, Mr. Gurdjieff.

GURDJIEFF: Philological question and . . . shit.

[*He shows a fancy Japanese box.*]

Look, America has such box for diamonds and Japanese have for
s . . .

[*Later.*]

Why you laugh?

[*Kanari explains appreciation of his sense of humor.*]

Sense of human? Not mean nothing.

KANARI: Humor—for laughing.

GURDJIEFF: Ah. Even too much I have. No, I had. Once in Tiflis I
had three shops, and for each one I make such comic drawings that
everybody come order—so much so that I decide leave that place,
something else do.

Monday, April 12

GURDJIEFF: How are you, what notable change have you felt?

KANARI: I have one small strong place no subjective state can
touch.

GURDJIEFF: Perhaps you mean that center of gravity is now in
your nature, not in your mind.

[*He asks Alice if she will have a second helping (of a fourth course).*]

ALICE: [*alarmed*] Oh, no thank you, Mr. Gurdjieff, I have *no* place
for it.

GURDJIEFF: Look how she is egoist. [*He puts his hand level with his
chin.*] You speak from here up, you not speak for tapeworm. *Tapeworm is in your presence*, you must not make angry, you must with
him be indulgent. Who be kind to tapeworm, who satisfy, tapeworm
help him achieve what he wish.

[*Later, Miss Gordon is telling him something and uses a fuzzy word
which she tries to explain and says, "I think . . ." and then says something about English words analogous to thinking.*]

GURDJIEFF: You have think, ponder, meditate—but not this word
(which he gives in Russian) which mean mentation. Mentation
means exact—divide, take, and not take.

Wednesday, April 14

He has (for a treat!) American canned beer, "Pabst." Georgie is
there and to her he directs his beer talk.

GURDJIEFF: In truth, this American beer is best beer, after Germany. You know, beer is German-American mind business. Americans,

when they make, they all put, they pay millions for réclame and new invention but later they will collect, because they not pity what must go in beer. Americans, when do, do *all*. They not pity, like English. English also have beer business; is elephant, but they make fly.

He tells us about the chain of beer gardens in Tiflis where, for réclame, owners gave all you could drink, and how people went drunk, from beer garden to beer garden, drinking till bust; but this was *real* beer, and the beer garden owners knew they would collect later.

GURDJIEFF: Was good thing, of course man must early-lately recognize such.

KANARI: Germans, Mr. Gurdjieff?

GURDJIEFF: Of course, these beer gardens were German.

Monday, April 19

Alice wears new Easter clothes to lunch.

GURDJIEFF: Look how she is *chic*. Yesterday she saw me in new suit and was jealous. Jealousy can be good thing, can be holy impulse. Man see something higher than himself, wish to be such, so make effort. Jealousy can be factor for cunning. Of course, not the dirty kind, not man-woman jealousy. (Greek selos, meaning zeal or eager rivalry.) Sardine, must now plan cure your hemorrhoid now and forever. You have not enough of this liquid for life—you know this liquid from which all life come, which give all.

SARDINE: Blood?

GURDJIEFF: No, not blood. Blood dirty thing is. In blood too many things is. This what I tell is in that other liquid.

[*When Krokodile's turn comes to go down the hall, he says—*]

Please be so kind, be object for my sadism. You *can* say such in English?

KROKODILE: Oh perfect, Mr. Gurdjieff. But only you can think such things to say.

[*At table. He drove to and from Le Havre yesterday and now is tired. Moreover, he did not sleep.*]

GURDJIEFF: Truth, I tired. My poor planetary body, he service me well and I make him object for my sadism. Once sadism mean only sex, but now for all things we use this word—new word only has been in my lifetime (Marquis de Sade). About twenty such words

147

arise since I can remember, even your "okay" and "cocktail." [*He picks up his glass of Armagnac.*] Now in truth he deserve such artificial help for strength, he tired. You know, I am like one barrel with small hole in bottom through which all pass out slowly. How you call what happens to that barrel?

[*Krokodile says, "Leaked out the bung-hole," Miss Gordon says, "Empty," and Kanari takes the palm with "drained."*]

This is the right naming of the barrel's state.

[*He talks about various "pick-ups" and speaks of that American cocktail, wondering innocently how the word originated.*]

GURDJIEFF: From where come this word "cocktail"?

KANARI: Nobody knows in America, Mr. Gurdjieff, but it's a new word; when I was child they began to use it. But cock-tail means tail of male chicken, and perhaps from this it comes; many colors in tail feathers, like all things you mix for cocktail.

GURDJIEFF: No, must come from kaka-tooloo. (The sacks full of contents of cesspools, carried off in the night in Eastern villages; if seen in the moonlight, with a hat put on top, is exact representation of man, he once said.) Those liquids Americans mix and make merde of. In Armagnac is represented years of man's labor and preparation, also brandy. These Americans spoil. Cocktail have such sound—like French kaka, child's word for merde. Kok is root from old word—vowel between consonants not make any difference; is kak, kek, kik, kok, kuk, all means same thing in all languages.

KANARI: *Caca*phony.

GURDJIEFF: This also and your Thomas Cook. People think only means merde. True, but bigger thing than they think. So your cocktail—head of merde, tail of merde. Go in behind, come out behind. There is formulation: "Nothing is behind tail."

Tuesday, April 20

He has a "Greek lunch"—seven different courses laid out. Kanari begs off from his special roasted sweet potatoes.

KANARI: I am afraid will make fat, Mr. Gurdjieff.

GURDJIEFF: Potato not make fat—potato have in him —— (Russian word). [*He tries to tell, touches his collar.*] What make hard? [*Starch, we say.*] Starch. This is what potato have.

KANARI: But starch makes fat.

GURDJIEFF: Excuse, not make fat if know what to eat with, with what combinate. Starch is very important thing, is one of the seven divine things for man. Without it, he could not even breathe. Always this has been known but now nobody know this, now starch is used for (to make stiff) collar for pimp and this thing (petticoat) for prostitute. And this, one of the seven divine things, people are afraid eat, afraid make fat.

MISS GORDON: Sugar also, Mr. Gurdjieff.

GURDJIEFF: Excuse, sugar is cheap thing, is svoloch thing found everywhere. Everybody can have sugar.

MISS GORDON: But sugar makes heat, isn't this bad in the body for making heat?

GURDJIEFF: Sugar gives by the way heat. Starch gives everything—body heat, material, even God thing.

[*When he returns from a prowl round the kitchen he hears Alice admiring Solita's scarf and says—*]

What you speak of Mees?

ALICE: Wool, Mr. Gurdjieff.

GURDJIEFF: Ah, wool. We know much about wool, eh Mees Gordon? This is also *my* specialty, about shearing I know all.

ALICE: I also have sheared, Mr. Gurdjieff.

GURDJIEFF: [*standing over her*] What you do is children play, Mees. Suppose you are in strange place and must have forty-two thousand dollars and this you can have for three days only, then again must have not forty-two thousand dollars but forty thousand more besides, because must live for several months—*this* is shearing what I know about. Not your children's play. Your shearing was accident—accidentally you learn make hat and there arise around you people who wish hat. You are there among them and can do, all result of accident, also your shearing,

ALICE: [*who has waited for the pause*] But I mean *real* sheep, Mr. Gurdjieff, with my father.

GURDJIEFF: Still this is children's play, I am specialist for wool. About this I know *all*.

Wednesday, April 21

Before lunch, Alice is speaking with Gurdjieff and tells him that Krokodile is upset, having realized that day that the separation will be nearly six months.

GURDJIEFF: [*to Krokodile*] We not be separate as long as with inside same idea have. This going not will touch your inner world. We are together. Soon again we will meet.

[*We have the vermicelli from Siam, and he asks Miss Gordon if ever she see in England.*]

MISS GORDON: Never, Mr. Gurdjieff.

GURDJIEFF: Still, in England they have. English never see what should see, only see what should not see. Everybody imagines he have knowingness for life. For this knowingness he is nonentity. Life is big thing and what each man have is only one small piece. [*To Alice:*] Now everyone imagine he can shear me; you for example. But I make naïve while you shear and at end I shear you, even of last hair, while you sit like dog in street that have lost hair. You represent yourself what you are not. You not know enough not to trust people. I wish you not be such. Here among us you can be off-guard but not in world where you soon will be. Now you are in scale of nonentityness. You will go, but we not will be separated as long as with inside we same idea have. Separation not touch your inner world, because we are together there.

Small thing can be big thing. All big things come from one small thing.

[*He explains the two objective hopelesses to Georgie.*]

Two kinds of hopeless idiots, objective and subjective. Objective, he is merde, nothing never he can do. Subjective have possibility not be merde. He already come into place where he himself know he is hopeless, he realize his nonentity. He possibility have not be merde always such as he is. Every man have moment when he can imagine that he is God.

[*He excoriates newspaper articles and the nonentities who write them.*]

They are nothing, but use words to cover nothingness. I, from nothing, nothing can take. Normal man cannot take where is nothing. But psychopathic man can take, with his wish and imagination he see something where is nothing. This is fault of your language, because no meaning have in its roots like Greek. Even Russian, of which some words come from Greek, have more meaning than languages in Europe which make themselves on dirty Latin. No meaning in roots, so no meaning in words. That is why life is such empty thing. Kanari, you rice wish? Then I will give you independent. I know you like, but pratique show that man that eat rice in those countries where you lived takes force only for working like donkey with body. But for man's mentation he must green things eat; vegetables, for making active his mind.

[*We have the Tibetan tea.*]

Tibetan tea very wise creation. From centrum come and little by little through the ages man learn about this. Two days boil bones of yak, put in grains of wheat and butter. All is here what man needs.

[*Later.*]

There is such custom about food—each day of year is for one special dish. Only next year can you repeat, not next month, if you are not educate man who can compose something different.

[*Later.*]

Fat never depends from what you eat, quite another reason is; when you make inner effort for your exterior body exercise, this effort blends with chemicals I give you and both together make yet another new chemistry (created by your will).

[*Miss Alexander asked about drinking toasts in water.*]

MISS GORDON: Only water you can drink for health of wise men.

GURDJIEFF: *No.* Can wine be, or coffee, what you like. Only not this Armagnac. This too expensive for wise man. Clever man, wise man, he drink only water. Only idiot drink this expensive thing, only man can be idiot.

*Friday, April 23–Sunday, April 25. Vichy.**

We start after 6:00 p.m. on Saturday in the car loaded with his Easter gifts; first for the Fontainebleau family, then the Moralines of Vichy. Alice and I are jammed in the back with a sack of tinned foods.

He doesn't speak until we are rolling over the hayfields just before Fontainebleau, the vivid green at sunset. He looks back and says, "Summer green." Coffee in Fontainebleau, then on for Nevers, for the night. Bright full moon—the most gorgeous night ride. We pass a frog pond—the car is creaking and the frogs are croaking and the croaking wins out on the instant we pass.

GURDJIEFF: [*with joy in his voice*] You heard? Oh, this noise I very much like. [*A rabbit runs across the road.*] Oi-oi!

[*Then another hour of moonlit silence till we come to his lookout over the Loire at La Charité.*]

---

* Katie's Vichy notes.

Even here we can stop, we not need broken our custom.

[*He gets out to walk along the moonlit path, we hear all the night birds and he returns to the car.*]

KROKODILE: Never have I heard so many birds singing at night, Mr. Gurdjieff.

GURDJIEFF: Of course, is just season. Everything live.

[*We spend the night in Nevers—midnight supper in his room—Pâté de canard de Rouen! In the morning we start early.*]

GURDJIEFF: So clean is air.

[*He speaks about the Fontainebleau family where last night he passed out big bank notes, a sack of food and a stiff suckling pig.*]

ALICE: I begin to understand what satisfaction you must have.

GURDJIEFF: Not necessary philosophize. Their emanation, vibration go out—some of total go to you. This is indirect food. Even this expression comes to me from Bible, is early Christian word—indirect food. If I am not happy, I can be made so. If people around me happy, then I can be. In indirectness, mechanically, does such force show. It comes to you without your consciousness—undirect.

Same word can be about sin—undirect sin, unvoluntary. So this indirect food is. Same thing also can be voluntary. You think, you make consciously.

[*In a café en route we speak of New York.*]

KROKODILE: Mr. Gurdjieff, last night we spoke about how New York will be a foreign country for us after you are there, such things you will find.

GURDJIEFF: Truth is. In New York is everything. Not first day I can cook but second day there I can cook more better dish than anything you have had my table in France. There, *all* can find, from *all* country. Only, must know where look.

[*By association we speak of Father Divine.*]

GURDJIEFF: About him I know. Now he have trouble.

KROKODILE: Because he is rich, Mr. Gurdjieff, and nobody can find his source for such richness.

GURDJIEFF: Why wish know?

KROKODILE: Because it's the custom in our country. If a man has automobiles, yachts, airplanes—he must show to the government what his source is. But this Negro cannot show, Mr. Gurdjieff, because his source is one very long procession of church mice.

[*Then Alice tells him about another such, in Los Angeles—"Aimee Semple." She tells him about her orchestra, her stage, her full moon backdrops, and colored lights.*]

GURDJIEFF: This show how people are hungry for something more (than life). Every year on earth there appear such; last year was one in Russia. This is not bad thing, you know, even with such misunderstanding, is better thing than your foxtrot and cocktail. Not matter how little it have, is not bad thing. Already it have some reality for people. Is not masturbator thing like foxtrot.

[*We have dinners for ten and twelve; processions of hors d'œuvres, processions of trout. Once I offer him carrots—a mound of baked ones on a symphony platter of vegetables.*]

Carrots I never eat. *Yellow is a dangerous color*—you have this understanding even about Orient. Never I eat cooked yellow, because we not know totality of what transformate when yellow you cook. Only fresh yellow can eat.

In Café Gambrinus. Our Big Talk.

GURDJIEFF: Already you decide to go out from average-ness.

[*We speak of the impossibility of turning back. He speaks for twenty minutes then tells us to spend the rest of the day and all the next, thinking only of what he has said.*]

Even if you *too much* spend for this, no matter. Later you can rest. But now must put *all* aside and concentrate only on this what I just now tell.

[*A pause for rest, then he laughs to himself.*]

One association just go automatically in my brain. You know, this is *first time on earth* such thing is told in such place. This has been told, but in one year's time and with big preparation—prayer, fast, even enema make before. Also special costume. Here in twenty minutes, in such dirty place, we have told.

KROKODILE: And with such people, Mr. Gurdjieff. (Alice and me.)

GURDJIEFF: Yes. Each thing such as now I just tell, have one *theme*. And you know, every one such theme have special incense. You must know from old ages man use this incense for make arise state for prayer, for thanksgiving, for Athenian night, for business even. Man long has known which incense make arise impulse for each state.

[*Alice speaks of Egypt; amber, peddled there chiefly as an aphrodisiac.*]

GURDJIEFF: They not know all. Amber is first thing in all incenses. Is base for every kind. Egypt uses amber; in Persia and Turkestan, the rose; in China, "anasha," from what come hashish (hemp). On earth this has always been so divided—different base for incenses which produce same results. One other thing also man uses; this poison mushroom, red cap, very beautiful. Everywhere he grow. And when is ready, on red cap from these (pimples) one liquid arises—this man freeze and take. This more strong poison than all what exist. More strong even than opium.

[*We speak of sources for amber.*]

ALICE: Origin of the ambergris of the whale?

GURDJIEFF: Amber is also from sea; when it make so, like cream, like egg white when you beat (sea foam). This foam stay long time then from this two things come; amber, and this what you clean with, what is principal industry of Greece. [*We think only of the pumice-like sponges. We cannot clarify more with him because the word sponge is unknown to him.*]

Feeling is more near to nature. Mind is nothing, in this case is only policeman, and only important as such.

We drive back to Paris with the Countess added—we have our senna tea dramas and a fifty kilometer drive at 6:00 a.m. from Vichy to Moulins where we gulp one great Armagnac before the ham and egg breakfast. We run out of gas. We run for bushes. He buys us each a box of pralines in Montargis.

Saturday, May 1

He has his Easter lunch with Knachtschmidt—twenty-four inch long suckling pigs, couscous (curried and peppered to choking degree), strange tropical fruits (which Sardine "veer-ifies"), and Russian Easter pudding and cake.

GURDJIEFF: Ach, now my tapeworm think what sing—he wish something more high than your "God Save King."

KANARI: Hosannah?

GURDJIEFF: No, that is dirty word, only use for marriage and business you make after.

MISS GORDON: Hallelujah?

GURDJIEFF: Is big word. Have in three things; Amen, God help us, and I am you and you are me. Very old word. Jewish take, but not is Jewish. Jewish not understand what means this, not even your Pope understands. Includes all scale from merde to God. More high expression not exist because in this is everything.

[*Sardine is given a mysterious fruit to identify (is possible) as Floridian.*]

SARDINE: [*after much mincing*] Is like pear, Mr. Gurdjieff.

GURDJIEFF: *Like is suspicious word—anything can be like one another.* Jam can be like merde—is wet . . . soft . . . Also coocumber can be like . . . such form . . . [*He has the look in his eye of being able to go on indefinitely . . .*]

Monday, May 3

[*Before lunch.*]

GURDJIEFF: Now Russians feast for fifty days until this day when He go up—Ascension Day. Such custom is. For everything in life there is custom—only in Europe and America not know. America have custom only for foxtrot.

[*At table.*]

I glad some of you went to service Russian church, participate in such good thing, for feeling experience. All Christian church ceremonies derive from old Greek church. Once in Jerusalem I saw such ceremony as must always remember. There were nine different kinds Christians all together in one place for Christmas, even Abyssinia. This Greek ceremony open up all your feeling, you forget why is, for whom is, you forget even Christ—such knowledge they have for composing ceremony, for psychology of people.

ALICE: Bible also taken from Greek?

GURDJIEFF: Of course. Everything Christian came from old Greek, then they spoil. All, all comes from Greek. Even from before time when was Bible. Your Bible is new book, composed four or five hundred years after by fisherman. And you know what understanding have fisherman.

ALICE: But before fishermen, what happened to knowledge?

GURDJIEFF: Nothing happened.

ALICE: But where was it?

GURDJIEFF: Was with initiate people, as always. They always go in one stream, it still flows today. You ask question from one stream, I answer from other, then you go back your stream with answer. Before there was nothing for man in ordinary stream, but fishermen who knew nothing, so nothing could tell but their wiseacrings. You remember the two streams I write about? Difference between two streams is the difference between interpretations of events on earth. One make elephant from fly, the other make fly from elephant. Events have two explanations—one for mankind, one for me. My stream is initiate-ism. You know what is in hypnotism. With that you can make water of wine for some people. For others you can make wine of water. I tell about my stream. What happen before not interest me. Remember my chapter on Maralpleicie—also Konuzion and poppy seeds. This is what happened before.

MISS GORDON: But there have been messengers like you.

GURDJIEFF: Many such there are, even you have in America. For English and Americans they are something, but for me they are merde, objective sense. . . .

What you learn from bible you wish believe, but your bible is one thing and my bible is quite another. Nobody now believe in Christian thing, not with inner world, especially young ones. Nobody but English old maid and your American Lesbians. In General, man over there not believe. Your bible is hodgepodge.*

Friday, May 14

Miss Gordon telephoned that he had telephoned from Cannes that "something was" with his car, and that he was taking the train. This noon, still in pajamas and typing, he sent me word he was downstairs. I threw on topcoat and descended. He was pacing up and down, his arm in a sling. Before explaining, he asked all about each patient to whom I had been giving piqûres in his absence. Then he said he had left his car on a steep Alp, engine off, handbrake only holding, while he went to look at the view. In the car there was a woman and children. Suddenly the car moved forward toward the curve and precipice. With one gigantic bound—"never was my brain so quick"—he leaped on the running board, put his arm inside, and steered the Buick straight off the road downhill to the only tree in sight. The car was smashed to bits, but the occupants were saved.

---

* End of Katie's notes.

He was thrown into the air, turned over several times and fell on his shoulder. "Almost all was finished; me, my work, all of you."

At luncheon were Miss Gordon, Sardine, Gabo's "fiancée," the Persian musician who is copying Gurdjieff's music, Kanari, and a guest from old Prieuré days—the Englishman Pindar. Miss Gordon asks permission to drink first toast to "thanksgiving" that Gurdjieff is safe. He accepted. Then he asked Pindar's opinion about potatoes.

GURDJIEFF: I can see from your answer which way you have gone since you were Prieuré.

PINDAR: I want to ask you a question. I want to know why the French cheat one.

GURDJIEFF: Now more than ever I can see which way you have gone, you ask such question.

PINDAR: What do you mean?

GURDJIEFF: Tell, Kanari.

KANARI: Elephant from fly.

PINDAR: What's that? What elephant? What fly? [*Pause.*] Don't you think, Mr. Gurdjieff, it's a good thing to learn languages? Wouldn't you advise people to learn Russian? Isn't it worth the effort?

GURDJIEFF: *No!* You must have big aim, what you learn is *by the way*. If you can't learn by-the-way, then you don't fulfill. Not man's center of gravity to learn languages. Either man must *do*—or have fly business.

[*Later he remarked:*]

Conscious labors and intentional suffering are the same thing—they cannot be separated.

Saturday, May 15

In the Café de la Paix, he gave the following exercise to Miss Gordon and Kanari, in nearly perfect English.

"Take any object and put it to your feeling; represent it to yourself with feeling. Then answer these questions. Remember, you must *experience* these feelings, Kanari. And you, Miss Gordon, you must stir (up) your mind, and police with feeling. As you continue this exercise, you must diversify your objects. Here are the questions.

" 1. Its nature and beginning.

" 2. The reason for its arising and the aim of its service.

" 3. Its dependents and if anything else can be used in its place.

" 4. Personal opinion of it and objective opinion.

" 5. Its end and its following actualization.

" 6. Its legitimate use and the most great and most small use to which it can be put.

" 7. Its objective inevitability and its subjective property of service."

At lunch later were Miss Gordon, Comtesse de Messey (Lolo), Georgie Lyon (English painter and friend of Lolo), Georgette Leblanc, Sardine, Kanari.

GURDJIEFF: Well, esteemed guest, how is sweet potato?

INNOCENT GEORGIE: Oh, it's delicious.

GURDJIEFF: What word she tell? Often I hear that word but don't care to remember it.

MISS GORDON: She means she finds it very good.

GURDJIEFF: Such word she use every day for everything, for merde thing. Yet now she use automatically for such thing as she eat at my table. This word is merde and he who use is also merde.

MISS GORDON: She hasn't had education like us, Mr. Gurdjieff.

GURDJIEFF: No, not even for merde has she education. Even words not have in English, whether is hard merde, soft merde, she thinks all is one kind.

GEORGIE: Is there more than one kind?

GURDJIEFF: Is seven kinds, of course. You think the English when they eat Australian frozen meat have same kind merde as when eat *my* food?

Monday, May 17

To lunch at two, which we had at three. While waiting, we read "The Herald of Coming Good," because there was nothing else. He called me into his room for examinations on all patients. Only Miss Gordon, Louise, and I were at the table, more were eating in the kitchen. For dish of the day was a new composition which he said he made for the first time. It is a dish from old times for the first occasion that a young man is invited to the home of his fiancée. Afterward, he never gets it again, apparently. "Happy day when parents of such doctor give her to household of young rich man." When I think that perhaps she has never seen him before! First were usual hors d'œuvres, a thick soup. After, many fruits and some to take home. About the exercise, "Valuable thing for your future, you will see how have lived—" I supplied, "With eyes bandaged, plugs in ears." "Yes, like in box, like piece of merde. After you do, then you will come to me with different intonation to ask me for instruction."

Tuesday, May 18

Café de la Paix.

GURDJIEFF: Ah, Kanari, as my secretary I now commission you somewhere find me frigidaire for apartment. Or else all spoil, such heat is. For buy or for rent. (But he did not trust me and came along all the Boulevard Haussmann until one pleased him.)

KANARI: If automatos in Greek means impulse in English, why then does this Greek word, automatic, taken into English, have exact opposite meaning?

GURDJIEFF: Word means same, only in your idiot understanding you have transformed it. Means in both language, from-self-arise. Only man in his mentation think he has consciousness, thinks that from self can arise something conscious, when can arise only unconsciously. (He might have continued if the taxi had not stopped.)

Lunch. Miss Alexander is there, to whom I have been giving piqûres also. Her chosen idiot—compassionate—had been changed by Gurdjieff to round, the last time she had come. To see if she remembered, I asked her before I gave the toast.

MISS ALEXANDER: I don't know. Was it changed?

GURDJIEFF: To round, I think, eh, Kanari?

KANARI: Yes.

MISS ALEXANDER: I don't remember, but it wasn't round.

GURDJIEFF: [*studying this situation*] What idiot you think you are today?

MISS ALEXANDER: Oh, eternal.

GURDJIEFF: That is round; sometimes I call from birth. Now, if you ask my opinion, what you need is to eat much of everything and— [*He stopped because she had turned away and was not listening to him.*] Now I am old man and must slowly eat.

KANARI: I could never relate such word as slow to you.

GURDJIEFF: When I tell, it means something. Never I tell something without a meaning.

159

Wednesday, May 19

Lunch. Miss Gordon, Sardine, and Kanari.

GURDJIEFF: Never use word "very" because it means "too much." Fruits in your Florida have auspicious exterior but what is interior is another question. There is reason.

KANARI: Soil? Too much artificial manure?

GURDJIEFF: No. Reason is emanations from sun. Not come direct.

KANARI: Because of tilt of earth's axis?

GURDJIEFF: Is exact.

MISS GORDON: Such a good lunch today.

GURDJIEFF: Yes, everything I have, except of course, one thing. Everybody has many wants, I have only one. I need only one thing. This end of stick not correspond and even I can tell reason. Is my organic weakness of mind, I had this even when young. Is because I waste my time trying to make people understand. So everything I have—except. Why I have all except is because I have knowledge. Now about this weakness that consists in trying to give understanding to people—this weakness is only this much. (He measures off a quarter of an inch between thumb and forefinger.)

KANARI: Then that means you are just that much lopsided, Mr. Gurdjieff.

GURDJIEFF: Yes. Good, good. See, Miss Gordon, how she understand.

MISS GORDON: I'm afraid I didn't understand what Kanari meant.

GURDJIEFF: Truth, English are hopeless, such sheep, donkey understanding have. Truth, pity you are English. That story about looking at sky for fifteen minutes before replying is for you and all English understanding. Reminds me of a story of a cart to which was put a horse, a goat, and one tortoise. Of course all could go only as fast as tortoise. The horse very nervous. He said, "What is this destiny which is written on my forehead?" The goat also spoke his opinion. And the tortoise who nothing understood except that every day the mountain before them seemed as far as ever, became very angry. He cursed and complained, "Go, go, at all times we go, but stay nearly in same place." So, Miss Gordon, never will you understand the two ends of stick.

Now look her face. In one place she love me, in another she hate me. Unconsciously, of course. If it was consciously, long ago I would chick-make. Now why we sit? As for me, I have eaten justly. Now, Kanari, why you look on me? Something you notice?

KANARI: Always I notice a new word.

GURDJIEFF: And you, Miss Gordon? You notice? Of course you not. "Justly" was word.

MISS GORDON: I didn't notice because you always use "truth"!

Friday, May 21

He persuaded me against my better judgement to go to Vichy in the car with him, Miss Gordon, and Gabo. "Mountains we will pass, and in such surroundings you will have material for third food." We started at five o'clock, Miss Gordon and I in the back seat with luggage and odorous food packages, piled to the roof. Once on the road to Fontainebleau he let out the car, passed by fractions everything ahead, or when half passing, fell back to the horns and screechings of cars behind. I was so terrified that I told him so and begged him to slow down. He said he had to test the car. "Must make one constatation. Too much money I pay for this car." I said, "Then stop and let me out." A trifle more slowly, we went to his brother's house. No one there. I took my traveling case and got out.

"How now, Kanari?"

I said, "I'll take the train here and meet you in Vichy."

"No, no, now you sit beside me, slowly I go. Moreover, never I go more than ninety."

"No, you go a hundred and twenty."

"How you know?"

"Because I see on speedometer."

"Impossible, never more than ninety. Now you sit till Montargis and if not like, there you can go and sit in train."

It was better after that. We arrived at Nevers at ten, the diningroom was closed, but they opened it and we had a cold dinner.

GURDJIEFF: Curiosity is a dirty thing. That is why I am always angry for idiot questions, why philosophizing makes me nervous. In English not exist two words for two kinds of curiosity, as in other languages. Word for other kind of curiosity is needing-to-know. For this needing-to-know you must have material. Then you will not receive something empty.

[*Near Vichy on the road there was a new lighting system.*]

KANARI: You say in your book such use of electricity is a bad thing. Yet more and more is used.

GURDJIEFF: The more they use, the greater will be the catastrophe. [*A cat crosses the road.*]

KANARI: Why do cat's eyes shine at night?

GURDJIEFF: All that family have such property.

MISS GORDON: To make other animals afraid? Mesmerize them?

GURDJIEFF: Yes.

MISS GORDON: Snake also?

GURDJIEFF: Yes, snake also have. And this same property man can achieve also.

Vichy, 1:30 a.m., Hotel Mondiale. The sleepy night clerk was delighted to see Gurdjieff who at once ordered *three* rooms, two with a bath. I followed him upstairs and ordered a single room, Miss Gordon regretted the loss of a bath. I said to her, "Sorry but it would be impossible for me to share a room with anyone unless it's an absolute necessity." We were called to his room, adjoining was a small one for Gabo, and we had to eat yogurt. He ordered us to take baths the next morning. I was too exhausted, anyway I had spent all day before in the baths. I did not go, but at noon took my work to the Gambrinus. Soon he came along with Gabo. I had to admit I hadn't taken massage sous l'eau and he was a little angry and made reproaches all the way back to the hotel. There were many hungry Russians, the usual family and others new to me. He went on and on about the bath I had missed.

GURDJIEFF: Now our Kanari look on me like dog on stick. Love, hate, at same time. Fear will be put galoshes.

KANARI: No, only afraid of showing my stupidity more than necessary. I don't mind galoshes anymore because I learn from them.

GURDJIEFF: You are joppa. My speciality is about joppa. Especially when connected with galoshes. And especially in public. I like undress you in public, to public I like show. [*Whispering*] Did you understand this morning why I wished you to go have massage?

KANARI: No.

GURDJIEFF: Then you are joppa.

KANARI: Of course. Not understanding is property of joppa.

GURDJIEFF: Yes, yes, now tell all what good thing you say. Tell in French. [*Everybody laughed when I told and he explained something in Russian.*] I take material from all what happen in you, Kanari. For

162

instance this morning in café when we speak concerning bath, I collect material. You are in truth squirming idiot.

KANARI: You change officially?

GURDJIEFF: No, not official, I speak here. [*He was quite feeling the Armagnac now.*] Look, look. [*He pointed to an empty fruit dish.*]

KANARI: One would say a wolf had passed there.

GURDJIEFF: Or a canary.

He went up to his room for coffee with everyone. I escaped, sat in the park and thought, will I or not take the damned bath. After an hour I decided to. I had the bath. I went to the park café, Miss Gordon was waiting and then he came.

GURDJIEFF: What you titillate? What you tell, Kanari?

KANARI: I tell how the Church of England forbids the royal family to go to the wedding of a man who was king.

GURDJIEFF: All that is work of dirty Jesuits. One special man work under in England, he back of all manipulations to make church powerful, such thing I know now is building as to make coronation wedding children's play. But like such (plotting) that happened in Russia, Russian church now quite finished. Correspondent saying: "He who digs hole will fall into it."

We went in his car then to the trout breeding grounds. Tea in the cold mountain air. We arrived back at the hotel at eight and there were ten Russians waiting for food. Trout, chicken, and two bottles. Two children were there, one daughter is of the nice Russian girl, the other unknown. He drank too much, made a fuss over the children, and then turned to Miss Gordon and me:

GURDJIEFF: This child was not yet born the time I came here with—ach, I forget name. Was English writer, now dead.

KANARI: Katharine Mansfield?

GURDJIEFF: No! Of course not.

MISS GORDON: You don't mean Orage, do you?

GURDJIEFF: Yes, Orage. Name quite forgot. Her father was Russian waiter. He heard me speak Russian and had sickness for home, so spoke with me. I tell about her child so understand everybody who not know this story. People with dirty mind could think something about how I am with her here. (His hand was on her head and sometimes on knee.)

KANARI: Oh, no, Mr. Gurdjieff. (He was looking at me.)

GURDJIEFF: I know man mind. Apple from apple mentation, merde from merde mentation. English, American, have merde mentation. Also French, of course, and sometimes Russian.

Later he was telling questionable stories, mama-papa business about chicken to the children.

GURDJIEFF: Now, Kanari, why you look so?

KANARI: Just my data. Can't get used to hearing such things said before children.

GURDJIEFF: My idea is every child should know such at eight years. Such education I give Nicholai and Michel. Do you think now that they would ever drink Armagnac or love—be such slave? (I certainly do.)

I couldn't face a trip back in the car, so I decided to take the train the next day. I told him at the Gambrinus after bath that I was going and he was furious. He said terrible things to me then, and at lunch. I said it was for an article, I had telephoned Paris and they had read me a cable.

GURDJIEFF: Such story you can tell Mees Gordon but not to me. You are joppa, you miss too much, truth.

[*At lunch.*]

Now I go lie—sleep. You will excuse?

KANARI: Not excuse yourself, I think, for such natural function. Don't all animals lie after eating?

GURDJIEFF: Not all animals sleep after eating.

KANARI: I think tigers don't sleep.

GURDJIEFF: No, tiger play after. Even like children among trees. No, not all sleep like sheep or donkey. Bear also sleep. Snake not sleep if a little eat, only if quite full, like if eat donkey. No, excuse, snake not eat donkey, is too big. Burro he can eat.

I hid after lunch and took the train at five o'clock. Margaret met me and came home with me. Miss Gordon telephoned and said, "Just back, he drove too fast and raced a motorcycle." They had no picnic at all instead of the two scheduled for today.

*No Date**

KANARI: Your friend, Rockefeller, is dead.

GURDJIEFF: Ah? Then many friends of mine, those devils, are glad. They will make him object their sadism.

Saturday, May 29

We went in the morning to examine his patient, Lolo. He asked and asked about interior feeling but she couldn't understand what he wanted to know.

GURDJIEFF: Two kinds of feeling has man. Physical, such as she told, and another kind for which no name in English or French— feeling-with-sensing. Perhaps all her life she never put attention on this normal thing. Now me, every day I can tell you difference in this feeling from what was yesterday. Yet if I should tell her she is uneducated, she would be offended. Cow with merde brain.

[*At lunch.*]

GURDJIEFF: Can good thing eat and still be hungry?

[*I nod, but I see that he is disappointed in me.*]

I speak about philosophical side of this. Tapeworm sing "God Save the King." Like English people. But while this they sing, inside quite another thing they tell, just opposite. They say to the devil with the king. Others sing Internationale and Marseillaise and that makes middle part.

KANARI: You mean that neutralizes the situation, like a safety valve?

GURDJIEFF: Of course. Just why such thing is of value. Then can starving people sing "God Save King" when such nonentity go by. Truth, nobody can have such fruit as this. Take, take, not pity.

MISS GORDON: That's what worries me all the time, Mr. Gurdjieff. To think we have such thing when others have nothing, are starving.

GURDJIEFF: Miss Gordon, Miss Gordon, may your mentation not be such.

MISS GORDON: But you tell in your book when some people have much it means that others must have nothing.

GURDJIEFF: Yes, I tell how is.

---

* Rockefeller died May 23, 1937.

MISS GORDON: But why should it be so?

GURDJIEFF: I not tell why. Eh, Kanari?

KANARI: You always say fact is fact.

GURDJIEFF: Is exact. Now explain.

KANARI: It is explained in a chapter of your book—"Man's Understanding of Justice is an Accursed Mirage."

GURDJIEFF: You see, Miss Gordon; not enough read my words, also must think about what read, otherwise empty will remain.

Sunday, May 30

Dinner. Olgivanna and Frank Lloyd Wright, their child, Miss Gordon, and Kanari.

WRIGHT: Very interesting, these idiots of yours. I've invented some also.

[*Gurdjieff did not reply.*]

WRIGHT: Mr. Gurdjieff, you're certainly a good cook. You could earn a lot of money cooking somewhere.

GURDJIEFF: Not so much as I can earn shearing.

[*After dinner he brought out a chapter of the Second Series and asked who would read.*]

WRIGHT: I read very well.

[*Gurdjieff left the room.*]

Damn, I'm sleepy. I can't take it. Still, I don't want to hurt the old man's feelings.

[*He began to read and Gurdjieff returned and sat down. Wright stopped reading.*]

You know, Mr. Gurdjieff, this is interesting and it's a pity it's not well written. You know you talk English very well, too bad you can't dictate. Now if I had time, you could dictate to me and I could write this for you in good English.

[*He read a few pages and stopped again.*]

Now I must go and take my little daughter home. She's sleepy and so is her father.

GURDJIEFF: Yes, for her sake stop. She is young. You, of course, are old man now and life finish. But she only begin.

WRIGHT: [*turning red*] My life *not* finished. I could right now make six more like her . . .

[*Olgivanna with tears in her eyes led the child to the door.*]

Tuesday, June 1

At the café.

KANARI: You said the other day that starch is holy thing, God thing. I wish to ask you if it is because, like amber, it has three forces in it—carbon, hydrogen, and oxygen.

GURDJIEFF: Now I not answer question because you go too far. You have one hundred kilos too much curiosity, your enemy. Before you had one thousand kilos, but still too much you have. I advise you recognize enemy and full stop make. Also another constatation I make. Something wrong your sex. Sex very important thing is, like light, like air you breathe, food you eat. If you are in five parts, two of your five parts depend from sex. You must more normal live.

KANARI: Cannot even think about such things. I do not wish, I have no time. In twenty-four hours I have only four hours for myself and I must use them for sleeping.

GURDJIEFF: Then lopside you will be and I can nothing do, for this depends only from you.

[*At lunch. Only Louise and me. Miss Gordon lost.*]

KANARI: To the health of hopeless idiots. And to your health also. [*To Louise:*] And—to both of us.

GURDJIEFF: Aha, you hear, Sardine? She philological manipulation make. Now I must give her mark. You know what is mark?

KANARI: I think so, Mr. Gurdjieff.

GURDJIEFF: Among initiates there is always mark. Once in old days there were *combats* (quite a long time we took finding this word, because he wanted *races*) on different days. One day would be cocks (cockfights), another day buffaloes, another day man and man, another day scorpion and falanga. Of course no newspapers, so to let people know they would put up flag of different color—yellow for cocks, red for buffalo, white for man and blue for falanga-scorpion. You see, Kanari?

KANARI: I'm afraid so, Mr. Gurdjieff.

GURDJIEFF: Then what you think about this? What you decide?

But I would not answer. I could have said, "Yes, and nine out of ten times falanga wins. But not this time. Of course Sardine understood nothing.

His apartment has been cleaned up and out, in honor new frigidaire. Miss Gordon, Louise, and I today for lunch, after I gave Alexander her shot. He was worried, hadn't slept all night. Galoshes in sight. He didn't say much, except, "Life is not always what you see for a person. Is like the theatre." I supplied, "Behind the scene." He said, "Yes. Also behind fact is always one thousand facts."

Friday, June 11–Saturday, June 12

He made a long speech today in Russian at his brother's face, on and on and on. When he went out to the telephone I said to Dimitri, "For heaven's sake, quickly tell me what he said, what was he talking about?" Dimitri looked at me sheepishly and said, "Vrai, je n'ai rien compris de tout cela."

I have been treating his patients with two electrical machines—very complicated and different adjustments for each. "Every person is not polarized alike," he said. The color in the tubes is beautiful—like xeon—even he admires it. "Something in color *is*—like life. And sometimes in colors, one color something of itself it even has—especially in electricity."

GURDJIEFF: Usually we constate with the mind. But in the case of constating with feeling instead of with mind, what would such word be in English?

[*About the Persian musician.*]

He is half woman. Such representative of art have too many "feelings." We have name for such in Russian, one word, meaning prostitute-in-trousers.

[*Later.*]

You must now have three states—active, passive, and *life state*.

[*Later.*]

Now I make them laugh about joke in Russian. I will tell. There is saying that a person look for pearl in merde. That means when he love somebody for no reason. (No good reason, no conscious love, just those imaginings that come with sexual attraction.) So I tell them in Russian, just this saying, but instead of telling word for pearl, I take my thought further, I tell word for that kind of bead that poor native women wear in India in necklace—not even piece of bread could buy with such bead.

Thursday, July 8

Lunch.

GURDJIEFF: Now I constate Sardine has changed. Not so much antipathicism as formerly when everyone wished to push her away. Sardine, something of woman you now have. You are not soft merde now—kind that is result in morning from too much eating some one kind thing because you like, not because hunger have. But not yet are you hard kind. You are in middle. Words exist in other languages for these different kinds merde. In some languages words exist also for different kinds of blood. Never word blood use alone, but one of these words to say what kind is.

[*Later to Sardine:*]

Today you eat like sparrow. You know sparrow cannot eat much, but peck, peck. Spoil for others.

KANARI: [*hoping for more details*] Like canary?

GURDJIEFF: Canary I not know.

KANARI: A little you know because once you said is svoloch bird.

GURDJIEFF: I know of course a little but I not know canary *behind* like sparrow. Sparrow I know like myself.

MISS GORDON: Yes, you used to paint them to resemble canaries. I always wondered if that was true or a fable like the ladder in the desert. Stilts in sand and ladder.

GURDJIEFF: No, those stories true, only ten percent is fantasy. That reminds me how I suffer when Soloviev died. For three months I was not myself. Such friend was—more than brother. I love him more than a mistress.

At Lolo's she asked him for her animal and he gave her, "Or Swiss or Normandie cow." Georgie came to lunch and she too asked for her animal.

GURDJIEFF: Also cow, but Tibetan. Pity I can't call you Yakina, but we have already one such. Perhaps you prefer other name? Swissina, Normandina? You know cow sit, eat what bring her, give milk, serve nature. One, two times a year when empty inside, no calf, no milk, she get up when nature calls and makes mama-papa business. Which cow you choose, Mees?

GEORGIE: Tibetan.

[*End of lunch.*]

GURDJIEFF: You all notice something fishy today with me?

[*He had been talking, he had mentioned the vibration chapter, pretending I had asked him a question I had not asked, telling me not to drink Armagnac, which I had not dreamed of doing, saying he had need of my clever mentation.*]

KANARI: Well, not fishy, just unusual.

GURDJIEFF: Unusual with me is fishy. Just today I carry (wear) corset, so all is changed, even my mind.

KANARI: Yes, today you talk.

GURDJIEFF: What egotist you are. Sincerely tell, how now your tapeworm?

KANARI: Is sleepy, but I will not let it sleep.

GURDJIEFF: I do not like your tapeworm, Mees. You understand why? [*Here he said something of a different gravity which I couldn't get at all.*] You understand what I told?

KANARI: First thing, but not second thing.

GURDJIEFF: Well, try to understand next thing.

He brought out a red pepper to show Georgie and told her about having made even easy shape for inserting. This would be good thing for Georgie to give Lolo to get her up in the mornings. I put it in my button hole and said we should wear them as the insignia of Mr. Gurdjieff, which seemed to please him, as he laughed a lot. Later we were all talking about Amelia Earhart having been lost and he had read it in a Russian paper.

GURDJIEFF: I not pity. Only fly should fly. Not man's business—is all vanity. Are two kinds of fly—fly that should fly, and when fly up chimney. (His expression for going bankrupt.) My experience with flying is with chimney. [*Advice to me:*] Have joppa, but not be joppa.

Sunday, July 11

Today he had thermos of iced water. He said, "Name is water Himalayas. I remember when tired, rest, drink from stream just such water, with one piece breath, one small pieces cheese. Never was such taste. This I always remember. Was thin then, very, could make places with feet that only goat could do. Goat can go such places, even when jump over (chasms) make so with horn to give momentum for going. Yak also good animal for carrying in such place." He said in Russian last night, but I understood, that twenty first idiot is God. Even God can be joppa.

Tuesday, July 20

Lunch. I asked a question in his room and he roared at me for using one of his words—crystallization. "After once we make picture, no more thinking of words, but *just do*, like normal man. Not your business this crystallization or whatever happens. You cannot know this, do as must be done and result will have in you. If fix on word, psychopathic result will be." I asked how many times to say "I Am" after the first part and he said, "Or once or a thousand times. When you feel I complete in you. Three kinds of satisfaction. One; from past, when some suffering or need from past is now liquidated. Two; for present—you eat good, drink good, and feel satisfaction. Three; for future, when you feel something good is now passing from you but will also be for all future."

He told Miss Gordon to remember our aim is to make tapeworm our slave, not to be commanded by him.

Sunday, July 25

Picnic at Vernon. I went in the car with Georgie and Lolo, Sardine went with Miss Gordon, and Gurdjieff with his tail from Rouen. All met in Vernon Café and then went to the usual high place, overlooking the wide valley and river.

He gazed a long time, sighed, and said, "Ah, great nature!" After a long pause he said, "What millions lie dead there from past times! And if all of you are such as they, you too will finish as such." There were cold chickens, fishes, loaves, the greens he calls "vegetables," melons and Armagnac. Gabo had not come, so Nicholai had to do everything and received all the scoldings.

He spilled his drink and blamed me. Sardine fed her dog and Lolo fed hers.

He said, "You know, some people not even have dog. Nothing they can put selves into." Sardine thought that this meant approval at last for Tuppy!

GURDJIEFF: Miss Gordon, you not eat vegetable?

MISS GORDON: Not today. I'll eat them tomorrow.

GURDJIEFF: Ah, tomorrow. Well I know this disease. Often I tell tomorrow not exist. Is only today. What must be done, must be done today. It is now or never. Next day twice as hard, day after four times as hard. Only you can count on today.

Thursday, August 12

Lunch. Mme. de Salzmann, Miss Gordon, a doctor for Dimitri who is ill, Sardine, and Putnam. There was fiancé chicken which was explained to Putnam—"not yet play papa-mama."

PUTNAM: You mean, it hasn't lived.

GURDJIEFF: I mean not yet has dirty psyche. You know, people can be exterior clean but interior dirt have. Such people as who do all dirty things only in imagination. Such people are one hundred times dirtier than person who at once do dirty thing. That is masturbation. So there can be chicken masturbator. Contrary case, can be people who have objective clean psyche, though exterior can be such dirtiness as even stink.

[*Later Putnam began "chatting" with me about boats. I knew Gurdjieff was listening, so led Putnam on.*]

PUTNAM: I had my honeymoon on the Bremen, it was terrible, third class and stormy.

SOLITA: Not a good idea when you're always seasick and have a bad liver.

PUTNAM: I am never seasick and never had a bad liver in my life.

SOLITA: You told me two years ago your liver was three times too large.

GURDJIEFF: [*who had cured Putnam of lameness, drunkenness, and his liver*] Now I listen to American chatter—from empty to empty. I hear Pachman say, "Never in my life," while Kanari heard him tell otherwise last year. Such empty talk can only be between Americans. Worse, it hinder other people who have inner life.

PUTNAM: But we're at table, eating.

GURDJIEFF: Many people mentate when eat, even choose such time, and those you hinder. This is American typicality. They have no education or even understanding of ceremony.

[*Later.*]

Other people read books, but I verify.

Friday, August 13

Lunch. The Englishman, Pindar; Miss Gordon, Sardine, and Kanari. Mr. Gurdjieff's brother is very ill. "He really die three weeks ago—now is only artificial."

GURDJIEFF: I am unique for the number of books I have read in my life from all countries. When could not read a language, I had someone translate. Five or six a day I read, often before sleeping. Now I nothing read.

PINDAR: I feel I deserve this dish because once for three months when I was with the army I had only a plate of beans three times a day. So now I deserve this to make up for that time.

GURDJIEFF: No, not deserve. If once you unconsciously had such experience and then if you consciously again repeated experience, then you could tell you deserve.

[*My toast is drunk and Pindar asks exactly what is compassionate idiot.*]

GURDJIEFF: Everyone is idiot, even God. But when these idiots see another who is another kind of idiot from themselves, they become angry and curse him. This is very characteristic of these idiots. Now compassionate means that among this company can sometimes exist idiots who know that all are idiots together so they pity all and not become angry. These are compassionate. I am unique idiot so I am no more this idiot compassionate.

PINDAR: I am too fat, I eat too much.

GURDJIEFF: Eat, eat, man is not pig. Man has as much room as his valise.

PINDAR: What valise? Leather bag for traveling?

GURDJIEFF: [*patting his stomach*] This is man's valise.

PINDAR: Why do you make me eat so much?

GURDJIEFF: Because I saw valise when you came in.

PINDAR: It's because you make me eat too much.

GURDJIEFF: You speak only of this moment, but what about past? I am not responsible. Exist twenty formulations about stomach. One I tell. Pig have stomach, man have rubber. That is why man can eat more than he can.

MISS GORDON: [*beginning to be angry, no one can guess why*] I've seen pigs that have eaten more than they could, Mr. Gurdjieff. Such fat stomachs.

GURDJIEFF: [*enjoying her anger and goading it*] Yes, you've seen— because pigs not wear clothes. Now you walk about apartment freely, before glass, without dress, before and after eating—and you look in glass, Miss Gordon.

[*Gales of laughter.*]

Now Kanari I can see by smile has idea for two articles, can write and make money. Perhaps you not know Mr. Pindar; she is writer, and moreover, famous writer. But with what kind of people she is famous is another question. Is that why you laugh, Kanari?

KANARI: I laugh at what you say. I think no question exists in the world that you don't examine from all sides.

PINDAR: Why am I so fat? Do I eat too much?

GURDJIEFF: Reason you have never heard of. Now I go lie.

[*He goes.*]

MISS GORDON: [*still mad*] I don't understand why you always say that about pigs. I have seen pigs. You, Solita, you just sit there and listen to him and laugh but you haven't seen pigs in the country as I have.

KANARI: No, but I see the idea that the pig eats to his capacity and man beyond.

Monday, August 16

His brother has two nurses. Cancer of stomach and intestines. Mr. Gurdjieff said yesterday, "By next week it will be finished. It is time, in nature, in any case."

We drove today to Fontainebleau to meet Gurdjieff and Pindar on their return from Vichy and picnicked in the woods.

At picnic there was a break in the toasts—I thought he had finished. He looked at me and said, "If we depend on such director, we could die of thirst." Then without waiting for me, he picked up his paper cup and said, "To hopeless idiots." Miss Gordon smiled at him lovingly and said with admiration, "Oh, he remembered this was hopeless." He just cast one look and replied, "But I was here, Mees Gordon."

He was telling Pindar he didn't even know his own language, English, but studies another. (Pindar speaks pretty good Russian and French.) He said, "Man not know his own nose and at same time wish to know God's tail."

Tuesday, August 17

At lunch today he said, "The difference between man and donkey— donkey eat only vegetable (greens). Man eat vegetable with something else."

Monday, August 23

Dimitri died in the last week of August. I was sitting in the Café de la Paix with Mr. Gurdjieff that morning and he told me the story. He had managed to keep the cancer inactive for twelve years, but when Dimitri quarrelled with him three or four months ago, he went to a German doctor for relief and that doctor had given him a medicine that was poison for him, made the "flower" grow on the cancer. "When they sent for me at last, it was too late. All could do was give such thing as keep him alive artificially. But he in truth died three weeks ago, and if today I joke it is because already I pass through experiences of his death. I will put him at Fontainebleau—my three near ones; mother, wife, and brother, all one place, and very original place. Nearly all family now dead."

KANARI: Your new family that loves you can never be the same.

GURDJIEFF: No. Blood thing so strong for me. But real family, sisters, nieces, not love but hate me. Because I am source, it must be so. Never I give them enough, and for this they hate me in their hearts. For what you can buy black dress, Kanari?

KANARI: If necessary, I can find for a hundred and fifty francs.

GURDJIEFF: Yet each woman ask me six hundred francs and there are eight women. I gave just half what they asked and all angry on me and curse me in heart.

Later at lunch with Pindar, Miss Gordon, and her niece. Mr. Gurdjieff would not allow me to refill Pindar's glass. Pindar looked at him suspiciously.

GURDJIEFF: Perhaps, Mr. Pindar, you think it is because I am Scotch that I not give you more—that perhaps because what I put in glass cost forty francs? Then look!

[*He lifted a full glass and tossed out the brandy into a corner of the room. "Not make dirty—with alcohol soon pass," he added gently.*]

September

After Dimitri's funeral, he went away till September fifth, and moved into his brother's apartment, leaving the rue Labie for Colonels Renard. I reported on all his patients and on my own exercises. He said, "Now you learn more in one month than in all your past life. From results from last exercise you can now understand what I told six months ago, that what you had done till then was all preparation. Now you can see why. All your life before was merde, now can be otherwise and can have hope for future. Think, if for past eighteen years you had worked like now, what could be today." Then I told him of the strange things that had happened to me in London in July. He understood but would not explain. He gave me a new piqûre on my right side with mixture for tiredness. The apartment is much better than Labie, clean air and carpets—for the moment. It's one he had four years ago. Gofeldt has gone, Valya is back; pictures from the Prieuré are on the walls and also the belled clock that was in the study house. At lunch there was a wonderful new soup with apricots.

GURDJIEFF: What call this?

KANARI: Pit. Also is called stone.

GURDJIEFF: Stone? Such name of dead thing give to this? This is heart of fruit, all life is inside, hundred trees can grow from just one such. Who give such name in beginning is merde and he who repeats it is also merde. Now collect these hearts and after we will open, you will see what taste can be.

Man is such that he can only be egoist. He is so made. But sometimes for an hour or two, what he can do is to look around him, see what is, how is, and make program accordingly. Only this will show him how he should be. I hate man. He is merde. Because he has brain, he philosophizes with it. Give him a rose and he thinks it is merde—not recognize. Give him merde and he says it is rose. He has lost good clean instinct that even animals have. They know the difference between rose and merde. Now because such day I will drink Armagnac. In mornings with such troubles as now, I make nervous, make elephant from fly. But with this Armagnac fly is not elephant. Fly is—fly.

KANARI: I hope you are not angry, Mr. Gurdjieff. (Forget the reason for the question.)

GURDJIEFF: Angry? No. Long ago I lost such property. Now I have quite other factors.

Monday, September 20

Miss Gordon returned from London. He said, "Now you are home again. Only here do you all feel at home in true sense." Louise (Sardine) served as example for all of us for Americanism.

She selected "best pieces" of everything on the table and offered them to everyone, not remembering there would be evening guests. "You choose and give as if they are your own and not my pieces. Even under you go, looking for best pieces. Parasite, nonentity, and by the way merde!" Later he gave a toast and said, "You notice my voice, how I make like priest? High priest make so when he praise God. Like merde making réclame for diamond."

Tuesday, October 19

Just two years from the first evening with him and one year from the day he told me to go review all my science studies and report.

I had written out a report on my year's work, my conclusions and "discoveries." I took it to the café and he gave permission to read it, and looked at my chart of head and body systems, to which I had applied his law of trimonia for certain exercises. He said nothing when I finished reading, so I asked, "Perhaps I was impudent to compose such paper for you?"

GURDJIEFF: Not impudent. Even I thank you. You have unconsciously given me answer something I was searching for my book, about future of humanity. If you have found such thing, others of future humanity also can do. This is what you have enlighten for me.

KANARI: I can't believe it, Mr. Gurdjieff.

GURDJIEFF: You can believe. You have initiated yourself.

[*At lunch. For my toast:*]

May God and devil both help—not quotation mark devil but real one. With both God and devil helping, you can see what end must be and where—Karatas—could not be otherwise. On that planet everyone have tail, so you also. It must-it grow already and I sure everyone will great curiosity have—look, touch—because they know you are one of my people. Especially in America.

MISS GORDON: But Americans will not have eyes to see.

GURDJIEFF: Excuse, such tail, everyone can see. Even she will be unhappy, nowhere she can go in peace, they will follow in theatre, restaurant, try look. You understand, Kanari, what I wish you, what I tell? What we speak-ed this morning?

KANARI: Yes.

Later he asked before Margaret if Yakina was my friend, if I would take responsibility for her. I said yes. "Good. Better recommendation I could not have."

Wednesday, October 20

Lunch.

GURDJIEFF: This is dish of day.

LOOMIS: You can't say dish of day—it's not English.

GURDJIEFF: Kanari, what is your opinion?

KANARI: Dish of day is good expression.

LOOMIS: But it's not English.

GURDJIEFF: What would you call it, Loomis?

LOOMIS: In America we say—ah, ah, uh, uh—well, we say plat du jour.

GURDJIEFF: That is not English either, Mr. Loomis.

[*Great merriment from all.*]

Let it be dish of day, Loomis. She is my philological secretary.

[*This is too much for Loomis. He turns on me.*]

LOOMIS: How long have you lived over here?

KANARI: Sixteen years.

GURDJIEFF: She remembers English very good, Mr. Loomis.

LOOMIS: [*paying no attention to Gurdjieff*] Then you are an expatriate!

GURDJIEFF: This fruit, you notice, have no seeds. Then how grow tree? Wind blow fruit when small far away, even kilometer. But no seed for growing. How then grow?

[*Silence.*]

KANARI: You not tell?

GURDJIEFF: Such secret cost me millions and my time. Why tell for nothing? I not give so cheap. Use your brain. Read book.

A few days later we were sitting in the salon, he and I. Suddenly he asked, "What was with Kanari?" I knew somehow what he meant and answered, "Jewish." "Well, now is just Kanari."

On my birthday he gave me an enormous basket of all kinds of fruit and candies.

Saturday, October 30

KANARI: May I tell philological surprise? Root of word vegetable means lively, to quicken. But when people are slow, we call them vegetables, while real meaning is opposite. Why?

GURDJIEFF: Some vegetables, yes. Two kinds there are. One kind slowly grow, others like cress and mustard and Russian kinsa, can grow in one night or two, three days, such very green ones. For feast days we used to plant in dishes of black clay the night before and next day put on table before guests to eat while growing. You remember at Prieuré, Miss Gordon? Ah, such feasts we had Easter! You must remember all your life. Who was not there miss too much.

MISS GORDON: There was also other end of stick.

GURDJIEFF: Of course. All great things must have two such end of stick.

Thursday, November 11

GURDJIEFF: There is voluntary and involuntary sin and there is also voluntary and involuntary goodness, or good deed. (He wanted a word, one verb, in English that means "take blessing from above and pass to someone below." I couldn't find it. He says it exists in Greek in the gospels. He said that Jesus knew his own nonentityness and should he return, he would be very angry that people thought he had said he was God.)

[*Later.*]

Pray today that God sleeps—then only can the devil and his friends help me. I have more friends among devils than angels. When God sleeps is the only time the devil is free to do what he wishes, for good or for evil.

[*Later.*]

Sleep is a strange thing. I very sleepy, my brain needs because not enough I have these days. I am, yet I am not.

At Lunch One Day

GURDJIEFF: Kanari, how much was what put kitchen box? Was twenty or fifteen francs?

KANARI: Not quite remember, think was fifteen.

MISS GORDON: Fifteen, Mr. Gurdjieff.

GURDJIEFF: How you know, Mees Gordon? You never put. Kanari, you must calculate how much Mees Gordon owes, two years kitchen box plus two zeros. (Roughly a million francs.)

Monday, December 13

Lunch. He shows a bit of the inside of a seedless orange and says, "Is sperm part. Only one orange in many have this part from which grow new oranges. Sperm is good word for this—sperm can be male or female, not only male. Old Turkish word is "soil" and truth good word is. If all *real* words and meanings in each language were taken, and from them one language created, no more necessary it would be to go to school.

KANARI: Yet instead man makes Esperanto.

GURDJIEFF: Yes, and such man make as masturbate all life, and when can no more, he make this artificial language.

About something I forget, he said "Logic cannot go further—logic is greater than God." I whispered to Margaret, "Logos *means* God." He asked, "What you tell?" "I speak of roots to Yakina. She will now begin word-study."

Later Margaret laughed at something he said, thinking he meant something else. Then defended herself by saying, "Well that would have been funny too." He said, "But not in this place." He teased her again about her plumpness saying, "Around donkey (ass) is fodder. So much fodder he cannot all use. And from another side, must be something under of valuum (value) because often nature protects specially good thing, or with thorn or with thick skin." Now I remember what he said: "Let grass not grow even, but I will lie." Yakina heard the word grass and thought he meant the grass would not grow under his feet. That's why he said it would not be funny in that place.

The next day Yakina was also there. He spoke again of logic.

GURDJIEFF: I can make of logic what I wish. Such idiot thing is logic, can make five times five equal one hundred and thirteen. Can also make two and two equal six or seven or eight. Such sh—— is logic.

[*Later, speaking to Miss Gordon about the slowness of the English.*]

Mees Gordon is one end of stick. Yakina also, but miniature.

MISS GORDON: Do you mean opposite?

GURDJIEFF: No, miniature—same but small.

MISS GORDON: We all know who is middle.

GURDJIEFF: Yes, I am middle—also Kanari. English boast at all times what control he has, how he is so and so, but not. Only English have no nerves. Italian other extreme—only *too* quick, even take knife if angry.

YAKINA: I don't think I am English, Mr. Gurdjieff.

GURDJIEFF: You are only quick theoretically. Otherwise you are late.

KANARI: I know one anecdote. Two Englishmen, one old, one young. Old one tells story for half hour, then second, to punish him, tells him the same story back again for half hour. The first Englishman said, "Bless my soul, what a good story. Where did you hear it?"

GURDJIEFF: One mistake you make. Second man not English. Never would English be bored with such story, even if three hours take to tell. Must-it he be from another country.

1938

Wednesday, January 12

He talked in Russian to Dr. Hambachidzé, laughing and turning an eye now and again to Yakina. I heard the word joppa and knew he would tease her again. (Russian name, one of many, for derrière.)

GURDJIEFF: Pity you not understand what I tell Dr. Hambachidzé—a Russian saying which could offend in English. This expression means thick-ass, and when is thick in that place, everywhere take on such thickness, even brain and of course understanding. Not bon ton, this word, so in my book I call such cook, thick-neck. You remember? Was in American chapter [*Miss Gordon does not remember, I finally remember cook.*] Such thickness always means round idiot, same thickness on all sides. Yakina, objectively you are round idiot, but subjectively sometimes something you understand in life—something else you have—you can make stop on round before continuing. So let you be official square for toast. This objective round is not altogether your fault, is result of your education, your past life. Fault is in your past, how you lived gives such result today.

[*After, to Kanari:*]

You now in galoshes. Look, Mees Gordon, Kanari sit in galosh for being astonish my formulation. Kanari, long time ago you should habit take for my English.

Thursday, January 13. Russian New Year.

The "tree" is drooping somewhat in places but is still magical. European branch of Knachtschmidt is there, his family, old friends, the Vichy "general." Caviar, hors d'œuvres, piggies with stuffing, lamb, fruits, sweets, much Armagnac. At arch idiot toast, he began again on joppas, speaking of arch kind that is morse.

GURDJIEFF: What is morse in English? [*We supplied: walrus.*] Walroos, yes. And what is joppa, Kanari?

KANARI: Can't say in English, not bon ton word. (Of course he knows it.)

GURDJIEFF: Ass. Ass of morse. Ass of walroos. Walroos ass.

Above and right:
Gurdjieff's Christmas tree

"You can't even get a vague idea of the enchantment of this tree. I'm sending you his words on the subject among the notes of the Russian New Year's parties."

"The décor on the floor is from one wall to the other —he knows I'm sending you these photos."

KANARI: Very funny because half of walrus is that.

GURDJIEFF: Excuse, not half—all. Rest of him is only by the way.

[*At squirming, he began to address his brother-in-law, who indignantly replied. All in Russian. Then he said to me in English:*]

I tell him he is such because he ——. He ask why I say such thing, is he not married? I say it is logical he make this, because now his wife is too fat. He tell, how can you say such thing to me when my wife is your sister? But I say what is sister to me when there is a question of logicality? You all know my principles.

[*At square idiot toast.*]

Yakina, pity such fat you have. You had once divine thing—divine possibilities. But now is too late. You have terrible ass.

[*To his sister for round idiot toast.*]

De naissance, from birth, is now as was always.

[*Looks at his Christmas tree.*]

In general such tree is merde. Anyone can make, only when *you* make is subjective, you lose something of yourself. But when I make, is objective for all humanity. Can be like medicine for you. If you sit and look for two three hours, you can remember all your childhood. From such merde thing, I make butter. Same thing what I do with my music and my kitchen. I make another vibration from these ordinary things. Truth, after look long time at this tree in beginning of new year, you can have food for whole year. Man can look and not be just animal.

When once you are initiated for one thing, it is like a chain—one link flow to another. And then whole chain flows.

Monday, January 17

Lunch. Georgette, Monique, Miss Gordon, Sardine, Yakina, Kanari. Make a circle of these names, put his between Georgette's and mine, and you'll have the order of our sitting at the table; he at one end, Miss Gordon at the other. This was the day when everybody was well dressed down—or tightened up for 1938. There was only one yogurt on the table, near his place. I passed it to him for his kasha and this is what I received:

GURDJIEFF: Aha, she wish remind me, but not for my sake. Is because she also like. Look how she manifest her ego, wish for herself and not will think pass to neighbor. Kanari, this dish is for all, not just for you. If such ego you manifest, you are candidate for hell. Here, take and pass—joppa.

KANARI: [*whispers to Yakina*] I see I'm to serve today for the joppa link.

GURDJIEFF: [*to Georgette*] Not eat such food with fork—must finger use for seven day pig, for birds must always be finger. Ancient people all this custom have. Why you smile at me, Miss Gordon?

MISS GORDON: I was smiling at someone else.

GURDJIEFF: No, on me you put attention, on me you smile. Even was psychopathic smile. Was logical it was for me.

MISS GORDON: No, you had only end of my smile. It was not for you.

GURDJIEFF: Then I am sorry for you. After all these years you must manifest either logic or idiotism. I not wish you to be idiot.

[*About something else:*]

Now you can article write, Kanari. She write article and truth is not bad thing, at any rate, is profession. Moreover, American article not so harmful as here. Other countries write and make suggestibility. But in America article such as go in one ear and out other. Your friend (poor J.) also write article, but I have seen her and nothing from such as she could be otherwise than empty. I am very patient. In two or three years she will be candidate such place as I write about in book (dog pound) where put in machine and result come out in two places—one is soap and other is manure.

[*To Monique at her toast:*]

Let God or devil help you. Choose.

MONIQUE: What is the devil?

GURDJIEFF: Whatever you wish. Everyone thinks of the devil in a different way. Choose how you think of him now, not what you will think a month from now.

[*To Yakina at square idiot:*]

Let devil help take you from your present center of gravity. I wish devil help you put this another place. You know what place, yes? Let be such conjury. Ass also is question of taste, like devil. Half of humanity like only such as yours, other half just opposite. Understand, Yakina?

YAKINA: No, I don't think so.

GURDJIEFF: Kanari, not explain her. Only scientific man can such thing explain. You have not science for such explanation. You understood what I told? Not altogether I think, only almost. Is life thing, not such idea with which you write your article.

[*Later—about some Greek root.*]

I was God forty-three languages—*was* God, now I forget. Languages my pastime in past. My past was till accident, then I begin my real life. I am only boy of twelve.

[*He looks carefully over each person's melon rind and points to Georgette's, at which she desperately begins to peck with a fork, saying, "Je n'ai pas fini, je n'ai pas fini!"*]

Such thing makes me nervous. Nowhere on earth now can such melon have, no one today can eat such, each one cost not less than three hundred and fifty.

[*Kanari begins to saw at her rind, Yakina has virtuously dug into the deepest places and so has a clean conscience.*]

Most active element is under, close to skin are the mineral salts. And this you would defile.

[*After coffee, Louise has passed near him, clearing away plates. He seizes her and slaps her hip.*]

You see how was before? You have all perhaps noticed how was and now how is?

LOUISE: [*with confidence*] Is harder.

GURDJIEFF: No, not harder. Is another kind fat. Shape also is different. Fat she take in three places. I know what this symptom means. Ordinary doctor not know [*he makes a motion like hammering*], but empty make because not have this knowledge. Now go, I not wish feel another place, might give another idea.

Wednesday, January 19

From the steam bath to lunch with Yakina also invited.

GURDJIEFF: How you, Yakina? Hungry after bath? Then with such dish as we have, all is roses roses.

YAKINA: Yes, too good, I suspect.

KANARI: [*seeing he has not understood*] She means she is suspicious that soon must be thorns.

GURDJIEFF: Always is so when too many roses. Roses roses. Now must begin to make only roses rose. Then rose rose, rose thorn, thorn thorn, thorns thorn, and thorns thorns. I will begin to make and you; Kanari, Miss Gordon, and Sardine, think how can make for her also, each one of us one part. I have thought, that is one-fourth part; Kanari also? That is one-half. In Yakina's past, all her can-ness (ability-to-do) was in her. [*Makes downward gesture.*] When I first saw, I thought was only such representative of art as have will-less-ness in one place. You understand what I tell, Marguerite?

YAKINA: Yes.

GURDJIEFF: No. If understand you would not carry (wear) such thing.

[*He looks at the rows of bracelets she wears on each arm.*]

Eheu! Life such idiot thing. What good life has dog. He at all times wish only eat, only one tapeworm has. But biped-man has three tapeworms to satisfy. But some people have two tapeworms atrophied. What was that saying—blessed he . . .

[*We supply—Blessed is he who has a soul. Blessed is he who has no soul. But grief and sorrow to him who has its inception . . .*]

Saturday, January 29

I pointed to Yakina's arms to show she had left off all ornaments and he smiled and said, "Little by little." After lunch he went over to a pot of dead flowers and smelled them.

GURDJIEFF: Finish. Nothing they have. Involution. Never was otherwise. Never active element they have, such dirty thing. From birth was only involution. Always they are false.

Monday, January 31

Nicholai's father is dying. I tried to get him a job at my bank, so I was late for meeting Gurdjieff at the café. I found Yakina sitting with him. Her face was so distressed that I waited until she left. The previous day she had said to him, "I see I irritate you, Mr. Gurdjieff, so I will go."

GURDJIEFF: I nervous and your friend come talk empty to empty. So I tell her I explain to Kanari who know my language. She too light for this work, too American. In life she perhaps have something good. But not for our work. I thought when she first came that after she had contact with me, something would collect in her empty place, but now I see is not so. Such empty life leave empty place. In fact, I could tell is piece of meat with emanations. Good formulation, eh?

KANARI: I think the reason is result of philosophizing for years with Orage's New York group.

GURDJIEFF: Yes, like that she is victim of self-observation.

KANARI: Perhaps not too late, Mr. Gurdjieff. She has such wish to work, be different. She truly knows there is nothing else in life but your work. Don't send her away.

GURDJIEFF: Well, I will see what I can combinate for her. She must all stop make, wait, begin again another way. She has only automatic mind, she not understand that of mind is two kinds and she quite not have real mind mentation. You explain her, but not use my words. (Yakina was stricken and cried, then rebelled, then said she "disliked that man," then decided to face him the next day and ask again for some task.)

Wednesday, February 9

Lunch. Yakina, Georgette, Miss Gordon, Sardine, Kanari.

GURDJIEFF: [*pointing to small black olives*] Is exact like merde of sheep—small, neat, clean. Very convenient for flies to lay eggs in, raise family. Not all is merde and finished, something good remains. Is best manure. But merde of man is worth nothing—is good only for cabbage. All from sheep is good—wool, food, merde—all.

MISS GORDON: [*happily*] But you say English are sheep.

GURDJIEFF: [*scornfully*] But that is for English psyche, Miss Gordon.

[*Then to Yakina he gives a description he used to use for Krocodile and "butter" derrière. How fat collect behind, reserve fat, on certain sheep, how a barrow is necessary sometimes to carry rear end of sheep. They get fat because they eat too much when there is summer food to guard against the lean months. To Georgette at squirming idiot:*]

God or devil. Choose.

GEORGETTE: Both together.

GURDJIEFF: Excuse. Cannot have both. How can be Paris and Berlin at the same time? Devil help small things, only so much he can do.

Tuesday, February, 15

Lunch. Stanley Nott, a friend of his, one of Jane Heap's group who is a painter, and Miss Gordon.

THE PAINTER: Why do you close the shutters and keep out the light?

GURDJIEFF: Because sun pass from there in street. And at all times my principle is—all or nothing.

SHE: [*pointing to yogurt*] What is that?

GURDJIEFF: Fou-fou.

STANLEY: I think you have great patience.

GURDJIEFF: I not have patience—I have practice.

STANLEY: I have patience.

GURDJIEFF: Of course. You are English. All English have patience.

STANLEY: I am ordinary idiot and round idiot. [*Laughter.*] But I prefer ordinary because we hardly ever get to round. So I am ordinary idiot.

GURDJIEFF: How can be ordinary? Not have ear or taste. You hear one-tenth like normal person, so rest must also be such. But you happy (lucky). Not hear at all times what makes nervous.

MISS GORDON: Perhaps he is tense at all times, trying to hear.

GURDJIEFF: No. I see that after tenseness to hear he sit back, rests, dreams, is happy.

STANLEY: What can I do about it?

GURDJIEFF: Go Place Opéra without trousers, with peacock feather in certain place and there walk.

In the café one morning he had told me about the ridiculous occult exercises practiced by ignorant men in India; one exercise is to put a feather in a "certain place," climb a tree and sit there, trying to feel like a bird.

I was taking off plates so I missed what proceeded, suddenly I heard, " . . . careful not be number eighteen, idiot that has stink coming from him which I call harmful idiot."

KANARI: [*involuntarily from sideboard*] But that's number nineteen.

GURDJIEFF: Er—er—is number seventeen.

Wednesday, February 23

Lunch. Miss Gordon, Yakina, Kanari. Gurdjieff soon began again on Yakina's plumpness, asking me to supply a word which I refused.

GURDJIEFF: When have money will find new secretary. Your obligation is to help when I look for word. Yakina, you were perhaps a beautiful child? You can thank this you are now spoiled. You are now receptacle for merde.

YAKINA: Yes, I know.

GURDJIEFF: Must be so with such child. Everyone spoil, parents, young man. Child not study, not learn. If beautiful face have man or woman, always I know is merde. If lawyer or engineer I need, never I choose beautiful face—merde is. I choose monster. He is not spoiled. He study when young, is clever. This is fault of education and parents. Now late, time has passed. You no longer are hard—just liquid now begin. Fault of your past that you are now empty.

YAKINA: What shall such a person do?

GURDJIEFF: Get on table—do some new titillation.

YAKINA: I don't mean in life.

GURDJIEFF: Ah, now very expensive costs such help. If for moving Kanari, castor oil costs twenty-five francs, for you will cost fifty francs. Now you must pay for your past.

MISS GORDON: What can she do?

GURDJIEFF: *Then* (in past) you must do—or your parents or guardian. Man must then, in past, take thought for his future.

Man is such that he wishes to live until last minute; such is his egoism. Let whole world burn, but let him live.

Animals and children only have property of pure logicality. They not philosophize. Only a philosopher can understand philosophers.

Who eats such food will die but who does not eat will perish like a dog. Another kind of man is also—who does not even perish like dog. If dog perishes in street, there is body, you can see, but cannot even see body of this other kind of man. He neither dies nor perishes—he disappears. Like the soldier of Arc de Triomphe, he is unknown.

Man is man. He cannot be otherwise. He is such that he can never change his body. He can only be as he is because he is the result of heredity. But his mind he can educate and with this control his animal body and not be its slave. He must at all times struggle and as his mind grows stronger, so will his weakness grow stronger. This is good thing, it makes for more struggle. It is not good if body at once lies down. He must command, he must direct. Easy not eat if not see. Only is difficult if he sees before him—and then not take. This will make something for him in another place, something he can use.

Man's body is merde and merde can never be diamond—not even merde of diamond.

Miss Gordon, please put off that light.

[*She searches for the button.*]

MISS GORDON: I cannot find it. I have never done this before.

GURDJIEFF: But one hundred times you see me make this. Such is automatism of man. Of course, if once he does, he can do it again. Is automatic. He must observe, look, know how to initiate what he must do the first time.

In Café De La Paix

Kanari's best friend has quarrelled with her bitterly over her devotion to Mr. Gurdjieff.

KANARI: Please tell me what is Miss X's animal?

GURDJIEFF: Ah, again, Miss, curiosity you have.

[*We sit for five minutes without speaking.*]

Now one secret I will tell. Not only is tapeworm in stomach of man, other worms are also. Perhaps you have seen in merde?

KANARI: No. Only in books as usual.

GURDJIEFF: Ach! Well, worms, such snakes as I tell about, is different kinds in stomach of man and of them all, one is always chief in this universe of stomach.

He commands all and from him, this chief in struggle of stomach-universe, from him depends of what consists the psyche of this man and what is his animal.

[*Then Mr. Gurdjieff talked on for twenty minutes, a monologue of which I could not understand a single thing, nor retain one sentence. When he stopped I told him I had understood nothing.*]

Of course not. Only I tell you this to give you taste of such thing. Not use word "*wish.*" Man not has possibility for wish.

1939

Wednesday, March 1
Trip To America—We Sail Alone On The SS Paris

He confesses on the train that he has spent all the dollars I had collected for his tipping on the ship and now has nothing. He takes out his watch and studies it.

GURDJIEFF: On boat, time will change each day. Already I prepare for this.

KANARI: *Prepare*?

GURDJIEFF: Of course. Necessary think of functions. They change if hour change when take lunch or dinner, even five o'clock tea. Not good if automatically this changes, so I prepare consciously the rhythm for functioning. Now I not remember such long tunnel, already long time we are underground.

KANARI: I have a special illness about being underground.

GURDJIEFF: Yes, air is different. But you must not have illness. For such unsatisfaction, you will later have satisfaction. When air change again, such satisfaction body has! Necessary make this changing with satisfaction for body. Always be just to body.

[*Dinner. First night on the Paris and he is already passing bonbons.*]

GURDJIEFF: Truth, my tapeworm not satisfied.

KANARI: No, for seven days he must do penance.

GURDJIEFF: What is this word?

KANARI: Is church word—punishment for sins.

GURDJIEFF: Not correspondent in this case. Church business is for psyche thing. Moreover, is all imagination, such manipulation. I speak only of real things—and of the heaviness my tapeworm must carry.

[*In the night the purser tried to change Gurdjieff's stateroom and he told him if he didn't go away from his door he would break all his teeth.*]

GURDJIEFF: After I told him with loud voice, they let me sleep in peace.

Second Day

We sit in deck chairs from eleven to twelve. He sees a woman pass, wearing trousers.

GURDJIEFF: She not can wear. There is old Russian word for such specific fat. All meaning in this one word. Old countries use few words but those make pictures for compact understanding. Ass is projector for understanding all other parts of a person. Always look in root to see what is, how is, all other parts. Ass is root. Also, of course, navel. Any navel I can look and tell what person is like.

Each night he attended the concert in the salon commenting how terrible it was. On the walls were scenes of Paris, Saint-Germain-des-Prés. The sea was very rough and many were seasick. When fewer and fewer people appeared, Gurdjieff said, "They are such people as not like this motion but for me is good thing when ship make so, because we must know we are in such place as we are."

In the salon this second night, he ordered Coca Cola which he called, "Kola Kola."

KANARI: I await your opinion of this drink.

[*He tries it.*]

GURDJIEFF: Ah, one bouteille enough for lifetime. I can smell and taste nap. What word I wish? From ground come—black.

KANARI: Tar?

GURDJIEFF: Yes, one drop this they put. Even liquid take this color.

Third Day

He is uneasy. Passports to fill out. One cable to send, composed and recomposed in the morning, and he choose to change it again at 7:00 p.m. At night, I promised to have cocktails with the Ogden Nashes.

We finish the cable at eight o'clock and he wishes to dine at quarter past eight. As I had to dress, I was a half hour late and only half in order. When I came to table, he asked, "What happen to you? I was just going down to see if you sick."

After dinner we sent the wireless—six hundred and sixty-five francs. Then we went up to the concert. He constated with me that the musicians couldn't be worse. But he said, "Truth, Tchaikovsky write such beautiful things, pity these men spoil."

Fourth Day

Sitting on deck, a thin woman passes. "She suffers to be thin because is fashion. This is the only suffering she can do. And just this kind suffering spoil her objectively. The only will she have is for this kind of suffering. Such woman will suffer and cry to pull out hairs from over eye, but if from leg must take, she will manipulate for one week, even ask for anesthesia."

At lunch he sees a woman two tables away, so overdressed that everyone was looking at her.

GURDJIEFF: This woman remind me of gypsy in Russia and by the way—is two kind gypsy—real and jump-up.

[*Later.*]

Tapeworm still not satisfied and by the way, Miss, tapeworm is only true representative of man's psyche. He eats like man, sleeps like man, is angry or glad. Only if is *near* man's stomach, is different. *Then* something proceeds automatically.

He says he feels well now and not seeing people every day allows him to keep his energy.

"Even I can tell you I feel today like impudent hooligan. Is two kinds of hooligan—impudent hooligan and ordinary unconscious hooligan such as breaks everything. I can now enter room and say 'Beware!' (I gave him this Shakespeare word for his French *attention!*) Even if you wish, Miss, I can give you example of impudent hooligan. He sit in restaurant. He call head waiter. He ask to try his peppers. He says, 'Now *you* try,' (to head waiter) but instead of putting this pepper in mouth of head waiter, he turn him around and put in quite another place. Another example I will tell. He come in salon where is many people. He walk to piano. But instead of playing such piano, he make pee-pee in it."

He sees a very fat man. "Ach, his valise is bigger than mine. Such man sits at table all day and all night he sits on water-closet. Next morning he forgets his night's suffering, only thinks to eat again. Makes program such as astonishes even head waiter." He says of a woman at the next table, "She is combination herring and leech." After dinner he sees me talking to the Ogden Nashes and later sends me the length of the salon with bonbons for them and their guests. Of course they want me to explain him to them. All very embarrassing!

We play the horse races every night. He always bets on number three and so do I and often we win.

Fifth Day

He remarks, "Time slowly pass." I tell him how extraordinary are the three Russian-Greek anatomical books he has lent me for my work at the Hospital St. Louis.

GURDJIEFF: Just from those books, I studied for my degree. Old German printings and some diagrams, very rare. But of course I found later much better in one Chinese monastery. Such for detail as you could never see even in dream. Only they were hard to learn to read because they not show negative picture, as all other books, but in this case, positive. Must study positive while holding always picture in mind of negative. Not one of your western scientists can even know there is such thing. This book also show at same time function. Also this, not one of your idiot doctors can understand.

KANARI: I know, even when I ask them such questions—after you told me about this thing—they do not understand what it is I wish to know.

GURDJIEFF: Of course not must ask doctor. Even they will think you quite idiotic for asking. When scientists wish know rays of sun and study rainbow (prism) they not even know they only study negative aspect of ray—as from distorted image in mirror where left is right and right left. What can they expect to know from that? Now continue such studies and remember—photograph everything on your mind.

Sixth Day

We have piqûres every day before lunch. This day he dropped a new syringe and broke it. I had to go to the chief doctor and make up a story to get a new syringe. Fog and icebergs.

KANARI: I organically hate that foghorn.

GURDJIEFF: Yet without could be unhappy situation. You *must* like instinctively because is good thing. But you have wrong instincts and impulse for disliking because you not have education. Everything mixed in you of feeling and thinking. Of course everyone hates such noise—you are not the only one.

[*At dinner.*]

What is what saw with?

KANARI: You mean saw for wood?

GURDJIEFF: *No.* I was going to tell one thing but with you I must always spend time looking for word. [*Silence.*] What man do in field?

KANARI: Sows?

GURDJIEFF: With what?

[*Makes cutting motion.*]

KANARI: Oh—scythe—for cutting.

GURDJIEFF: Yes. Well, I wish tell that those two men there who invite those two women dinner eat last night, now no more sit together. So I tell I think scythe meet stone.

[*At the concert he hears the music of Debussy for the first time.*]

GURDJIEFF: For such music I can say is like shadow of sex organ seeing shadow another such opposite organ. This is not simple onanism like most musicians, because everything is involved—mind, feelings, all psyche.

KANARI: Yet French consider Debussy a solid musician, he is their modern genius.

GURDJIEFF: Yes, not everyone can make such. Necessary much manipulation and compromise.

*Seventh Day, New York**

Sardine, Theen One, and Krok await the 11:00 p.m. landing of the Paris. We wonder who else on the pier belongs to him. Then we see Lillian and Donald Whitcomb, Carol Robinson and Rita Romilly. Also Mr. Wolfe. But the Rope doesn't mix. We all pick different gangways for the expected landing. I see first. This is what I see. In the practically solid surge down the gangway—Kanari chic as Paris being pushed ahead and looking back. Four layers of people behind her is Gurdjieff—a too-small beret perched on his bald head, with the leather band out—and the little yellow silk bow (on the band—for tightening, ordinarily) sitting on his baldness. Somehow we join. Gurdjieff looking like a happy baby in that beret (which Kanari tried to separate from him during all the voyage because people laughed) sees his Knachtschmidt and names each one.

Gurdjieff has seven pieces of luggage. I take charge with Donald. Meanwhile, Donald's wife Lillian and Rita Romilly are commis-

* I have to go to Grosse Pointe to my family for a fortnight. Following notes are Katie's—Crocodile's.

The SS Paris arriving in New York

Hotel Wellington, New York City

sioned to find a hotel. Romilly tells me he can't go back to anywhere he was before. (Carpet and furniture disasters.) So they choose the Wellington, Seventh Avenue and Fifty-fifth Street. Telephone for a suite. Meanwhile, Gurdjieff's seven pieces of luggage are together and the custom man comes. I unlock the pieces. A suitcase filled with eyelashes is the only declared material. Gurdjieff, passing out bonbons, is treated gently—instead of one hundred dollars duty, they settle for one third, which he pays. He goes off to the hotel, telling all to meet afterwards, in Child's. We help Kanari get through, put all the luggage in the car, and go directly to Child's.

After midnight. About fourteen are with him at table. All who were at the pier, plus Muriel Draper and an escort. Everyone orders—everything from fried eggs to scotch and soda. The bill comes to six dollars and fifty cents which Kanari and I pay.

Wellington Hotel. He has a bedroom, bathroom, and living room—a very correspondent place for him—shelves around for the cooking things which shortly are to collect.

There are several days of meeting at Child's, but the restaurant annoys him. They are not used to a half dozen chairs being pulled around one table which becomes strewn with lichee nut shells and loucoum. Finally Gurdjieff says categorically he will go no more in the café but will receive in his hotel—midday to two o'clock and six to eight o'clock daily. Every day some of us are there, but seldom any of the others, though Carol Robinson had commissioned Kanari to ask him if he was going to "begin anything." The old crowd doesn't seem to know anything about going and sitting. They wait to be invited. Meanwhile, we go and sit.

He starts out with a Sterno, making his own coffee, then Thin One brings him a big electric grill. Next day, some gallon cooking pots appear. Forks and knives. Watermelons in the bedroom, cheese on the fire escape, bread in the desk, and pickles in the bookcase. We eat on paper plates from Woolworth. Alice went up alone on Friday (the day before his bath) and rolled two hundred meatballs for his Saturday night bath party. He steamed over a gallon of wheat kernels—and threw two pounds of butter in the pot. When I saw that I said, "Just now I think Miss Gordon feel something, even across the ocean." He laughed and said, "Not *only* Miss Gordon but you all, I think."

Sunday, March 12

At the Wellington Hotel. We have a terrific lunch so that even he says, "Now I am so full that even if God put something before me, would smell like gasoline."

Alice is candidate for idiot.

From a sequence every one of us has forgotten, he is talking about honey. "From sh—— to honey," he says, "Man can transformate sh—— to honey, *with knowledge.*"

Discussing the crisis in the USA, which he has constated through the lean pocketbooks of people, we tell how taxes take all, even tax what you work to get. He says, "Now for this there is one formulation very correspondent—they wish take three skins from one donkey."

Gurdjieff has Armagnac trouble. His Château de Larresingle brand is no longer imported. We look everywhere. Meanwhile we drink whiskey. Then from whiskey to his own home-brew—triple-distilled alcohol (from his perfume industry) shaken up with lichee nuts and small pieces of toasted lemon-skin. This is a frightful drink, so strong it eats varnish off the table.

Alice and I bring him the underwear we brought across for him two years ago. He had forgotten about that and is pleased. He unpacks it and comes out from the bedroom saying, "Look," with a pink embroidered nightgown held up against his front. Each one he brings out this way. He tells for whom is each piece. Alice says, too bad, she could have ironed them, not have returned them to him so mussed. He says, "No—better like this." I forget how he explained that ironing would make a different thing of each piece—remove all value—all creases and folds of a long voyage. "Quite another aspect gives." As he arranges the nightgowns and embroidered pillows, he says, "Now already I more solidness have for hotel. Moreover, with nothing, man cannot borrow. But when he merchandise have, then can he take."

One lesson for me I tell—revealing my crocodile mentation. In Child's he commissions me to find a needle for his German Syringe—he is badly in need of piqûres. I run the length of Fifty-seventh Street to Liggett's—they have no such needle—only ordinary kind. They tell me about adapters—which fit any needle to any syringe; only must be ordered in advance. I run back to the café, empty-handed. He waits with Kanari, counting minutes. I tell him about the adapter. Then he says, "But for now. You not bring even ordinary kind?"

So I beg him to wait—just three more minutes, I will get ordinary kind. As I go out, (Kanari later reported) he says, "Truth is crocodile mentation. All or nothing." I meanwhile taxi to another drugstore, get hypo needles—short and fine, also the other kind they carry—very long. One of each to be safe. First I give him the short fine needles which he wanted. Then I bring out the long ones. "I bring all they have, Mr. Gurdjieff, not knowing exact which you prefer." I know something has been said by the way he smiles at Kanari. He fingers the long needle. "With this you can make injection in brain, through navel."

In the hotel, meanwhile, we develop a technique for garbage disposal. After dinner, we empty the wastebaskets into boxes and bags, wrap neatly and tie, and each one carries out a package of garbage. The first night we did it without asking him, feeling only that the hotel people must not see those bones and rinds. When he saw the package going out the door, he asked—and we tell him we're taking it away.

"We will place in the middle of Times Square, Mr. Gurdjieff."

"Of course," he says, "most important place put in."

Sometimes we look at our Rope going down in the elevator, each with a bag of garbage folded to look like a gift. Sometimes we can put them in the refuse bin on the corner of Fifty-fifth and Seventh—but when the doorman is looking, we walk proudly to the car with our bundles. Once we had to drive four blocks before finding a refuse bin along the curb, and by that time the fumes in the car were unbreathable.

Now, lately, the situation seems not so acute. Gurdjieff told Alice that the hotel housekeeper took him out to a movie. So now he has a relation with the hotel staff. We often wonder though what people in the hotel across the street must think when they look down on Mr. Gurdjieff's fire escape. Crocks, jars, pots and bundles, all out to cool—and four tins of caviar gathering soot. He has never opened any of this for us.

He finds his greens here—taragon, mint, etc. Also, from time to time, some Armenian friend delivers a sack of cheese.

Also, in one bureau drawer he keeps a great roll of that unleavened Turkish bread—lavash. It doesn't look unlike flannel underwear rolled up in the corner. He holds the roll against his chest and tears off pieces, piling them in the middle of the table for us to eat. He has already at least once produced a gallon of his chicken and apricot soup . . . and his salads taste just like Paris's. He keeps the salads in glass jars under the window in his bedroom next to the watermelons. All the Woolworth cutlery is in the bottom drawer of the bureau. The plates are all paper—except the soup dishes. We never say specifically that we are coming, but always when we go in the door, we see the four (or five if Sardine comes) places already laid, and his welcome to us is generally a wave of a ladle.

Diet note: We sat down to one of his wonderful grape-leaf spiced soups with meatballs. He rolled cheese and greens into lavash and ate this first, whereas Alice began with the hot soup.

"Not begin with hot thing—always first make foundation with cold thing. Then hot come down and mix with cold, help transformate."

Once Kanari and I saw a bathroom scene. These were the Sterno days, before the electric grill. I made him use the Sterno on the tiled bathroom floor—too dangerous for the table. He was making coffee on the Sterno. The pot wouldn't boil. He hovered—first sitting on the toilet seat, watching the small pot intently. The strain of getting that coffee to boil was too much for us. We waited in the other room. Then I tiptoed back to look in the bathroom. He was on hands and knees on the bathroom floor, blowing into the Sterno stove. A Sterno set-up is about six inches high so you have to lean low to blow. His rear pushed against the basin, his head against the toilet seat, and he seemed to be shouldering the bathtub nearer the wall. An elephant kneeling. I whispered, "Kanari, come look."

Once he counted heads before eating—Thin One, Kanari, Sardine, and Krok—but there were five places at table. He counted again. Four people—five places. Then he laughed—"Me, I forgot." That reminded him of a story—a man had six donkeys to drive to a market place. Night came and he had to sleep with his animals in a mountain place—carefully he herded his donkeys and counted. Only five donkeys he could see. Very worried, he looked every place. Only five donkeys could he count. Finally a man came along, and the donkey driver told him his predicament. "But you're *sitting* on the sixth donkey," said the newcomer.

The meatball soup (for which Alice had rolled the balls). We sit and he tells Kanari she owes this soup to the labors of Thin One. "Then I am grateful to Thin One," said Kanari. Gurdjieff—"Grateful—what is this word you use in this sense? Not you have right be grateful. Only *she* have right be grateful. Ach . . . your American mentation."

One Sunday, Alice and I drove him down to Atlantic Highlands to the Whitcombs—to bring back a trunk of books. The Whitcombs had prepared a roast lamb—but he refused to remain for lunch. They had everything prepared—even boiled eggs for his salad. Only coffee he would take. But then Donald showed him on the roast his special part—the tail. So Gurdjieff took a knife, cut off the tail piece, also several chops, and brought them back to New York—where the Rope ate with gusto at the dinner in his rooms. (Alice kept the lamb hot in the back seat under blankets, and then continued in his room, keeping it warm on the radiator.)

In a day or two, he says he is going to Phoenix, Arizona. He has had telegram from the Frank Lloyd Wrights.

Friday, April 14

I go to dinner at half past nine. He is lying on the bed. I tell him how it was. Then we eat. "One soup never before seen in America." Near the finish he says, "My tapeworm call cara-ool"—then a long discussion to find the meaning in English. He tells how in old villages man in black cape come down from hills and all villagers, when see, cry out, "Cara-ool." Cara-ool means black wool. This he implies means all's well—I tell him about the Town Crier and he says, "Correspond." (Two days later, at the appropriate time in the after-dinner talk, I say, "Cara-ool." He is pleased I remember, only this time not told right for the meaning I wish to convey. Cara-ool can also mean "Help, help." He says it for me—"Cara-o-o-o-l," long rising cry on the o-o-o-l. This way it *"has accent for local morality*—psychopathic thing is, local morality. Must learn what is local morality, then only can say so they will understand . . ." (That the meaning "help, help" is implied.)

He says, "Tonight, I drink like bourjui. You know what is?" I do not reply for several moments. Then he continues, "Bourjui seven aspect have; one, he have wishing eat, and *will* eat, even if grass on earth burn. So tonight, I wish drink—like bourjui."

We speak of Theen. "You wait . . . you will see the *mechanism*" (of remorse, I think he means). When I tell him how the baggage was put outside the door and the lock changed, he says, "So much the *better* for us." We take coffee in his bedroom only he does not drink.

He asks me to sit on the bed and tell one story—"with *tzimuss*." He says tzimuss so it sounds like quintessence. I say so. He says, "Not tzim*uss*—tzim*ess*—nearly same sound have, only quite another meaning. Tzimess mean sperm." I tell him my ear is uneducated for sounds. He says, "Nearly same sound have."

He tells if I would lie beside, would bring *fulfilling*. I tell I not have education for understanding such. He says, "Not mama-papa, you not understand. Man when tired sometimes can fulfill, having passive beside him. Then can *he* be passive. This very complicate thing I tell. Woman all is same. Man can *be* woman. Just this fulfilling when rest together—without mama-papa business. You not understand. I far go." He leads, I don't remember how, so I speak of cow. "I Swiss cow perhaps," I say. Gurdjieff—"No, Normandie cow. You not hear about Normandie cow? All world, in all language, know is *normal* cow. Not have big here (where udder would be) or here (where other organs would be) but all same—though average have—still give big. In Tibet, one normal cow give one liter daily. This one liter what one Normandie cow give equal five liters what ordinary cow give daily. You have such for me. You are here—friend. I not feel I must be so-so (gestures politeness)—or nervous. Even I can eye keep shut. No one come in door to kill. You sit, you are near."

I felt importance about everything he said, only could not understand. Then I put cigarettes near, and prepared for going. I accept his invitation to come to dinner tomorrow night at 11:00 p.m. when all come from bath. "You prepare appetite—*even for beating*."

Saturday, April 15

11:00 p.m. All the men who went with him to the bath are around the table—Donald, Leighton, Stanley Speigelburg, Benson. No women yet—I arrive two minutes to eleven. He twits me. "Eleven exact, I tell. Then will women come." At eleven exact, Rita Romilly and Lillian come in. Special sitting for women; the men give up their table seats and occupy the lounge. A new atmosphere for me—different from what I have known in Gurdjieff gatherings. At first I think I don't like it. The men titillate about politics while Gurdjieff is talking. Once he interrupts his talk, listens to them in the lounge, then says to us, "Hear . . . how they beat each other!"

He asks Lillian how she likes the soup. She makes an answer couched in phrases of politesse. Her husband, Donald, says to Gurdjieff—"Look, she diplomat."

Gurdjieff looks at her a moment, then says, "She is *ass-ing*." So unexpected was this new word, and so exact, I laugh loud and congratulate. "Good, eh?" He says, "This you must remember tell Kanari. Ass-ing." Everyone comes in now for a discussion of ass-ing—much laughter. "From a joppa root," says Gurdjieff.

Later he is speaking of tapeworm. "Two kind is. One—eat all but no satisfaction have. Other, eat all—but have satisfaction. Today, all day, first kind I have in my house." (The people who came.) He looked at me when he made this gruesome formulation and I felt Theen had been there for lunch, but he did not say.

Sunday, April 16

Sunday lunch. Only Leighton is there. Leighton can tell good stories in Gurdjieff's way—making every word understood. He tells Gurdjieff how he read in a newspaper about one chicken that laid one egg, then ten minutes later, another egg, another ten minutes—another egg—so on until twelve eggs were laid, but toward the end the eggs became smaller and the shells soft. Then, when the last small soft-shelled egg was laid, the chicken rolled over on its back and died.

Gurdjieff—"If clever man there was, then could save chicken. Only one thing do. Very simple thing."

I dare—"Can you tell, Mr. Gurdjieff? If so simple?"

He waits a moment then says, "Camphor give. Small pieces in food." He explains how chicken comes to have so many eggs. "One small part inside make stop. Nothing can pass. Then all dirtiness go—in blood, or in organ, even in this place where make egg. Then suddenly break through. This why so many eggs at once. Could continue, many more than twelve."

Leighton tells how he saw one extraordinary photograph in a German book shop. It was a book on Malaya. A Malay sits so—knees at right angles to each other, feet on ground, arms out holding one small monkey which he has killed. He is removing the intestines of the monkey. Pulling the gut toward him. And position of monkey is exact same as position of man, only reverse. Legs fallen open at right angles to each other, arms out—exact like man.

Gurdjieff—"German. They wish *prove* something."

I wish to hear it again so I say—"For proving."

Gurdjieff—"Yes, of course. Even they cry—documen*tal*!"

We speak of matches. Gurdjieff recalls the time when only Swedish matches was, and after many light in room, must leave room. Sulphur smells so strong. Leighton tells how grandmother made light from tinder. Gurdjieff says he remembers farther back . . . when not even this was known. "I very old man." He tells of people he has known in life. Galvani, in Italy. "When I was boy, he invent electricity. Was holiday in school. Such excitement was for electricity. *And from this I begin my doctor business.* With leg of frog." Having done this in the lab myself, I picture Gurdjieff with a frog's leg muscle strung up, giving to the exposed nerve small electric shocks, reading the reactions on a kymograph.

Leighton remarks later (I forget the association) that he is like a chameleon. I think he was describing how Gurdjieff's food changes him instantly. He explains to Gurdjieff what a chameleon is, but Gurdjieff knows. Gurdjieff—"Better. You are like one paper. Intelligent paper is." I guess he speaks of litmus paper, turns red for acid, blue for alkali. Gurdjieff says, "Yes, only not called it such name. Even I know man what invent such—German was." He sounds a name like "Linmuss," inventor of litmus paper. "Never he thought, when he this invent, would be used as is today. For photography—such dirty thing."

Leighton mentions that "Linmuss" lived nearly a century ago. "But I known," says Gurdjieff. "Even I know this Morse. Telegraph inventor. Only he not invent. He take code from system which existed long, long before. Signal by light. "Heliograph," I say. "Yes, man in past have such system for speaking—with light."

Gurdjieff speaks of shipbuilding in the old days. He worked in a shipyard. Then, the most important part of the work was the drilling of holes in the iron plates.

"All ship work consist from this—making holes." He tells how they did it with *pressure*—not heat, as now. "One great apparatus, beginning with large wheels which turn, connecting with small and smaller wheels, then at most small wheel, force begin again go upward to more big wheels . . . then at last, force of this pressure comes into the tool—and he push into the iron, make one hole."

Leighton tells how he just talked with one man from New Mexico who witnessed the Easter ritual of the flagellants—men who beat themselves with cactus and crucify one (chosen the year before) on a cross. Only now they use rope, not nails. Sometimes the man dies, sometimes not. Leighton describes the organization of this group, very exact and honorable. Very democratic, too. From themselves each year they choose a leader. This religious idea was brought over by the Spaniards, says Leighton.

Gurdjieff—"Excuse, not Spanish is—long ago I saw in Persia. Many a time. They take knives, long and sharp, and with blade they beat their heads. Such terreeble blood flow—is all over man, all over ground. Cut, cut, cut. Then they wash away blood. And ten minutes later every man is well man. *Nobody die.* Only for three days after you can see marks on head. But all blood stop ten minute after they wash." (He said the Persian name of this, I said it back to him, to remember the sound. Now I cannot reproduce.)

Several Days Elapse

I have the taste of being in the sitting and waiting line. Small tasks I do—laundry, gold watch, etc. But no eating.

Then there is a lunch. The cucumbers are not good to eat today. He speaks of seeds. "Is mother cucumber. These mother seeds." He shows me some. "All melons have seeds but not *all* mother seeds. Only *some* have active element. Necessary know." (I neglected to mention the cucumbers were inedible because they had lain in a drawer beside the herring.)

He is tired this day. We make short work after lunch. I look in the door of his bedroom and thank him. He is stepping out of his trousers. His long grey woolen underwear! He says, "Krokodile, you excuse. I not waste time!"

Saturday, April 22

Another Saturday night after-bath dinner. I go to the café, planning to meet Rita and Lillian. We had spoken the week before about joining up for bath. I was not invited for dinner afterwards, and did not expect. So he looked surprised when I walked into Child's at seven o'clock. He is waiting for his men with Donald. He says, "Why you come?" "I wish go bath with women. Last week they invite," I say. "Invite? Who invite? You?" He asks Lillian, she says yes. "Why you not tell?" says Gurdjieff.

He invites me to sit at table. Restless, other men do not come. He goes with Donald, then five minutes later the men begin coming— Dr. Sapeshko, Leighton, and friend . . . so they follow to bath.

Lillian tells me that Donald said, when the question of women at dinner was brought up, Gurdjieff had replied, "Women not correspondent"—so we plan to have dinner together after bath, while she waits for her husband. Rita decides not to go to bath, she had been ill since last Saturday when she waited too long for food.

After bath, Lillian telephones the apartment, just to be sure we have understood properly. Leighton answers and asks where we have been all this time, Gurdjieff says, "Come immediately, we wait." So we go. I know I am included this time because Lillian said, "He says come and bring."

Leighton, Donald, Joe McClaffery, Tammany lawyer, friend of Leighton—first time at Gurdjieff's—are there, already at the soup course. Lillian and I begin with giant asparagus with red horseradish sauce. But we must drink full glass each toast, to catch up. I can, Lillian can't. Gurdjieff jokes about Lillian's size.

GURDJIEFF: Even for clothes she is Jewish. Always when she buy clothes is not child clothes, is now woman clothes. (Lillian wears size fourteen!)

LILLIAN: From remnant counter I clothe myself.

GURDJIEFF: [*to men*] Truth though, for one thing I pity her. For how she must carry life's carriage.

[*I remember rabbit and camel (she is rabbit, Donald is camel) harnessed together.*]

Truth, is most unusual combination. Even he sometimes wonders how could be.

[*Donald says they could be exhibit in World's Fair. (Rabbit and camel harnessed together.)*]

If I real truth from scientifique would tell, then all America would come to see. Such formulation could be . . . for welfare all America. But only *I* could compose.

DONALD: Perhaps you could be there, explain, announce.

GURDJIEFF: No, because then you could not know how many come see *her*. So many would come see Gurdjieff. Even animal in America now know this name Gurdjieff. Important I *not* be there, only then can you constate how many come for the exhibit! Only important thing is that I compose formulation—from scientifique. Then this exhibit would be known for foremostness.

LEIGHTON: You mean uniqueness.

KROCODILE: No, foremostness is exact.

GURDJIEFF: [*pleased, to Krocodile*] *Can* be—foremostness?

KROCODILE: Yes *can* be, and moreover, is exact. Only never before used this word.

GURDJIEFF: This you remember for Kanari—your reportage. New word.

[*Dr. Sapeshko goes on to explain why "unique" could not take the place of the word Gurdjieff gave. Gurdjieff quiets him in Russian. Donald thereupon tries to calm the doctor still more and Dr. Sapeshko resents this, saying to Donald that only Gurdjieff can speak so to him.*]

SAPESHKO: Not you can speak so to me, you are small man. But he—he can say anything to me and I can take. You know why? Because I love him.

GURDJIEFF: [*turns to Donald with a serious, gentle look and speaks in a quite different tone*] Truth, Donald, one fault you have. Though you are known as kind man, good nature, and though everyone know you not wish give offense, you do this unconsciously sometimes. Is fault that spoils all life for you. You have not considerateness for state of surroundings. Necessary always know what is around you—the state of man who is around you. With cow, you can shit on face of, and he not take offense. He lick, smile, shake head; not understand, not offense take. But man around you is already more high. He have states. You must know what is state of every man around you in room. Man, of course, is most of the time asleep, but this makes even more important that you be sensitive. Because when he is awake, even if only for one moment, he is already in state—and for this one moment is delicate, sensitive. Perhaps is only moment in his life when he can be enlightened. So you must consciously try to understand, be sensitive for him. I know what is state of each man around me, because I am educated man, I have knowledge. You must try always to have considerateness for state of surroundings—if you wish be objective bon ton. Never can you offend one thing on earth. Even if you offend one worm, one day *he* you will repay.

Sapeshko—him I love. You know why? Because never me he need with egoism. All of you—many men—wish to give me your soul. But for something. Only one or two on earth love me without egoism. And Mullah Nassr Eddin, him I love. Every man must on earth for one thing feel holy—or else (he makes a gesture across his throat, for hanging). Never I put him in galosh. I could put—only not wish.

[*Leighton tells now in the West they have an expression, "Say it with a smile."*]

Of course, because then he think you joke. You notice . . . never anyone take offense anything I say? Even you know what words I use, but *never* you see man angry with me when *I* tell. You know why? *Because I am cynic.*

[*Leighton says he doesn't mean cynic, he is not a cynic. He is a skeptic.*]

Excuse—not skeptic. Skeptic means you believe, I not believe; you hope, I not hope. I know this word from Greek. You know I know Greek roots. Cynic is word. Perhaps you not have in English.

Leighton says it doesn't mean what Gurdjieff meant. Leighton doesn't want Gurdjieff to be a cynic! He says, "Perhaps iconoclast. You are iconoclastic. This word, you know what means—ikon-breaker."

Dr. Sapeshko comes in on the word ikons—there is discussion which Gurdjieff terminates thus: "In old Russia there is one question they ask—What is ikon? Answer is—bad art." He relates how man automatically paints ikons—is not painter, because painter is artist, he paints only what he *feels*. Ikons are children's play. Bad art.

Then Gurdjieff goes back to the word cynic. "Cynic is the word. Cynic means a man who is not afraid to tell truth, exact how is, yet never he offend people when he tell because he is so right, he tell so exact. Never they *can* be offended, *because the truth he tells*." (I learn from the dictionary at home that cynic comes from the Greek root meaning dog—cynical—dog-snarl!)

[*Leighton tells Gurdjieff that his guest, Joe, is Irish.*]

GURDJIEFF: Then because you are Irish, I must tell you, our guest, how I and my people (indicating all of us) look upon Irish. You know Irish are dirty people, not psychically, but organically dirty. In life, only two baths take—once when baptized, once when died.

He tells a story of young and old Irishmen at a river crossing, re-moving boots, and young one remarks to older how dirty are his feet—"Idiot, thirty years longer on earth than you I exist!" He goes on to the English. "Irish is dirty, Scotch is stingy, English is stupid." Someone asks about Welsh. "Is sh—— of all three."

He tells his English stories—marvelous, sitting there with his little feet (in new straw slippers) out at right angles, heels together, hands on spread knees, leaning forward, laughing. He tells a story about the Scotchman who wanted to commit suicide by gas, then after he begins, there comes by association "because never thought stop in man" the idea of how much cost; so he goes to neighbor's house to use his gas.

The story about the three Englishmen on the hill, discussing weather. This I have never heard told before with such humor, such acting. Sitting there, he is an Englishman looking up at the sky.

And a new one (for me) about the Scotchman who woke up one morning beside his wife, nudged her, no response, nudged again, then turned her over and found her dead. Scotchman gets up, puts on slippers, goes to head of stairs, calls down to cook, "Prepare only one egg this morning!"

And one more (for me new) Scotch story. Scotchman stands on pier near river. Sees man in boat prepare to suicide by drowning. Watches him remove coat and jump. Then watched man come up first time. Then go down. Then up a second time. (Gurdjieff—throwing an agonized face back and glugging like a drowning man is a sound-picture never to be forgotten.) Then he comes up for third, last time. As he glugs (this is my word to describe what Gurdjieff does) the Scotchman looks down on him and says, "If you die, may I have your boat?"

We all laugh so hard we forget to go home. At half past one Gurdjieff says with a woeful expression, "I sorry that your host bores you." This is his new way of saying, "Go, go," to guests!

I say, "Thank you, Mr. Gurdjieff."

"For what?"

Lillian whispers to me, "For everything," so I say, "For all."

Gurdjieff says to the men, "Listen how she tell *all*. Only one small part is."

I say, "One small your part seem *all* even to a crocodile."

Addenda

Several days ago, at lunch with Leighton only, Gurdjieff reminded me to be sure to tell Kanari his new word—"assing." I said, "Already I have told."

GURDJIEFF: [*to Leighton*] Kanari collect my new word.

LEIGHTON: Is antiquaire. Antiquaire, one who collects things.

GURDJIEFF: Antiquaire—not is. He collect only old thing. Kanari collect for future. Is *antiquaire for future.*

[*"Boswell," says Leighton, but Gurdjieff has already defined the situation and does not reply.*]

Wednesday Night, April 25

Tonight I wished to see him but didn't know how, so I wandered past the café—not there. Wandered in the hotel—not there. Wandered out the door of the hotel, and *there he was*. Standing on the doormat of the hotel saying, "Oi, oi, so hot."

Handsome, hat on back of head, overcoat over arm. I titillate about possible errands I might do, has he any? He titillates about rendezvous he has at nine o'clock. We titillate. Weather. (He knows how much I wish to be with him this night.) Then I prepare to go by placing one foot forward. So he says, "Telephone nine o'clock." So I say, "*Thank* you Mr. Gurdjieff."

I wander for two hours around Times Square, happy because I am invited to telephone him. Not one other soul in this crowd has that privilege. At nine o'clock I telephone. "If you wish come supper—you *can* come?" "In four minutes I'll be there." I run all the way.

Only Dr. Sapeshko is there with him. Magnificent sturgeon. I must drink one whole goblet of Armagnac, for harmony. I do. The doctor blinks. Later, we come to square, and I say, "And to my health also."

SAPESHKO: May God bless you.

GURDJIEFF: What tell?

[*We tell and he smiles on me and says—*]

May God merde on you.

KROCODILE: Already this big thing is.

GURDJIEFF: Of course. God cannot remember all who are on earth—two thousand million. So, if accidentalement he do—even one small piece of, fall on you—is big thing.

Next I remember—I hear the doctor say, putting up his glass, "Da Pianni." He receives it half full. So I say the same . . . and receive it full!

The soup is gorgeous. I say, eating the spiced black mud, "Is Third Series soup, Mr. Gurdjieff."

GURDJIEFF: No, even more far. Is for one hundred and one modus . . .

[*We struggle to find the equivalent of this word in English. What he says means "way of doing." I say it is Latin—modus. He checks with the doctor in Russian and says, "Yes, can be."*]

You not read my book—one hundred and one modes masturbate? [*He looks surprised.*] Is fashioned after one hundred and one tales Scheherazade. Is final for all Beelzebub series. One hundred and one different ways of doing.

KROCODILE: Such terrible picture this is.

GURDJIEFF: Why terrible? All will laugh when read.

SAPESHKO: Some will cry.

GURDJIEFF: Psychopath is.

[*Later.*]

If you wish I tell first of the one hundred and one. Man in bath, he all around him have hot water. He lie comfortable, catch one fly. Take off both wings. Then suddenly out of hot water his mister comes up. He hold fly without wing in hand. He look at his mister. On end he put the fly. Fly, without wing, can go only round and round. So round and round he go. You can picture this man? Even now he can think. Even of business.

One hundred and one—but really is two hundred and two. Man and woman. Different for each because organs are different. You know, from navel to ass (he draws a line down his front) woman have twenty-eight gradations—and I can know, looking her face, how far must go, *for her*. In her face I can see. Harmony—exact correspond—how is her face and which of the twenty-eight is for her.

Saturday Night, April 29

At ten I meet Lillian in the lobby, we telephone to hear, "Come queecklee."

He has the table in the middle of the room, all wings open. His bath companions—Donald, Leighton, Sapeshko.

Before eating all sit hungrily at table except Gurdjieff. He goes in his bedroom and returns with something in his hand. He tells how today he went in one man's toilet and missed the train because he stayed there so long, because in the toilet was one thing he never saw before. He shows what made him miss the train—three tin-types of self, all framed from a photomaton. The pictures are a fright. Of one he says, "Just out of prison." Then he goes again to his room and returns with something else—"This *absolute* new thing, never before on earth I see." It is his picture in the middle of a mirror, the mirror is blue with orange trylon and perisphere, Gurdjieff cap in hand, centered like a medallion.

LILLIAN: Like multimillionaire sportsman.

GURDJIEFF: No. You know what look like? As if just came from house (prostitution).

There is soup made from unlaid hen's eggs—webs of them as large as marbles. Only for me mentally squeamish to eat, the taste is excellent. First I thought they were little white dumplings floating. Everyone had at least eight in his bowl. Where on earth does Gurdjieff find dozens of unlaid hens eggs in New York? Then a second soup—lentils, chicken, nuts, spices—wonderful. He asked me, "What would name such a soup? Most famous name must be." I cannot answer.

GURDJIEFF: A la Mrs. Roosevelt.

[*He tells how she is most foremost. Goes everywhere . . .*]

LEIGHTON: In airplane. [*He toys with chicken bones.*] But chicken also have wings.

GURDJIEFF: Chicken also service nature. How you call Donald, for bon ton?

DONALD: Fertilise with manure.

GURDJIEFF: But *what* fertilise. Always you must tell what.

DONALD: Can't think what. I say pumpkin.

GURDJIEFF: No. Chicken manure for pumpkin is. For her, must be more high thing, as far as you can go from pumpkin.

[*None of us follow. Leighton tells how she always has itch, for going.*]

GURDJIEFF: Yes, but *where* have itch?

LEIGHTON: Well, she sits all the time in the airplane.

GURDJIEFF: And not always comfortable is.

LEIGHTON: No, because she doesn't have much cushion (joppa).

GURDJIEFF: *Now* you see? For *thees* she make . . .

[*I'll never know how Gurdjieff did it but I had a picture of Mrs. Roosevelt sitting in a plane on a cushion of her own manure. I laugh (nervously, I hope).*]

GURDJIEFF: [*to me*] You *see*?

KROCODILE: One picture begins to form, Mr. Gurdjieff.

[I know by how he laughs that I am right.]
KROCODILE: Now I see why not for pumpkin.

The table doesn't get all this. Some look at me as if I've gone loony, Gurdjieff is laughing so hard his eyes are slits. The men all seem to have a joke together. Gurdjieff wants to tell it but decides it's not correspondent for woman. One can guess what happened to him in the bath, from the way the men laugh. Gurdjieff even says—"In bath, such emanation come down on me . . ."

LEIGHTON: As from goddess.

GURDJIEFF: Yes, such was.

[He goes on to ask if I know this word umpf. He explains that all Hollywood actress have umpf.]

GURDJIEFF: Woman who is not umpf is sh——.

LEIGHTON: *[correcting!]* Who not *have* . . ."

GURDJIEFF: *Ees.*

LEIGHTON: In local idiom we say—*have* umpf.

GURDJIEFF: Quite another thing is. Have umpf is one thing. *Be* umpf . . . you see?

Gurdjieff shows us all the five and ten cent gifts he has bought for presents. Of one item he is especially proud. He has bought dozens. "Small thing is," he says, "but for them in Paris is new and wonderful." He illustrates how he will, with a bow, present this rare gift from America, how they will receive it, awestruck. He hands Leighton the gift. It is a ten cent folding bunion knife!

Sunday, May 7

Another Saturday bath night. I go to Ansonia with Draper and Rita, meeting them in the café first, where at seven o'clock all gather. Leighton brings Theos Bernard, as a guest. Bernard without beard—tan gabardine suit, corn flower boutonniere, tip tilt nose, a nice friendly little boy with lines in his face. Gurdjieff tells all to come to dinner at eleven o'clock.

Rita, Draper, and I arrive at eleven exact. Seven men are already around the table. Gurdjieff, Leighton, Bernard, Speigelburg, Benson (Rita's husband), and one other. They are at squirming. Food practically gone. Ladies eat melon and drink canned fruit juices of which Gurdjieff now has a gross of tins, ranged on the ledge above the tub in his bathroom.

Bernard, like the other men, sits in suspenders. Draper is magnificent. She "darlings" Gurdjieff and the whole center of interest goes to her. After a while, Gurdjieff remembers his guest. He speaks in general of one person there who for him is very important. Draper looks as if singled out.

Gurdjieff waves his hand—"Not *you*. I know you. I know *all* you. Of *him* I speak. He for me is like new lemon. I wish squeeze."

Draper—"I get two slices, darling."

She and Gurdjieff bargain over the division, finally decide to go fifty-fifty on Bernard. Bernard laughs, as if jolly part, but watches.

Then Draper bewails Bernard's fat . . . tells how four hours ago she saw him come in the café, with color in his face, light in his eyes, alive, gay, and with a future . . . and now . . . now . . .

Bernard laughs at her picture, then says, "But I'm still *alive*."

Gurdjieff—"But how you tell—such *cheap* life. Man must at all times mathematically hear, mathematically understand, mathematically answer. Only *this* is life. Always he must be with his I. Only then is he man not in quotation marks. No matter what he have in surroundings—people, noise, alcohol—always he must mathematically understand. Never lose self, even when drunk. *He* can be drunk, but never his I be drunk."

Leighton claps for Gurdjieff's speech.

Gurdjieff to Leighton—"You are joppa, moreover . . . morse"

They wait for "morse" to be elucidated.

I say "Walrus." I formulate for them: "Walrus is all joppa with whiskers at one end." Gurdjieff enjoys that.

Rita reads the American chapter. Gurdjieff laughs so hard he gets red in the face. Leighton nudges Bernard at the "good" parts. They laugh a lot with Gurdjieff, while those of us who have heard this many times wish to cry, it grows more terrible with each reading. Meanwhile, Gurdjieff leans forward on his paunch and watches Bernard's reactions. But he never gives any indication of what he sees, if anything. His attitude—benevolent.

At parting, in his bedroom, however, he says to Bernard:

"I will tell you one prayer you must say tonight. This most holy. Is initiate thing." Everyone hearing the word "initiate" moves closer. Also Bernard, now standing squarely in front of Gurdjieff.

Gurdjieff then crosses arms across breast and looks up. "First you make so." Then Gurdjieff puts his index finger in mouth, takes it out and with a sweeping gesture brings it slowly around to his backside, but from the other side.

"And third time, you make so." He wets finger, bends, brings it down between his legs, toward backside. "This initiate prayer. This you do—and *then* you can sleep."

1948

Gurdjieff arrived on the SS America with Mme. de Salzmann, Lord Pentland, another Englishman, and a Mr. Walton who was at the Prieuré and who is now "tamada."† All the old group are at the ship or Hotel Wellington to greet him. First coffee and Armagnac at eleven o'clock, then lunch at two o'clock for twenty-five or more. He told us the English (old Ouspensky group) had paid his debts in Paris, millions of francs; that he was to buy a large château for his headquarters; that his health is now even better than before his accident. "All debt liquidated in France; I come to you pure, like new-born baby."

A big suite at the hotel, prepared and stocked for him with his kind of food and drink. When Alice burst in, he said, "What! You not afraid to come?"

"No, Mr. Gurdjieff."

"Why you not afraid?"

"Well—because I have known you many years."

Alfred had flown to New York earlier and had already begun to re-hearse the new group of sixty at Carnegie Hall; Gurdjieff went there on the first evening to supervise the exercises.

For the toasts—at Alice's announcement that she was now square idiot having been changed from squirming, he said, "Ha! Was automatic changed." At Enlightened, tamada asked, "Anyone here?" Gurdjieff said, "No. Yet have been times when everyone at table was." Then he formulated second series "mesoteric" toasts and gave the first two:

(1) "To health of all hopeless idiots, both subjectively and objectively; that is to say, to the health of all candidates for an honorable death, and to the health of all candidates for perishing like dogs."

(2) "To the health of all candidates for all kinds of idiots."

GURDJIEFF: [*to Carol Robinson*] If you wish, advice I give you. Now must begin to eat for quality, not quantity. If not, you will soon re-

---

* Notes of Solita Solano.
† Toastmaster.

Above and below: Gurdjieff, 1948

semble wife of merchant—each time see, more big is. And for your profession, think how will be if fingers four times bigger, like elephant. You know even elephant have five fingers. [*To all at table:*] If you wish help me, every hour you must say *I am*; *I*, with feeling; *am,* with sensing.

DONALD: I need help, Mr. Gurdjieff. No use to struggle without help.

GURDJIEFF: You shall have help. I have brought help, all kinds— even physico-chemico.

S: One request, Mr. Gurdjieff. New friend's mother wish to see you, just look at you five minutes. May she come?

GURDJIEFF: Yes. Mother is my weakness. I loved my mother very much. I invite come lunch.

[*Then he went out with Donald to shop for salad materials, Donald carrying a shopping bag.*]

Next Day

He once said, "Scale is from merde to God." Now, about toasts, he said, "Unique idiot is highest thing and in stone or static thing is the lowest; between the two is our scale or measure. First time one starts up, the scale automatically proceeds as far as number sixteen. This is easy, easy to go up. For going down, is difficult, because go down with consciousness. Second time go up, can go beyond sixteen—even to stink idiot."

S: Is stink idiot same as harmful?

GURDJIEFF: No. Sometimes stink idiot can be made clean. But harmful never, in objective sense.

At The Wellington Hotel

GURDJIEFF: Do you understand what I said?

S: I'm trying to.

GURDJIEFF: Not enough to try. Must understand without trying. He who always try and never do is onanist. Must at once *do* in life, if wish normal man be—in all things. There is no "nearly" in real understanding; is or is not.

Gurdjieff, 1949

1949

On October 25, 1949, after many days in bed, Mr. Gurdjieff finally consented that Dr. Welch be sent for. When Dr. Welch arrived in the evening of October 26 and declared to Gurdjieff that he could take care of him much better if he would only allow himself to be hospitalized, Gurdjieff refused no longer to leave his flat.

As soon as the ambulance had delivered him to the American Hospital, Dr. Welch tapped him for water and removed thirteen liters. On the twenty-seventh I telephoned to Gabo for news: "Il est très faible, mais il y a de l'espoir." I rushed to the hospital to find Valya and Gabo in the salon. They told me that Dr. Welch had slept—when he had slept—by Gurdjieff's side; that Gurdjieff was being fed anally by glucose; there's a mysterious issue of blood that may mean only a hemorrhoid; that he is so weak that he just lies there without speaking. I sat in the salon of the hospital all the afternoon.

Friday, October 28

No change in his state since two days. We all sit in the hospital every day, waiting for bits of news. Valya was sent to find the softest possible sheets for Gurdjieff's bed. The atmosphere now is that of doom, though one cannot bring oneself to believe it. Jeanne de Salzmann, Gabo, and I were the last to believe that there was little hope.

Saturday, October 29

I telephoned at 10:30 a.m. for news. "He is just the same." Les imbeciles! Half an hour later he died. Unconscious. Russell telephoned at one, just as I was preparing to leave for the hospital to sit out the afternoon again. As soon as I could move, I went to Neuilly. Jeanne, Vera, some of his family, several others, were already there. We waited in the salon while he was being embalmed. Vera said, one; he had cancer of the liver, two; the French doctor had raised Gurdjieff's eyelids while he was supposedly unconscious and said that Gurdjieff had looked back at him, three; that four hours after his death his forehead and neck were still warm—a curious phenomenon that the doctor said he could not understand.

When we were called, our little procession walked out to the hospital's chapel about a hundred feet away. Gurdjieff was lying on a divan, wearing the suit bought for the American trip. His "valise," which he always called his stomach, was as flat as a young man's. He was covered to the shoulders with a pale brocade cloth on which had been laid red roses, pink orchids, and white flowers; on either side of his head were two large bouquets of violets. In the candlelight his face is like a statue's. The first day his face had a slight lavender tinge and the mouth was almost smiling. The next day he looked darker and the smile had disappeared, he was already far away, the eyes had begun to sink and the lips had a grave line. Perhaps taking the death mask had made this change. He looked as if he had just said, "Now I go away with my secrets and my mystery—my work here is finished." For two days and nights people streamed to the hospital, stood in line to see him. They stand about him in the most complete silence I have ever known and just stare at him. Nearly all of them are crying and yesterday when Bennett came he burst into such sobs that he had to leave and go outside, where we could still hear him in the distance.

Monday, October 31

He has turned to gray stone. Carnations have replaced the violets and roses. Gabo has brought the brown and gray icon of St. George from the apartment and placed it at Gurdjieff's feet. The English groups and many Ouspensky pupils arrived in the night. Many went to the chapel directly from the gare carrying their bags and rugs and sat along the walk outside on the ground like Mexicans. All groups took turns to make the veille and change over every four hours. There is a service every day at four o'clock—a priest and his assistant who chants the prayers in Russian. Russell tells me that Gurdjieff once said to him, "I wish I were *real* man who need to sleep only one hour each night."

Tuesday, November 1

I sat by his side, near his face, for two hours; he is more gray today and the skin is tighter over the immense intelligence of his skull.

Someone has made tiny bouquets of red roses and yellow daisies and strewn them over the pale brocade. Russell and Valya were absent, having gone to Fontainebleau to prepare the plot in the cemetery which has been rather neglected. A small choir came from the Russian Cathedral and sang the responses. The chief priest was dressed traditionally—robes, silver cross and chain, long black hair and beard, liquid black eyes, and a honey voice. His sister Sonya sat beside me, crying, and Luba arrived from her job in England. Crocodile dared to kiss Gurdjieff's forehead to say goodbye and so did Gabo, but I neither dared, nor could I have done so if I had dared. Jane Heap said, "He doesn't look dead." Vera said, "Today is his birthday, where he has gone." I forgot to say that on the day before he died, Jeanne de Salzmann, standing by his bed, had spoken to him in Russian. He did not, could not reply, but he lifted his hand and held it out for her to take. She has been superb. She sits by him with closed eyes from which the tears slowly flow, her face without blood under the skin; and when away from him, she makes all the arrangements with Bennett. The movements group meet and practice as if he were alive. Jeanne has had people for readings, I was told. Louise March flew from Vienna—another stricken, marble face. The chapel is so small that most of the people must stand outside to listen at the services; we crowd together with our lighted tapers until we are touching the bier. The grief is silent and terrible to see as we all gaze at the noble beauty of his dead face.

Wednesday, November 2

Today was the mise en bière. I did not go as I was told that only the family would attend it. But Jeanne, Louise March, Russell, and others were there.

I with many others waited at four o'clock for the arrival at the Cathedral. We stood for two hours until he was brought there. (I was told the casket was too small and something had to be done about it, I don't know what.) Six bearers carried him in—Valya, Michel, Gabo, Russell, Sonya's husband. The lights were dim and lovely, many flowers already, vested priests and small choir for the service. The church was crowded, all golden under the high dome and filled with incense smoke. The catafalque was covered with black, embroidered with silver. Not a sound ever comes from any gathering of his people—neither footstep, rustle, cough, even a sigh. The quality

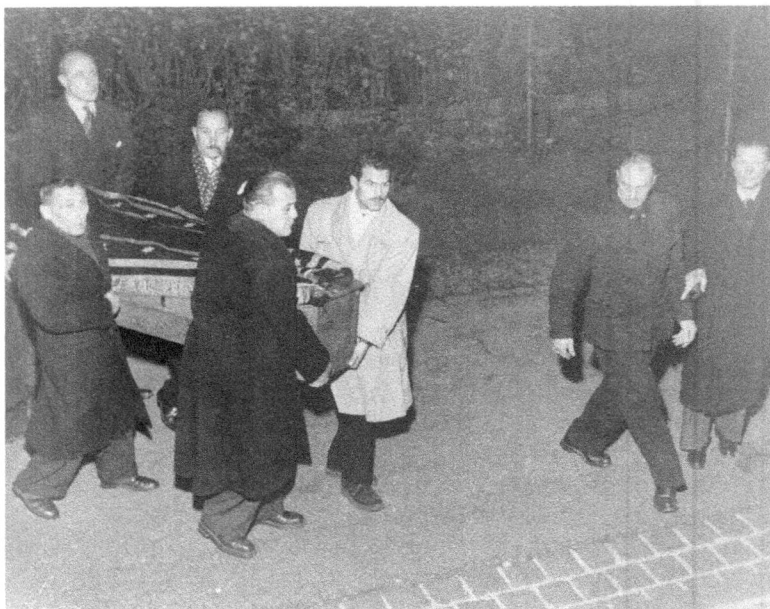

of silence is unique. No veille is permitted in the church. We all went away and left him alone.

Thursday, November 3. The Last Day.

The high requiem mass began at half past eleven. Entirely candles, masses of flowers, the voices of five white-and-gold robed priests, a cantor with a divine breaking voice. How beautiful is the Russian language! The church was packed with all those we know and with people whom I had never seen in all those years near him. After the chanting, the prayers, and the singing were finished, everyone passed singly by his coffin for an hour, from the right to the left. Each mourner made a genuflection at his head, stepped up to the icon at his feet, kissed it, stepped down and passed to the left, taking leave in a farewell of ceremonious simplicity that tore one's heart open even wider, if that were possible.

At two o'clock we all returned to the church. Crowds lined the sidewalks to watch the casket carried out and placed in the great funeral motor-car. His family rode with him. Private cars and motor-buses made a long cortège to Fontainebleau. We drove for an hour and a half, first turning to pass through Gurdjieff's street, his flat, through all the old familiar streets, roads, forest. In a cruel icy wind we followed on foot into the cemetery to the family plot. I saw the grave that had been torn open in the rocky watery earth, deep, deep. The bearers lowered him into it. For the first time I heard a sigh, a sound like a sigh, from all the people there. The priests began to chant . . . We all passed by the terrible hole, cast a bit of earth down onto the coffin, knelt, signed ourselves—passed on. It was over.

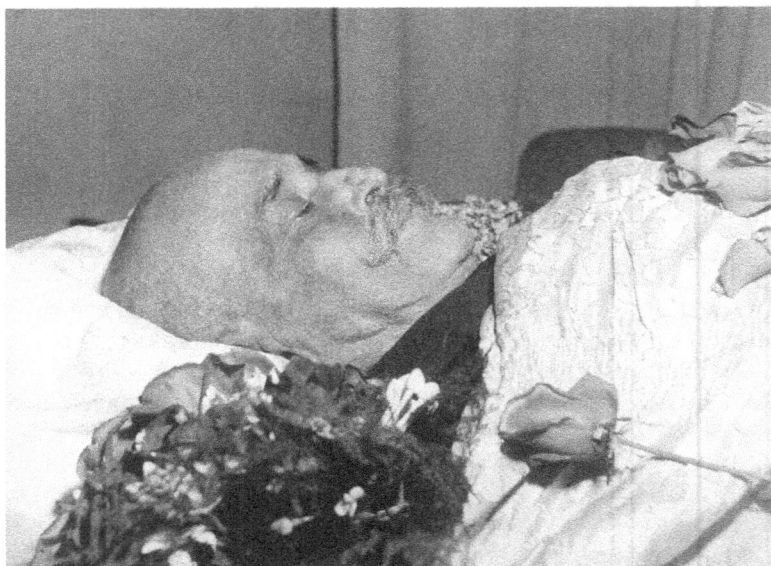
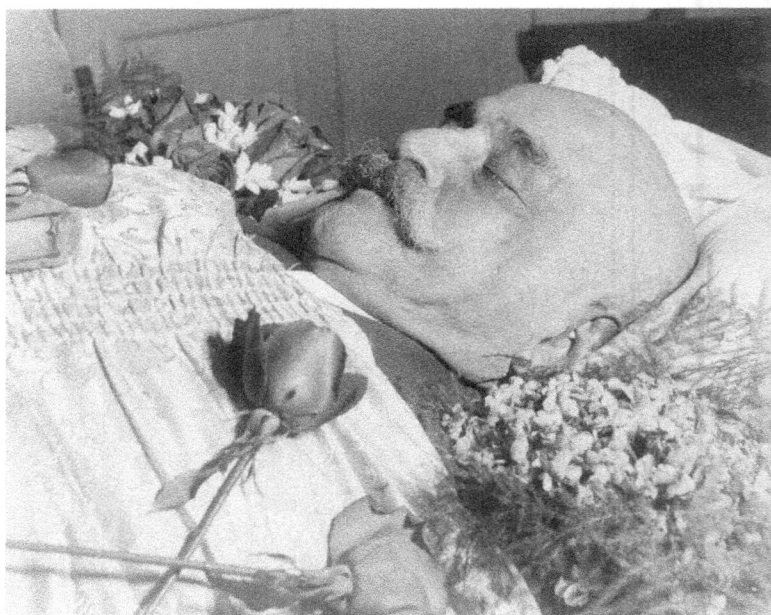

*Sunday, October 30**

For everyone.

He is lying on a divan, covered to the throat with a pale brocade couverture which is piled with red roses, pink orchids, white flowers; on either side of his head are two enormous bouquets of violets. The chapel is lighted with candles. He is dressed in his best gray suit. His face is like a statue's. Yesterday he looked alive still, a slight smile made him seem so; his skin had a most curious lavender tinge. Today he is darker, the smile has gone, he is already far away, the eyes have begun to sink, the lips are in a grave line, though not quite stern. Perhaps it was the taking of the death mask that changed him, but I think not.

He looks as if he had just said, "Now I go away with all my secrets and my mystery. My work is finished here." All day for two days and all night last night and still tonight, the people stream to the hospital, stand in line to go in to see him. They stand in the most complete silence I ever have known and just stare at him. Nearly all are crying; yesterday when Bennett came, he burst into such sobbing that he had to leave and go outside, where we could still hear him in the distance. He died at half past ten in the morning yesterday; I had just been telephoning for his news at ten and was told that he was the same. (I had been out at the hospital Wednesday and Thursday afternoons, sitting for hours in the salon.)

I was in the hotel with Janet yesterday, Katie having gone shopping, when Russell rang up to say he was dead. As soon as I could move, I went to Neuilly. Vera, Mme. de Salzmann, Gabo, Valya, and many others were there. Vera then told me that he was in the process of being embalmed, and that we could see him as soon as he had been taken to the chapel. While waiting, she disclosed that the cause of his death was cancer of the liver; that although he had seemed to be sleeping for hours before he died, the doctor had raised his eyelids and had said Gurdjieff looked back at him and was conscious. A most curious phenomenon; four hours after his death, his forehead and neck were still very warm; the doctor said he couldn't understand it.

On Friday Mme. de Salzmann had spoken to him in Russian. He did not reply but lifted his hand and held it out to her to take. She

---

* The letters from Solita Solano on the death of Gurdjieff.

has been absolutely superb. At the service yesterday, she sat near his head with white face, closed eyes from which the tears slowly flowed. Her son Michel stood by her side. She wasn't there today at the service. A Russian priest intones the prayers, his assistant sings the responses, we all hold a lighted taper in our right hands and just gaze and gaze.

The chapel is too small to hold all the people; we crowd together to make room until we are touching the funeral couch. Those who cannot enter stand outside and listen. Then when the service is finished and we go out, the crowds who are waiting pass in. Of course he is never alone, several people volunteer each night to watch; Katie has gone with Russell tonight; I shall go tomorrow or Tuesday night. On Wednesday afternoon, he will be taken to the Russian church and at eleven o'clock on Thursday will be the high requiem mass. At midday we all go to Fontainebleau for the enterrement. In the meantime, there will be a mass every afternoon, for the people who heard late of his death, especially for the English who will come. Louise March flew from Vienna, where she was editing his German edition. I hear Jane Heap is ill, so perhaps she will not be able to travel. I think he would be proud of the behavior of all his people. The grief is terrible, silent (except Bennett) and has a really objective quality of dignity. Janet was so moved that she took a taxicab out to the hospital after I left and went into the chapel to join me—and Russell and Katie who fortunately came in from her shopping and rushed out in time for the mass. It is very painful for her to leave tomorrow night for Germany and not attend his funeral and burial. But impossible to arrange, as she is now responsible—since four days ago—for all the German sector. Of my own grief, I shall not speak; it is a small part of the common catastrophe. The cable from Martie and Dorothy was perfect. I shall always be grateful to those powers that allowed me to be here to see him before he went away from the planet earth.

Thank you, Lib, for telephoning. It was a comfort. All future details will be written as they occur and I will tell even more when I return. But I shall never be able to describe the noble beauty of his dead face.

Solita

Midnight, November 2

For all: This is Thursday night, midnight, and at six o'clock we left
him six feet deep in the cold, cold ground at sunset, the coffin still
uncovered; the last of him I saw, and it was not he, was a long, pale
brown box, with a golden cross at the head, a few roses some des-
perate person had thrown in with the handfuls of earth each of the
hundreds had dropped, in accordance with the Russian custom.

But back to *Monday*. The previous notes I had sent to Lib, to
be copied by Margaret. In the meantime, Lib had gone to Boston
for her son's operation and the letter is waiting at Morristown to
be sent to Margaret to copy, as I was too overwhelmed to remember the carbon. So Monday, at the chapel of the American Hospital. He had turned to gray stone and looked even more "at peace."
His suit was navy blue, not grey, as I thought. His tie was blue and
crooked. Carnations had replaced the violets and roses. The brown
and gray icon of St. George (his saint) and the Dragon which Gabo
had brought from his (Gurdjieff's) apartment was placed at his feet.
As Katie and I were sitting, with many others, at his side (the condi-
tions were *intimate*) waiting for the priest to come, we looked up
and saw Jane Heap standing at the door. Gabo rose and gave her his
place next to us for the service which began in a few minutes. Katie
had "watched" (fait la veille) the night before until half past four in
the morning. She saw the English group arrive in the night, direct
from the gare with their little rugs and bags; they sat along the walk
outside between the chapel and the hospital, on the ground "like
Mexicans." Alfred also came from London, looking like alabaster.
At 4:00 a.m., the French delegation took over. Streams of people
came and went all night, as they did all day. Can't imagine what
the American Hospital thought of all this, the hundreds of peculiar
pilgrims who came and stayed and went away, all through the icy,
frosty night . . . (one day he said to Russell, "I wish I were *real* man,
who needed to sleep only one hour each night . . .") Forgive incoher-
ency, must put things down as I think of them, or you'll never hear
them. Lillian Whitcomb was in NYC when she heard the news, as
was Lord Pentland. Both flew at once. Where am I? Still Monday.
I waited for Jane in the hospital salon. She looked pale, but well;
beige cape, good English hat, since discarded, sad to say. She kissed
me tenderly and said, "And Martie went away!" I said no one could
have imagined a fatal termination, no one believed it until it hap-

pened. I couldn't really talk with her, nor have I been able to since, as individuals of her group constantly engage her attention more than I, and call her from me. We are still in the salon, as of Monday afternoon. Katie went back to the chapel to say goodbye to him again. She told me she knelt by him in prayer and then she dared to kiss him on the forehead, "Cold as marble," she said. I tried to dare, but could not. She left that same night in tears for Germany. During the days she was here, she waited in vain for some word of sorrow or sympathy from Alice, as I have; not one word has come from her, so I suppose her cable was not delivered; nor has anyone in the Gurdjieff family had a message from Alice. Of course, she must have sent something, so tell her that she must reproach the Western Union. What Katie really hoped was that Alice would fly to be with her—us—and go to the funeral. Mme. de Salzmann who has been a marvel of behavior through all this, is going to America in November, she says.

Now for *Tuesday*. I'm just back from the chapel. I sat by his side, near his face for two hours. (By the way, I've ordered a photograph of his dead face for all of you.) His sister, Sonya, sat beside me. Luba came from England, where she has a job with one of Jane's pupils, repeat, *pupils*. Russell and Gurdjieff's nephew, Valya, spent the day in Fontainebleau in the cemetery, cleaning up the family plot which has of course been neglected for years. Jane unfortunately did not wear her chic hat, but appeared nearly shaved. Today's her birthday, and Russell's too. A small choir came from the Russian church and sang the responses. The chief priest in the old tradition robes, silver cross and chain, long black hair and beard, liquid black eyes and honey-voice. There were new flowers over the tilleul silk brocade. Someone had made tiny bouquets of red roses and lake yellow daisies. Gurdjieff's face today is grayer and the skin is tighter over the immense intelligence of his skull. Vera said, "Today is his birthday, where he has gone." (You know that three days are needed to shed the body and today they were completed. Saturday to Tuesday.) How I wanted to kiss him goodbye like Katie and the Russians but I didn't quite have the courage . . . Jane said, "He doesn't look dead." But indeed he does, since two days. Martie: When Jane and I left the chapel together, we clasped hands desperately and walked like that, exchanging memories in silence for five minutes—no need for words. All her great gift for emotions was in her hand.

Wednesday. Un froid de loup, repeat, *loup*. Went in the morning to order our flowers. I thought one enormous piece would be better than six oddments. I spent ten dollars apiece for us—Dorothy, Martie, Alice, Katie, Lib, and SS "De la part de ses amies Américaines"—then Dorothy's name first. Hope everyone agrees. I had no instructions, so acted on my own responsibility. Oh, God, never to see that smile again, hear him say—well, no matter what—especially for me—"Kanari." Janet wrote about him in her New Yorker article; will they print it? She finished working at midnight, just as Katie telephoned she had arrived in Germany . . .

Now for the *last day*. No, Wednesday. So worn out I don't know what I'm writing. Wednesday, yesterday, the mise en bière. I couldn't quite go to hospital to see him put into box, and as I found out later, I wouldn't have been allowed to—only the men of the family. I went to the Russian church at four and waited there, debout,* till nearly six before he was brought. Six men carried him in—Russell, Valya, Gabo, Michel (his son by Mme. de Salzmann), etc. Dim lovely lights, many flowers which had arrived early, vested priests and small choir for the service. Church was crowded even for that small ceremony, all golden under the incense-smoky high dome. The catafalque was covered with large black cloth, embroidered with silver. Not a sound ever issues from any gathering of his people—neither a footstep, a cough, a rustle, or a breath. A remarkable quality of silence which is so rare as to be noted as unique. (Martie, thanks for the clippings and don't believe in those last word records, as no one thought he would die until he was so weak that he never spoke again, only held out his hand to Jeanne when she spoke to him. But shall inquire when I see her in two days, as she has asked me to.)

Last day. Janet went with me this morning at half past eleven to the high requiem mass at the Russian cathedral. There had been no veille permitted last night, so he had been alone till the church opened. Entirely candles, flowers, the voices of five white-and-gold robed priests, a cantor with a divine breaking voice. How beautiful is the Russian language! The church was packed—not only with those we know, but by hundreds of his followers whom we never saw, whom I had never seen in all my years near him. After all the chanting and prayers and singing were finished, for an hour everyone passed by his coffin, one by one, from the right. Each mourner,

---

* Standing.

streaming with tears, made a genuflection at his head, stepped up to the icon at his feet, kissed it, and walked to the left. Each, un-self-conscious, took his and her private and sorrowful farewell to him with a ceremonious simplicity that tore one's heart open even wider than before, if possible. Then everyone went away to breathe, have a drink or coffee, and at two o'clock we came back to the church. The crowds stood along the street to watch *him* brought out and put in the great funeral carriage, his flowers placed on the top. The family rode with him. The hundreds of others rode behind in the cortège in many private cars and four enormous autobuses. The streets were jammed, closed to traffic for blocks around the Russian church, and other crowds gathered to watch the spectacle. The drive to Fontainebleau took an hour and a half. I went with Lillian and some very rich, silent, chic, tiresome English, old followers of Ouspensky. Through the old familiar roads, streets, towns, turnings, forest, to Avon. In a cruel sunny icy wind, we walked by the hundreds through the cemetery gates, following *him* to the family plot. *I saw the grave* torn open in the rocky, watery ground, deep, deep, horribly deep . . . The porters let him down into it. A great sigh came from the people—the only sound they had made since he died, when they were together. The priest came to the rescue with his chanting. Later everyone passed by the terrible hole, cast a pinch of earth down on to the box, knelt, made the sign of the cross, passed on. It was over. He had disappeared from us forever.

Back in Paris—I don't remember coming back—we were all asked to come to the rue des Colonels Renard for supper, as usual after a Russian funeral. The family received us, gave us—what? I don't know. You will all know how impossible it was to walk up those stairs and enter that sacred place. But it was done. Then I came here to write you, as is my duty. Done now.

Lib, I hope your Joe is all right. I will write you when I have recovered a little. Glad Dorothy's back will be all right. Will send or bring a photograph of him as he looked in death—and if I can, a death mask. (Copy, of course.) Can make only three copies—one for Katie, one for Dorothy and Martie, and one for Lib and Alice, to be kept for my notes.

Your loving, more dead than alive, Kanari.

Thursday, November 10

For everyone: Here are some addenda to the former notes which I must put down as quickly as possible, before Janet drives me away from her typewriter.

It's evident that some "highly placed" person has decided not to tell that Mr. Gurdjieff had cancer. Even Lillian Whitcomb, near him from Prieuré days, did not know last night. I now have the complete medical report: Besides the tumor, his heart was dilated and his lungs were "raddled" from the bouts of coughing, bronchitis, from which he had suffered for thirty years. Only to Gabo did he speak of his pain; made him bend down one day so the others could not hear, and said, "Very, very bad pain" in Russian. (Ochen, ochen.) The night they punctured him for the twelve liters of water, he sat up in bed, accepted the local anaesthetic, smoked a cigarette while they worked on him, and said he felt relieved. He wore on his head the old red fez! as there was a draft from the window on his baldness. Two days before he was taken to the hospital, he called in four people who happened to be sitting in the salon through the night—Salzmann, Russell, Vera, were three; I suppose Gabo was the fourth—and just looked at them for a long time, saying not one word. They believe he was saying goodbye.

The priest at the Russian church stated that there has never been such a funeral before, except Chaliapin's; that he has never seen such mass grief, or such a concentration of attitude, he said, on the part of the mourners. Even the undertaker who had never seen Gurdjieff before he saw him dead, broke down at the grave and wept! Just from the vibrations, I daresay.

He left a lot of money—in Switzerland, three Paris banks. His sister, Sonya, is having a full-length statue made of him, to be kept in the apartment. It will be dressed in his clothes and on his head will be placed his fur cap ... The French group are going to keep the apartment as a sort of shrine to which we may all go. The group dances and readings are continuing. Salzmann goes to America first part December, with daughter Boussik and the three children. She will carry on his work as best she can and I suppose we will all help her. Katie has so pledged and so shall I.

I am lunching with Salzmann tomorrow and will have further news then to send you. I sail a week from today. I still have bronchitis from the cemetery blasts; I expected pneumonia.

APPENDIX I

Letter From Kathryn Hulme To Jane Heap
Sunday Night, October 20, 1935

Dear Jane:

When I waved you off two days ago I had no idea, that the next step and only possible step was toward Gurdjieff. You went at 10:17 a.m. and at noon, without knowing how it took charge of me, I was walking alone into Café de la Paix. I saw him instantly and went to his table. He was alone too, at first he didn't remember me, but as soon as I said Child's Fifth Avenue and "drive behind you Fontainebleau," he seemed to remember. He invited me for coffee. I told him I had just waved you off. Then he looked at me, said I was thin in the cheeks and that I was changed. He said I didn't change; *it* changed for me. He said, "Now I think you smell my idea. You smell, so, my idea." I have to tell you step by step. Then he went back to my change; he said, "You can change like that ten times, each time more strong, then maybe next change, not *it* changing, *you* changing." "Maybe perhaps," he said. He said he was sitting there thinking. "Now I must have rest, and then you come in, *you* rest." Then he talked about the crayfish club, and how he sheared people. And he said, "You be candidate," and I said, "Yes . . ." then he explained it would cost thousands of francs. "Six thousand," he said, but he reduced it to three thousand before the hour was up. Then, it was two o'clock of the day you left. He said, "You come hotel," and I went. He had a secretary waiting for him. His room is small, three people seemed to fill it. He asked me to read for him a new translation in English, then he ordered lunch. We had it in his room; he had a herring and some cheese in the armoire, and ordered two plates from downstairs. He talked often about money, and about his need for rest also. "You understand what I mean rest," he said. I didn't but said nothing. Then he said we would have a crayfish dinner that night; he would invite friend, I would invite friend. I was planning to see Louise, so I said my friend was one who wanted to see him, one he called "orphan" once. He didn't remember but said,

"Bring her," and made me promise that afterwards she would go and I would be with him. I promised.

At the hotel, Louise balked, she wanted Solita in it too. I said I had promised one friend but if either she or Solita wanted to walk in and say, "I come too," and take consequences, all right. Meanwhile, completely aware of having brought upon myself the chance to part with a thousand francs, I borrowed it from our hotel patron. We three then went to Café de la Paix. His friend had not come, he seemed glad to see all of us. So we went to Brasserie Excelsior for crayfish. You know the kind of dinner—cook, patron, etc., helping to polish off a quart of Armagnac. Afterwards we returned to Café de la Paix. We sat on the terrasse and he talked, and he told Solita she was Jew and canary, and me, that I was Jew and crocodile. Something to Louise—we've agreed each would tell you her own story. So I just will tell crocodile. He said, "I give one analogy—crocodile. Example, crocodile walk down street, more influence than ten—what you call your president, Roosevelt? Yes, more influence than ten Roosevelts." He was in a good mood and we left when he had an eleven o'clock appointment, but I had promised to return, and he held me when the others were behind and said, "You come back?" We three went around the corner and dropped into a café. I told the girls I couldn't go back—I had been with him from noon till nearly midnight—I was completely lost and stupid. After having kissed a thousand francs goodbye (in mind) I hadn't been allowed to pay for the dinner, and so I didn't know if he expected me back (for that) or if it was all joking. But I did go back, alone, as I had said. He was waiting for me. He asked if I was tired and I said that I was, and that I wanted to go home. But first, I wanted to pay for the dinner, I had listened to his story about owing him, each day it was a cipher added, and told him I wanted to pay. I was half joking, half serious. Maybe I wasn't anything. Anyhow, he said, "How much you bring?" I had five hundred francs and he took it. He said, "I take this for *you*, not for me," and said, "Come," and stalked to a taxi. The girls were waiting around the corner but off I went. In the taxi, he told me he was going to take me to a place that would astonish me. "But you not show astonishment," he said, "you and me not show astonishment, only inside show astonishment." I didn't know if I was riding to doom or what. Jane, I really was paralysed, but could not have stopped going. We got off at Café Select and walked down Montparnasse. He said to me, "You funny person, I not understand you." And we walked on. At a corner near the Gare he turned abruptly, said, "No, that place too strong for you, we go other place." And so we walked beyond the Gare and came to a house which I spotted instantly as one of the so-called hot spots of Montparnasse. He said, looking up at the shuttered windows, "Nice house, new house," and in we went. It was packed with men and naked girls dancing together with only a twist of silk about the loins. He was watching me in his way, but I truly was not shocked or astonished; I've seen things in my time and felt nothing inside which would have told itself to him. We took a small table and had two Perriers. It was strange being in a place like that with him. I can't tell you what all my thoughts and emotions were, they went so fast. Naked girls brushing buttocks past our table, and men reaching out to them, that sort of thing. He watched everything. I never felt so safe or so secure in all my life, and yet, all the while, he was baiting me. He said, "What is your taste?" He wanted me to pick the girl I would choose if I were man, he said. I simply could not, I said, "They all look alike to me, smell alike." "Choose," he said, "Which one?" I spent a time in anguish. I couldn't know what he wanted. Finally I took our two Perrier bottles and stood them side by side and said, "It's as if you ask me to choose which bottle, both are the same." He liked that, I think. He smiled, but pointed to his bottle and said, "But that have more liquid." It had a half inch more than mine. But he was easier after that. He pointed to the hostesses of the place—slightly more elevated hussies in black silk dresses. He said, "If you man and want for animal purpose, you choose any girl on floor and can have for thirty francs, *but* if you choose manager woman, she cost fifty francs." Then, after a long time of staring around, he turned suddenly and said—"Suppose, example, you out there, no clothes, I here; I choose you, why? Because I see (and he put his hands over his eyes and gestured inwards), I see something else," he said. Soon after, he paid the bill and we went out. I was falling to pieces by that time but I walked steadily and still felt "safe." We walked down past the Gare and I had it all around me, that place, those awful naked girls not even pretty in body and being there with him and feeling as if I were there with God . . . well, nearly that, and once he said, "You funny, you not astonished?" I said, "No." He said, "Other place, very bad, only you and me not can be together there—ten men, ten women, do things, we watch behind glass. I said, "Too strong, too big stink for me, remember I am baby crocodile." And so we got in a cab and he dropped me at the hotel with the command to meet him today at eleven and go to Fontainebleau.

I was in the café at eleven and he was waiting. He brought me one of his books. We were to go by train and could work, he said. We missed the train he wanted to get and took a taxi across town to the autocars, missed those, and returned to Gare de Lyon and took the next train—half hour in the station café. He gave me a translation of his work written in Child's, Columbus Circle, dated November 6, 1934, asking me if the French was readable. I read it; I could understand the French, the ideas. In the train we sat opposite and he read newspapers while I read his book. He dog-eared a certain chapter, author chapter, the last in the book, the epilogue. He said, "You smell my idea, I think this best for you to read first." It was his statement of the three-centered being, his analogy of the horse, the cab, the cabby, and the fare . . . you know it. Kundabuffer and the river-branching analogy. After a while in the train, he spoke to me. He took a rod from his pocket, asked me the word for wand, and said this was his wand; it would make magic, he said. He explained it had a core of platinum which would sell for millions of francs, *if* he would sell. Then he went back into silence, though I positively believed he could wave me off the earth any moment with that wand, if he wished. You know the surcharged emotional state after practically a whole day with him, and half of the next.

We arrived in Fontainebleau and went to his brother's house. They were not expecting him but got together a grand luncheon by 2:30 p.m. Then he showed me his "machine"—you know about it, I'm sure, and have doubtless seen it work. But Jane, it paralysed me when he stuck that metal wand in a corner of what looked like a radio, and himself stood on those wood pedals on the floor, and made vibrations go into the wand, and then drew them out and threw them back and made such strange high stinging sounds with that hand movement and the awful intentness. I was frightened to death but very peaceful, some kind of impossible combination like that. The quality of those vibration notes took my ears, I thought I couldn't stand it. But all the while I sat quietly, watching how beautifully his hand worked in air, drawing sound from the rod, putting it back . . . it's paralyzing. Then there was lunch. Once when he left the room, his sister-in-law talked with me about you—remembered you spading in the Prieuré garden and how fine you were, and wanted to know all about your health now. She was comforting, a kind of laughing physical center, the only easy one around Gurdjieff it seemed to me, in that family circle. His brother looked at me once only, when we were taking the trolley back to the station. He was watching me watching Gurdjieff who was sitting on a bench, gone. And I think he, the brother, knew I felt a kind of love and safety, for suddenly he gave me a smile; it nearly cracked my heart, and he never again met my eyes, nor Gurdjieff's.

Train home; "Very very sleepy," Gurdjieff said and pulled his hat over his eyes and slept most of the way home while I read his book. Now and again he opened his eyes and looked at me without seeing me. Back in Paris I said I would take the Metro home, but he said, "No, you go Café la Paix with me, then take bus home." So I went. He knew (and *how* did he know?) that I must take an AM or AF bus; he pointed it out to me from the corner after I had refused his coffee invitation. I told him I was tired and my feet were cold; also that I knew he had a seven o'clock rendezvous. I shook hands with him and said, "Thank you," but couldn't know for what. There are no words for it. And he said, "Thank you for *com*-pany," and so we parted, and he said if tomorrow I wish, I can find him in his room working at one o'clock. Jane, this is going on four pages and I'm ashamed I could not say it in less. Your eyes!

I needed to tell you, Jane, because all this is a direct outcome of the month you spent here, a kind of finale if you wish. What he wanted to find out about me, God only knows. But he seemed satisfied. At the crayfish dinner party he looked at me and then said to Solita, I could write her diary. And I knew he could. Beyond that, I know nothing; that's why I had to tell it step by step . . .

He does want money, at least, he talked about that rather continuously, but didn't paralyze me because he talked of so many zeros and I told him at the beginning I was only church mouse, had no job, had nothing but the daily bread etc. and told him the five hundred francs I had in my purse was for the dinner he had not let me pay and that I didn't want the debt to triple, a zero added each day . . . He took the five hundred francs and said I was a round idiot . . . of the three kinds, round, zigzag, and square, round was the worst. Jane, I'm too tightly wound up now to be able to tell you anything more coherent than this. But I *do* need help from you. I did have help from you today and yesterday—those long hours of uncertainty, my first time alone with him and not knowing even how to answer him when he asked a question. My help from you was simply in remembering you and how you had said, "Each person we bring into the method is our responsibility." And somehow remembering that, I could know how to walk with him, not talk, but watch and listen. And I had a feeling he was comfortable and satisfied and liked my company which I learned by an intuition to make visible or invisible, as he wished. All that I could do because I remembered your words and deliberately set myself not to be too great a damned fool . . . and maybe succeeded a little, because he never got angry or impatient though I was a stupid blank often . . . not knowing where we were going nor why, nor what he wanted . . .

Can you know from any of this what he wants of me? What I should do, or not do next? Is there *anything* you can tell me? I have a fearful temptation to run over to London to hide behind you. I understand now why there had to be garden and scullery work at the Priory. Two days continuous with Gurdjieff are almost too much to "take" without the relief of scrubbing and spading. I'm a little beside myself, but calm. I *think* I've had my money test and my sex test and come out not too badly, for there was another invitation for tomorrow, which I cannot take up—I'm too dead, and he said, "If you wish," which makes it not exactly a command. Meanwhile, if you could find an instant to send me a word, counsel, or condemnation, anything . . . it would help enormously.

Love to you Jane, and to Elspeth.

APPENDIX II

New Year With Gurdjieff
Thursday, January 2, 1936

I want to tell you about it just the way it happened, because seeing him made the day for me, and perhaps will make the year. Gloomy yesterday and rainy, I had no feeling it was the beginning of a new year or the beginning of anything for that matter. Mi-chemin with every one of my problems, yesterday was just Wednesday, no different from the previous day, Tuesday. I phoned Solita, she had to go to his house around 1:00 p.m. but I said, "Maybe if we tried to catch him in the Café de la Paix, I'd have a chance to see him too." Solita said, "Yes, but I'll need a half hour to dress etc. . . . Then I haggled. But in a half hour perhaps he will have left the café (been leaving before noon these days) and we'll have made the trip for nothing . . . back and forth, haggling and debating, no direction, no action anywhere (in me, I mean) and finally hung up deciding not to go to the café . . . Then upstairs in my room, walking around aimless and indirect. Some of his chapters walked back and forth in my mind—remember the "gallery" chapters, people who were "turning points" in his life and how he traveled days and miles to find them? Prince Liubovedski, Skridloff, etc.? Remember the twenty-one day ride through Turkestan, blindfolded, when he went to a monastery where he thought he might hear something? I thought of those chapters and suddenly the shocking shame of my attitude came over me—me, unwilling to take a bus ride to the Opéra on mere chance that he would be in the café, unwilling to give up half an hour and three bus tickets on the *chance of seeing Gurdjieff*.

I was out of my work clothes in three minutes, two minutes later—dressed and going out the door. It was just eleven when I walked in the café. He was sitting there, alone. I sat at a table near, waiting until he would see me. His eyes examining every person who came in the café found me quickly, "Crocodile," he called and I went over to his table, straight into the most beautiful smile I ever saw. I felt his mood, friendly, glad for company, and touched with a special kind of gentleness he has on holidays like Christmas and

New Year—it was the perfect moment to find him alone, like the first time I found him alone after Jane left . . . and I was so surprised that at long last an impulse had been correct, I kept saying to myself, "Well, Katie Hulme, I beat your inertia that time, I put it over on you, Katie Hulme . . ." and felt near to tears just for the emotion of having made Katie Hulme do a right thing at a proper moment. Tears of victory maybe.

"And how your New Year?" he asked. "No party last night," I said, "No feeling of holiday, yesterday like any day, Theen One (Alice) and myself go home eleven o'clock." He teased me for not being able to make something on New Year. "I have beeg party," he said, "beeg party, many people, and champagne, veritable champagne." (Solita had seen one mangy little bottle of champagne in his house, but he was making his story beeg.) Then he told me how his Fontainebleau nephew "met a beeg year" having a breakdown coming to Paris from Fontainebleau and not getting into Paris until 10:00 a.m. New Year's Day, and how he sent his nephew right back to Fontainebleau for a task, laughing and saying, "Idiot, idiot, he meet beeg New Year." Then we were silent a long time. Then he said, "Ach, holy-day, idiot day, look all those people (in street) asleep. Asleep, once could *make* something, for holy-day, now nothing. Ten year, twenty year ago, holy-day was important day, could *feel* holy-day, New Year Day people could *make* something, could make begeen new thing. Now no more. All dies—all this (indicating the drowsy few over coffee in the café). All this die too. There again he struck the what I call world-note. Remember a crayfish night when he talked about the reciprocal relations of Individual versus Society, but he didn't call it that. You hear that world-note often these days when he talks, the dead weight of the universal idiocy that drags us all down . . .

Then more silence, then, "What you do now?" he asked. Work, I said, "Still same book, not finish yet, not important work (I meant not for any Being purpose of mine), but I make exercise of it, I work, I make exercise of my work." "No good," he said. "You make exercise, spend energy, and it bring no good." "Even making exercise of concentration?" I asked. "Yes, even concentration," he said. "Leesten, I tell you some thing, leesten, this important. You make exercise of all these things, you spend all energy and have nothing left for self. Must know *how* make exercise of things, then can build something for self at same time. How you do it bring no good, only leave you feenish each day, nothing left for self. Once you learn *how* make exercise, then can continue aftomatically (automatically, re-member?!) like Canary, you see leetle change there?" I told him I saw a "beeg change." "No," he said, "not beeg, I just tell her how do one little thing, how make one little exercise; she have seven parts, just say for example seven parts—I make something for *one* part, she have six parts must do for self, if *can* do, then can build something for self—once she learn *how* do, then can proceed afto-matically in her. Then will see beeg change . . ."

So that my darling was New Year. It's the last clod cut away from under my feet. And I like the feeling. You know how we've talked of effort, of making exercises of all our difficult tasks, etc., but you see, *none* of it, not even an effort that cracks the three centers can be of any use unless you know *how* to make it, and that knowing has to be *told* to you by one who knows. There is *no* knowledge of that kind springing spontaneously in the human brain. All this back-break-ing effort, if not done with self-observation, does nothing more but wear you out, reducing you simply to the "planetary manure" for which use most of us are doomed.

I suppose when he took away my last clod, I should have fol-lowed it up and asked him to give me one thing, one beginning clue about how to make effort and save something for Being at the same time . . . but I couldn't. I don't feel ready for it. If I *had* asked he would have known I was just "philosophizing" and wouldn't have told me anyhow.

There was silence again. Then he said, looking at the clock, "Twelve o'clock I must go home, but must do something on way home, cannot remember what must do—ach, my memory go these days. I know I must do something, but what is, cannot remember. Have *taste* of it (he touches his tongue) but cannot remember." He concentrated. Then he said, "It is something in life." You know, when I heard that—something *in life*—I felt as if he were light-years removed from me . . . something in life, he kept saying, a Being from the planet Karatas trying to remember some idiot business he had to do among the three brained beings of the planet earth. It gave me the strangest feeling I think I've ever had beside him.

He had some more merry moments. He looked at me, nodded, said, "Knachtschmidt & Company perfect correspondence for you. You *know* Knachtschmidt?" he asked. I laughed and said I remem-bered how he used to call all of us Knachtschmidt & Co. when he wasn't calling us church-mouse, and then I asked him exactly what it meant. "Knacht," he said, and tore at his clothes, "no clothes," he said, "how that word English?" "Naked," I said. "Yes, yes, naked . . . Russians say Knachtschmidt, very funny how they mean it. Example—many peasants with no shoes come together in group for company, wish make some thing together. Knachtschmidt & Company," he laughed, "perfect correspondence for you." The more I looked at that analogy during the day, the more perfect it became! Barefoot, stupid, poor, coming together for company to *make something*. Well, at least, *this* peasant knows enough (sometimes) to "come together," and sometimes something is "made" too! But I feel from the way he laughed that he likes his Knachtschmidt and Company that used to come together to make something in room number six.

Gordon came into the café then, he had to speak to her for business. I got up to leave; thanking him, I said, "You have made my day, Mr. Gurdjieff." "How?" he asked, "How make your day? Idiot, all I do is disillusion you." (I wish I could write out how he said disillusion!) "You mean about effort and exercise," I said.

"Yes, I take all away from you, how then make day?" He "twinkled" at me. He knew damned well he had made it for me.

Solita came to the café then. He invited Gordon and myself to go to his house for lunch, with Solita. "Small things left over from beeg party," he said. The "small thing" was a four gallon pot of soup, an enormous plate of roasted grain of some sort with grapes and apricots and God knows what else in it, bear meat, cheese, and yogurt which he had made himself, and then platters of loucoum and apricot paste in strips, and fruits, etc.—so much that I couldn't eat but half, and he picked up a plate I had tried to hide, some kind of baked rice and meat, and said, "You know how much cost make that dish? One hundred francs—and now you have defiled it . . . must eat," he said, "or if not, then must take home with you, because anyhow I put you down for one hundred francs, owing me . . ." There was a new table cloth for the holidays, and a Russian woman doing kitchen work so we had no dishes to wash, but could listen to his music afterwards . . . and I was so glad to "be back" I became quite "psychopathic" within myself, with my emotions manifesting wildly . . .

We left at three. At the door he said, in return for our thanks, "You see, Gurdjieff New Year not tail of donkey." A short paunchy man in suspenders and dirty carpet slippers with a most beautiful smile. Indeed it was not tail of donkey!

APPENDIX III

Letter From Janet Flanner To Solita Solano
Thursday, December 14, 1944

The old gent said that the objective was the last stage of attainment, with subjective being previous if indeed not too low to be part of same scale. Poor Gordon rather drunk and drawn and very thin, devoted and inadequate and earnest, kept saying, "Oh how true sir, oh how very important that is Mr. Gurdjieff." She seemed still, to be hoping for some sort of heaven to be included in his pattern, wanted it so much for others that she was willing never to go there herself: strange mixture of masochism and Christianity: he was very gentle but hopeless, about heaven and her too, I felt.

Treated me with great love and gentleness and esteem. There is no other set of words that suit except those three. I was touched and at ease: no harem, no hysteria, no ogling. Only a very wise old man sitting in his rich pantry of foods and thoughts. He said he was finishing his book in one more month and then would see no one, ever. She cried out, "Oh, sir, not even me?" and he said, "Why you different as any other, Mees? Eef do not know how to be alone now will never know how." You recall how his "H" always included a "K."

I had to recall you all by your animals names which was ticklish, at first: he knew I was Canary's friend so that was easy. Then I recalled Yak for the Lolly, and Crocodile; Gordon supplied for Alice, and Rita R. he recalled by name. He was deeply glad to have money, tell her; tell you all, was touched to have communication from what he called outside places.

I shall go again next week or later: asked me which kind of lamb I desired for my next meal there, I chose married, he roared with laughter, said I chose well, very fine brandy he gave me. We polished off close to a bottle. I was careful to drink very small doses so emerged soberer than he or Gordon. He gave me nuts as a present, I gave him candy bar from PX and bar kitchen soap and package cigarettes: he had plenty of his own naturally but said it was thinking to bring gift that made for pleasure to him. Gordon almost wept at tea I gave her, also bar lifebouy soap from PX, and PR woolen panties: those she clutched to breast saying she had wondered how to continue without any. I shall give her one full set with shirtsleeved shirt and panties, thick ribbed kind. I shall have enough without. If that sounds crass and selfish I can only say that unpreparedness of Europe in general, even after it is all over is so much result of stupidity that survival of the more intelligent even in matter of woolen drawers, seems basic.

I shall have to write a number three letter, I see, too. I was so panic stricken and addled as to what to write for New Yorker that I could not think to write you or anyone darling, forgive. I wrote one whole piece then tore it up. What I sent is at any rate true as far as I go: I could have gone farther and found the same selfishness, greed, dishonesty. On a small group of Maquis and Resistance, a whole France has heaved itself up to glory and rehabilitation. It's true darling. Only Germaine asked me how goes England. Not one other French person asked, nor about America. It is really abnormal. Their only question is, "Do you love France and do you know how much we have suffered?" The Dorés are different because they love you Katie, Alice, Louise as individuals: I saw Louise's beautiful desk still in her room now occupied by H. Hessel, recall her? I refused to look at our rooms or furniture stored in Louise's room. Too sad. Hotel dirty, shabby. . . .

Love J.

CHRONOLOGY 1935–1981

1935   November 23: Gurdjieff moves to eleven rue Labie.
1936   May: Margaret and Georgette return to Paris from the Midi and are invited to lunch at Gurdjieff's table.
       August 2: Alice and Kathryn go to America for three months and return to Paris on November 2nd.
1937   May 7: Alice and Kathryn sail to America.
       August 23: Gurdjieff's brother, Dimitri, dies of cancer.
       September 5: Gurdjieff moves from rue Labie to his brother's apartment, six, rue des Colonels Renard.
1938   July: Kathryn returns to Paris for three weeks.
1939   March 1: Solita and Gurdjieff sail on the SS Paris to America.
       May 19: Solita and Gurdjieff return to Paris on the SS Normandie.
       September 1: War is declared.
       October 5: Solita sails to New York on the SS Washington.
1941   October 26: Georgette dies of cancer.
1942   June: Americans in France are being threatened with concentration camps—Margaret returns to America and meets Dorothy Caruso on the SS Drottningholm. Solita, Kathryn, Alice, and Janet greet Margaret at the dock in New York.
1944   December: Janet returns to Paris after the Liberation and visits Gurdjieff, having promised the Rope to look him up.
1945   Elizabeth Gordon dies.
       July: Kathryn visits Gurdjieff while passing through Paris for her work with the United Nations.
1946   June: Kathryn visits Gurdjieff with Marie Louise Habets.
1947   *La Machine à Courage* is published.
1948   June: Margaret travels to Paris with Dorothy and introduces her to Gurdjieff.
       December: Gurdjieff sails on the SS America to New York.
1949   February: Gurdjieff returns to Paris.
       October 29: Gurdjieff dies in the American Hospital at Neuilly.
1950   *Beelzebub's Tales to His Grandson* is published.
1951   *The Fiery Fountains* is published.

1956   *The Nun's Story* is published.
1958   March 12: Alice dies.
1959   Warner Brothers release the motion picture, *The Nun's Story,* adapted from Kathryn's novel.
1960   Kathryn moves to Kauai, Hawaii with Marie Louise.
       Meetings with Remarkable Men is published.
1961   June 18: Monique dies in Le Cannet and is buried next to Georgette.
1962   *The Strange Necessity* and *The Unknowable Gurdjieff* are published.
1966   *Undiscovered Country* is published.
1973   October 19: Margaret dies of heart failure in Cannes and is buried next to Georgette and Monique.
1975   *Life is real only then, when "I am"* is published.
       November 22: Solita dies in Orgeval, France.
1981   August 25: Kathryn dies in Lihue, Kauai.

BIBLIOGRAPHY

Gurdjieff, G. I.
  The Struggle of the Magicians. The Stourton Press, 1957.
  Views from the Real World: Early Talks of Gurdjieff. Arkana, 1984.
  Beelzebub's Tales to His Grandson. Harcourt, Brace & Company;
  Routledge & Kegan Paul, 1950.
  Meetings with Remarkable Men. E. P. Dutton, 1963.
  Life is real only then, when "I am." E. P. Dutton, 1978.
  The Herald of Coming Good. La Société Anonyme des Éditions de
  l'Ouest, 1933.
  Transcripts of Gurdjieff's Meetings 1941–1946. Book Studio, 2009.

Hulme, Kathryn.
  Undiscovered Country: A Spiritual Adventure. Little, Brown and
  Company, 1966.

Anderson, Margaret.
  The Unknowable Gurdjieff. Routledge & Kegan Paul, 1962.
  My Thirty Years War. Horizon Press, 1969.
  The Fiery Fountains. Horizon Press, 1969.
  The Strange Necessity. Horizon Press, 1969.

Anderson, Margaret, and Mathilda Hills.
  Forbidden Fires. The Naiad Press, 1996.

Leblanc, Georgette.
  La Machine à Courage: Souvenirs. J. B. Janin, 1947.
  The Courage Machine: A New Life in a New World. Book Studio,
  2012.

Patterson, William Patrick.
  Ladies of the Rope. Arete Communications, 1999.

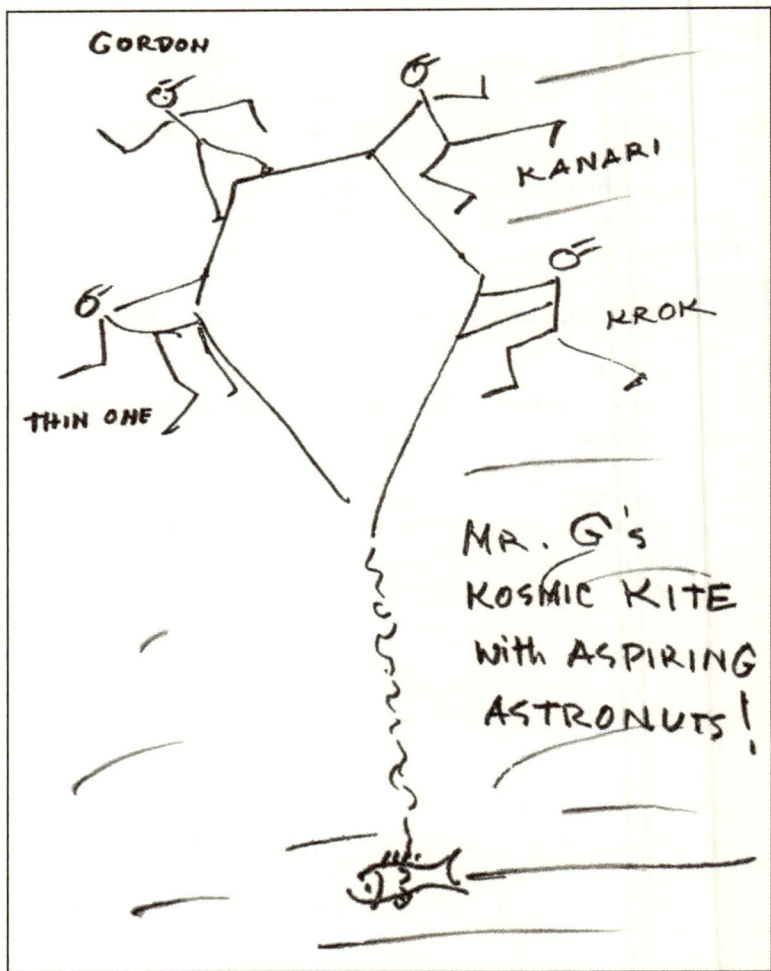

Drawing by Louise Davidson (Sardine)

INDEX